Margaret's Mission

Margaret's Mission
to Arabia, Africa, and India
1965-2010

Paul Heusinkveld
with Margaret Doorenbos

Van Raalte Press

A. C. Van Raalte Institute, Hope College

Van Raalte Press is a division of Hope College Publishing

A. C. Van Raalte Institute
Theil Research Center
9 East 10th Street
PO Box 9000
Holland, MI 49422-9000

https://hope.edu/vri
vanraalte@hope.edu

Printed in the United States of America

Library of Congress Control Number: 2021932815

Editor-in-Chief and Publisher:
        Jacob E. Nyenhuis, PhD

Project Editor
        JoHannah M. Smith

Layout and Cover Design
        Paul A. Heusinkveld

Missionary Memoirs Series Logo Design
        Marena DeLeau

With this issue we are introducing our Missionary Memoirs Series logo. The highly stylized "MM" is intended to suggest mountains, valleys, and broad plains, a representation of the variety of contexts in which missionaries have served around the globe.

Dedicated to

Mary Jo Hospers Kopp

The Missionary Memoirs Series of the Van Raalte Press

This series is dedicated to publishing the heretofore untold stories of missionaries of the Reformed Church in America and the Christian Reformed Church in North America and Hope College alumni who worked to proclaim the Christian Gospel, both at home and abroad. These books are the recorded accounts of their experiences, transformational for themselves and the people of the countries where they served.

Series Editor
>Donald A. Luidens, PhD
>Director, Van Raalte Institute

Project Editor
>JoHannah M. Smith
>Van Raalte Institute

Editor-in-Chief and Publisher
>Jacob E. Nyenhuis, PhD
>Director Emeritus, Van Raalte Institute

Editorial Board
>The Albertus C. Van Raalte Research Professor and the Senior Research Fellows of the Van Raalte Institute

Contents

Maps

Introduction of Series Editor Donald A. Luidens
by Jacob E. Nyenhuis

It gives me great pleasure to introduce to you both the new Missionary Memoirs Series of the Van Raalte Press and the series editor, Donald A. Luidens, director of the Van Raalte Institute and professor emeritus of sociology at Hope College. The publication of Don Luidens, *Seeds of Hope, Hate, and Change: Missionary Witnesses to the Middle East in Transition* in December 2020 led the editorial board of the Van Raalte Press to formalize plans for this series, with this outstanding two-volume work designated as the first in the series. Luidens brings a very rich experience and broad knowledge to his leadership of this new venture. He has built a substantial network among former missionaries and their descendants that will greatly expand this series. The Van Raalte Institute gratefully acknowledges the anonymous donor who is underwriting this series.

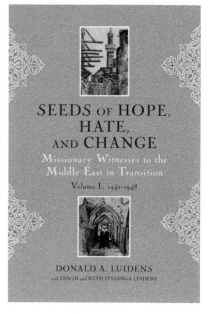

Luidens was born to his missionary parents, Ruth and Ed Luidens, in Bahrain. He subsequently lived with them in Iraq and Lebanon and attended boarding school in southern India. This rich background enlivened his interest in the world's treasury of contrasting cultures and led to a career as a sociologist of religion. A 1969 graduate of Hope College, he earned an MDiv from Princeton Theological Seminary in 1972 and both an MA and PhD in sociology from Rutgers University (1974, 1978). He served on the faculty of Hope College from 1977 to 2014. He held a visiting research fellowship at the institute in 2014-15, became a senior research fellow in January 2016, and has served as director of the institute since 2019.

The Missionary Memoirs Series
By Donald A. Luidens

The Great Missionary Movement of the nineteenth and twentieth centuries was one dimension of a world on the move. With advances in transportation and communication, millions of folks uprooted themselves and sought new lands and opportunities. Cultures collided and interacted in unprecedented ways, sometimes benevolently and at other times more tragically.

Joining this cavalcade of travelers, Christian missionaries ventured forth from Europe and North America into, what was for them, unknown lands. For the glory of God and the salvation of countless souls, these intrepid believers planted themselves in new soil, sharing the seeds of the Good News with all who would listen. Their encounters with new peoples, new religions, and new ways of doing things would transform their host countries as well as themselves. Moreover, when the missionaries returned "home," they would likewise transform their native countries.

Narratives of these extraordinary people are rich in accounts of this transformative process, often deeply personal and told with fulsome detail and complex texture. Drawing on diaries, memoirs, letters, and other contemporary documents, the authors in this series will bring to life particular times and places, stories that enliven all times and places. They stand as vibrant spiritual testimonies, as well as unique anthropological records, and are well worth preserving for future generations.

Preface

Margaret Doorenbos begins her story in 1965 when her family arrived on the little desert island of Bahrain. I remember well the moment the Doorenbos family joined the Arabian Mission,[1] in what we called "the field."

My family and I were already in the field. Having grown up in the Arabian Mission, I knew that one of our most anticipated events was a new family joining our close-knit mission family. So when the Doorenbos family landed in Bahrain, our whole mission was waiting anxiously at the airport for their middle-of-the-night arrival. I was more interested in meeting the boys—Dirk and Keith —than the parents. Like me, Dirk and Keith would become "mish kids" (missionary kids), sharing the strong bond—like brothers and sisters—we forged among ourselves. I could identify with them and the adventures awaiting them. Like me, they were destined to grow up in exotic lands, learn other languages, become bilingual, spend years away from their parents at boarding school in India, go to Hope College, and forever be aware of the unusual life they were afforded. But I looked forward to meeting Margaret

---

[1] The Arabian Mission of the Reformed Church in America began in 1889 and established mission stations in Iraq (at Basrah and Amarah), Bahrain, Kuwait, and Oman (at Muscat and Mutrah).

and Harvey, as well, and we youngsters immediately called them aunt and uncle, as we did with all the other missionary parents.

The lives of the Doorenboses and Heusinkvelds became closely intertwined as we shared the kinship that missionaries develop. My father and Harvey were professional colleagues and assigned to the same mission stations (Bahrain and Oman). In addition, my father oversaw the Arabic language school that Margaret and Harvey attended, and our families both vacationed in Kodaikanal, India, where we mish kids went to school.

The definition of an adventure—exciting, unusual, and typically hazardous—fits missionary life well, and Margaret has done a superb job of capturing those conditions. She accurately portrays life in the Arabian Mission: the struggles facing missionary kids; the pain of sending children off to boarding school; the challenge of learning Arabic; the exhilaration of a life of purpose; the pleasure of being part of the great missionary movement and philanthropic service to our fellow humans; the camaraderie of the missionary community; the sadness of long separations from family and relatives; the anxiety of having our lives severely impacted by political turmoil and revolutions; the apprehension associated with being forced to leave a country we had called home; the joy of seeing God's grace at work; the awakening realization of the inherent value of every life; the wonder of witnessing nations advancing from the Middle Ages into the twentieth century; the trial of having limited contact with individuals from one's own cultural heritage; the daily challenge of being immersed in another culture; the witness, firsthand, of having an impact on people in dire need; the struggle of sometimes having no clear answers for dealing with strange situations in different cultures and languages and religions; the reward of saving thousands of lives; the growing understanding that one is desperately needed, while at the same time regarded with ambivalence; the wonder of venturing into the unknown; the gratitude of seeing lives transformed by healthcare and education and spiritual connection; the grim reality of suffering devastating personal tragedies; and the experience of utter joy and celebration in committing and recommitting oneself, throughout one's life, to the wellbeing of others.

For all the deprivations of mission life, one thing we had in abundance was a deep, abiding sense of purpose. And all of this I can relate to very well; Margaret's narration rings true with my own experience at every stage.

In this book, Margaret describes her adventures in refreshingly candid detail, providing authentic views into the missionary lifestyle, giving a flavor of both the mundane day-to-day events, as well as the unusual ones. In her diaries and letters home, she provides a vivid depiction of life in the mission field, and these sources form the backbone of the story that follows. She is a keen observer of a large swath of the recent past in the Middle East and Africa. In her writing, there is history, drama, success, failure, good times and not-so-good times, incredible challenges, and amazement at both the goodness and the darkness that humankind is capable of. This is what life is about.

From my perspective as a mish kid, I can say the missionary life was a good life. Being bilingual, experiencing different cultures and ways of viewing the world, and being brought up by parents committed to the wellbeing of others provided profound insight into the human condition. As Margaret documents, our missionary parents lived philanthropic, purposeful, and mostly contented lives, focused not on material riches but on the riches of mind and soul. For the most part, they lived the type of dedicated, purposeful lives most of us talk about but are too afraid to take the risk of living.

Margaret's frank, from-the-heart, narrative portrays missionaries and mission life as less than perfect. Indeed, the missionaries she and I both knew were far from perfect, and—like all humans—they made mistakes. Nonetheless, I believe what they did right far outweighed their mistakes.

Margaret writes during the closing days of the great missionary era, which I, as a child, assumed was permanent and would never end. In the new world order, the missionary calling has not ended, but its character has changed dramatically; its new form is virtually unrecognizable from what I experienced in my youth. Thus, Margaret's sojourn describes a world of mission that is no more. Her insightful journey into a bygone era informs, entertains, and touches our hearts, minds, and souls.

Margaret takes us into a world parallel to our own, a world mostly unknown from our Western vantage point, where the people of Arabia, Africa, India, and indeed most of humankind reside. By entering this parallel world, we gain understanding, compassion, and respect not only for that world but also for our own. It is a priceless journey.

Having been born into a missionary family, I was aware—from listening and watching the adults—that, to the best of our ability, our work as missionaries was to care for all our neighbors and to make the world a better place. This worldview is elegantly born out in Margaret's story.

Margaret begins her narrative with her family's arrival on the mission field. But what of her family before that? What of Margaret and Harvey's earlier years? What about the formative circumstances that brought them to Arabia? To put her story in context, something must be said of that which led them to the mission field and their life together as missionaries.

Margaret Grace and her identical twin sister, Mary Josephine, were born in Utica, New York, on March 28, 1934.

Margaret's mother, Evelyn DeVries, grew up in Holland, Michigan, and lived in the large, reddish-orange brick house that stood on Twelfth Street between Hope College and Western Theological Seminary.[2] She fell in love with Henry Hospers II, a student at Western Seminary, who later became an ordained pastor in the Reformed Church in America (RCA). Following in his father's footsteps, Henry attended Hope College and Western Seminary and had a distinguished career as a pastor in parishes throughout New York.

Rev. Henry Hospers was pastor of a church in Utica, New York, when their two daughters were born. He and Evelyn had no other children. In 1951 the family moved to Alexandria Bay, New York, where Margaret spent her senior year of high school before enrolling at Hope College in 1952.

Harvey's mother, Florence Kooi, had been a missionary with the Central American Mission in Nicaragua for ten years when she

---

[2] Known as Fried Cottage since 1990, this house was moved to 337 Columbia Avenue in August 2018.

learned that her sister, Edna, who was married to Jacob Doorenbos and had four young children, had passed away. So she left the mission field to help take care of them. She eventually married Jacob, and Harvey Edward Doorenbos was born on November 22, 1933, followed by his younger sister, Polly, making for a family of eight. Harvey grew up on their farm in Morrison, Illinois, with no electricity or running water, but as one of the youngest of six children, he had a happy childhood and was known for his sense of humor. Harvey did well in school and went on to Hope College in 1951 with the intention of becoming a physician.

Evelyn, Henry, Mary (*l*), and Margaret Hospers, 1950

Another of Harvey's goals in college—besides preparing to become a doctor—was to find a spouse. When Margaret arrived at the beginning of his sophomore year, Harvey believed God had led him to her, and they began to date seriously.

After Margaret graduated from Hope College in 1956, she and Harvey had a double wedding on June 21 with her twin sister, Mary, and her new husband Jack DePree. The twins had a shocking surprise on their wedding day when they learned that they had been adopted as infants. Although they had not known this family secret, it was known by others, including Harvey and Jack, who thought it best to tell their new brides on their wedding day.

Harvey and Margaret moved to Chicago, where he was enrolled in Northwestern Medical School. To take care of finances, Margaret taught junior high school classes in Evanston from 1956 to 1959. The couple then moved to Grand Rapids, Michigan, for five years for Harvey's surgical training at Butterworth Hospital.

During this time, Dirk was born in 1959 and Keith in 1962. In 1965 the young family flew to Bahrain to begin their missionary career.

I am fortunate to have had many sources for this book, most notably, forty-five years of Margaret's letters and, for three years, regular meetings with Margaret and Harvey. I also learned much by talking to Margaret and Harvey's family members, colleagues, and friends, including Keith Doorenbos, Maurice and Elinor Heusinkveld, Donald and Eloise Bosch, Jay and Midge Kapenga, Corine Overcamp, Donald Luidens, Paul Armerding, Peter Kapenga, David and Lowey Dickason, Lorraine Sikkink, Thomas Staal, and Timothy Staal. In all of this, my wife, Michelle, has been a coresearcher and editor.

Margaret and Harvey in front of Hope College's Dimnent Chapel at Margaret's 1956 graduation from Hope College

I must give voice of my deep gratitude to Jacob Nyenhuis, Donald Luidens, Donald Bruggink, and JoHannah Smith of the Van Raalte Institute for enabling me to realize my dream and calling of documenting missionary stories.

It has been an honor for Michelle and me to help bring Margaret's inspiring story to life in her own words, using her letters and diaries, and to make it available to a wide readership.

Paul Heusinkveld

CHAPTER 1

To Arabia—Life in Bahrain
1965-1966

Harvey, our two boys—five-year-old Dirk and three-year-old Keith—and I left for Arabia on Sunday, February 21, 1965, from Grand Rapids, Michigan. At 3:20 p.m., some fifty church people and friends came to the airport to see us off, including Dr. and Mrs. Louis Benes, who led the group in prayer. Their daughter, Dorothy Benes Weiss, and her husband, Raymond, were in the Arabian Mission in Bahrain.3 Mrs. Benes gave us Barbie dolls to take to her granddaughters there.

The Doorenbos family at Chicago's O'Hare Airport waiting for their flight to Bahrain, February 21, 1965

At the airport in Chicago, we were surrounded by Harvey's sister, Polly Doorenbos; Mother and Father Doorenbos; Jack and Mary Jo DePree (my twin sister); Dr. Fred Speirs (Harvey's colleague at

---

3 Ray Weiss was the pastor of the Arabian Mission church in Bahrain.

Butterworth Hospital in Grand Rapids), and his wife Carol. We left Chicago on the 5:00 p.m. flight to London, then from London to Rome and on to Beirut, where we joined Dr. Corine Overkamp, also newly appointed to medical work in the Arabian Gulf.

On all five flights, we were in the tail section of the plane. At times, the intense turbulence put my faith to the test that "underneath are the Everlasting arms." If anything, the bouncing around served to remind me that as one's faith is tried and tested, so also one's trust strengthens and rests confidently in Him alone. But lest I take that promised rest for granted, life's little "bounces" were sometimes necessary to rekindle my faith and trust in the Lord and His plan for us. With that in mind, I reflected on my emotions in that moment: Was I let down? lonely? disappointed? Not at all! It was a dream come true for us to be where God had placed us.

The American Mission church in Bahrain, famous
for its clock tower, the first public clock in Bahrain

When we arrived in Bahrain at 10:30 p.m. on Friday, February 26, we were greeted by intense desert heat and the warm fellowship of the whole Arabian Mission, children included. Before leaving us at our new quarters that night, Ray Weiss prayed with us, as his father-in-law had done in Grand Rapids, and included a prayer for those at home who were not "privileged to be here."

Harvey was eager to begin sitting in on the various worship services available through the mission, so he began with the Arabic worship service the next evening, Saturday, at 8:30 p.m. There was also a Sunday morning Arabic service, a morning Sunday school in English, and an afternoon Sunday school in Arabic. The Sabbath day ended with an evening service in English. Most of Saturday, the church was used by different language groups[4] among the expatriate community. The church was a very busy place, offering worship and fellowship in many different languages.

Life in Bahrain

On our first tour of town, we were surprised that cars drove on the left side of the road, even though some had steering wheels on the left side. Men wore suitcoats over long white robes, and women wore a head-to-toe black covering called an *abaya*, with a black cheesecloth veil over their faces and chests. Local Arab women appeared free to be out and about on the streets in this covering. It was a town of many nationalities, including non-Bahraini Arabs and many Europeans.

We missionaries were clustered at the northern end of the island, close to the water, so we could see and smell the salty sea. We settled in a first-floor, two-bedroom apartment in a four-apartment building. Our home was within walking distance of the church, school, and hospital. Our upstairs neighbors were with the British Royal Air Force (RAF),[5] and our other neighbors were both Saudi Arabian couples. The building had a strip of grassless ground in front and in back and was surrounded by a tall concrete wall. The mosques nearby used loudspeakers atop their minarets

---

[4] The Bahrain church has long been home for many congregations with different languages. This is still the case; in 2021 there were eight congregations that spoke Arabic, English, Tagalog, Tamil, Telugu, and Urdu, with over twenty-seven hundred parishioners worshiping at the church.

[5] Bahrain was still a British protectorate.

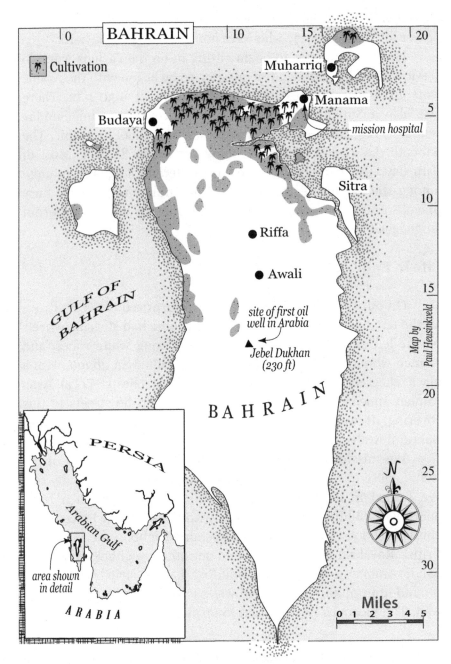

Bahrain Islands, with inset map of the Arabian Gulf
(also known as the Persian Gulf)

for the five daily calls to prayer. The loudspeakers were necessary to be heard over the constant noise of the busy streets below, especially the incessant car horns.

Bahrain is a group of islands, and the largest one is where we lived in the city of Manama, the commercial and international section of the island. The neighboring, second-largest island is Muharraq, where the international airport was located. The greater share of Bahrain's Shiite[6] population lived in communities on this smaller island, accessed by a bridge from the main island. The tension of these two islands was between the Sunni[7] Muslims and the Shiite Muslims. The two sects differed not only religiously but also in their ideas about which government should control the islands. Iran's Shiite government believed it owned Bahrain and the Persian Gulf between the Arabian Peninsula and Iran. Bahrain's Sunnis claimed the islands should be independent, and the gulf should be called the "Arabian Gulf."

The rules of residency were stringent. Bahrain's Iranian population was not allowed to return to Iran or to travel to either Iran or Israel. For expatriates such as ourselves, travel to those two countries required a second passport, without which we could not re-enter the Arabian countries. No Israeli goods or products were allowed into Bahrain, and the government's customs agency was keen to enforce that rule.

Manama is built up along the island's north-northeastern coasts. Sheikh[8] Issa's palace area at that time was mid-island, and farther south was the Bahrain Petroleum Company (BAPCO) settlement of Awali. The sheikh had stables and provided a racetrack for weekly camel and horse races. Sheikh Issa Beach was the closest and best swimming spot and one which expatriate families were invited to.

---

[6] Shia, one of the two main branches of Islam, followed mainly in Iran, rejects the first three (Sunni) caliphs and regards Ali as Muhammad's first true successor.

[7] Sunni, the larger of the two main branches of Islam, differs from Shia in its understanding of the Sunna—traditional Muslim laws based on Muhammad's teachings—and its acceptance of the first three caliphs.

[8] The official title of the ruler when we arrived on 26 Feb. 1965.

There was the British Club for the many company personnel of the RAF, BP Oil and Gas, and various banks and business agencies, as well as government advisors who lived in Awali and Manama towns. We went there occasionally and enjoyed British choral concerts, dinners, and movies by invitation of a club member. The US Navy had access to Bahrain's ports, so there was also a small expatriate group of Americans. The missionaries had a very strong fellowship and a good relationship with the British, but the British had to work hard to develop friendships in the Arab community.

The rest of the island consisted of sand and loose gravel over scrubby rock outcrops. Because the land in the center of the island was mostly nonarable, small villages dotted the shores where date and vegetable gardens did manage to thrive, sustaining life and providing income. There were no lamb, beef, or pork products locally, but goats were common in the villages.

During our first week adjusting to life in Bahrain, Harvey received word from the United States that he had passed his surgical boards and was now a board-certified surgeon. He began performing surgery at the American Mission hospital as the retiring missionary surgeon, Dr. Harold Storm,[9] was packing to leave.

The week we arrived, we had temperatures of eighty degrees at noon and high humidity. Dampness pervaded the house at night, sprouting mold on walls and furnishings and transforming the yard into a morass of mud and slush. Since the water table was so high throughout most of the island, when the boys played in the yard, they could not dig very far down in the dirt before sea water seeped in. A fan overhead in each room and one air conditioner made the apartment more bearable—and this was February. Even with each room's door shut tight, sand and dust somehow always got inside.

---

[9] Dr. Harold Storm, a legend in the mission, was one of the first Westerners to cross the Arabian Peninsula; he knew Abdul Aziz Ibn Saud, the first king of Saudi Arabia, as well as three of the rulers of Bahrain: Sheikh Hamad bin Isa Al-Khalifa, Sheikh Salman bin Hamad Al-Khalifa, and Sheikh Isa bin Salman Al-Khalifa.

We soon learned that the climate was at nearly 100 percent humidity[10] most of the year and over one hundred degrees for eight months of that time. Ice cubes seldom solidified if the freezer door was opened too frequently. When the electricity failed, as it often did, we went without lights, a refrigerator, ceiling fans, hot water, and an air conditioner. The cool cement floor and walls helped to cool us for the first hours of the outage.

Nights saw an invasion of cockroaches in the cupboards, dressers, kitchen, and bathrooms. They arrived via the pipes. Geckos—small lizards that hid behind the furniture, pictures, and mirrors during the day—came out to feast in the darkness. We could hear them as they crunched on the cockroaches—a gratifying, if unpleasant, sound.

Dirk attended Saint Christopher's, a British school adapted to the typical Arab school schedule, Monday to Thursday and again on Saturday. Keith was signed up in a Monday-to-Friday morning preschool program. The missionary fathers who had cars drove the children to their classes. Both of our boys wore school uniforms.

The boys were in school in the morning, but our designated study time for Arabic classes[11] was in the afternoon, a less-than-accommodating arrangement. That meant I would need a cook, babysitter, and housekeeper at the house when we were away. For our cook, we hired an elderly Arab man who had been with American families before. He made the main meal each noon and stayed as late into the evening hours as our appointments required. An Indian man collected our clothes weekly to wash and iron them.

It would be another week before our apartment was furnished and ready for us. Our belongings at the port were being cleared through customs and, once processed, would be unpacked

---

[10] The island of Bahrain lies in the middle of the Arabian Gulf, the warmest sea in the world; thus, it has extremely high humidity and one of the highest average dew points in the world.

[11] The Arabian Mission required new members to take two years of Arabic language training. It was believed that trust between the mission and the Arabs could be achieved only by using their own language.

and moved into the apartment piece by piece from the shipping crate stationed on the mission compound.

The mission women observed the World Day of Prayer at the Anglican church by the boys' school. The service was conducted in English, as well as Arabic, Hindi, and several European languages. It was truly an international service. Different ethnic groups lived in various areas of the city. Our home was in a traditional British area, along one of the main thoroughfares near the hospital. But it no longer housed as many British residents as it did Arab tenants.

The previous British owners of our apartment left a dog behind when they moved, so we inherited a guard dog for our front porch, which, however, meant that no one—friend or foe—could approach without his barking an alarm of warning. Arabs generally do not allow pets in the house, so there was no expectation to bring him in. But our boys, of course, wanted to feed him.

First impressions of Arabia

We had been in our home just two weeks when riots broke out. Restive crowds and hordes of students roamed the streets carrying placards that were strongly pro-Nasser,[12] expressed anger at the loss of oil company jobs to automation, and reflected a strongly anti-Western sentiment. When the riots moved into Manama's busy shopping district, the simmering antiforeigner resentment flared, provoking arson and attacks on shops and people. Schools were forced to close as the gangs went past, encouraging, as they did, even small Arab children to join in on the stone throwing. After one boy was beaten to death and ten people shot outside the hospital's main gate, the police were able to quell the trouble temporarily, but Harvey had his hands full with casualties.

As the rioting resumed for the next two days and the shopping centers remained closed, Harvey spent most afternoons

---

[12] Gamal Nasser, the president of Egypt, was viewed as the champion of Arab nationalism, leading the way to returning the respect to Arab culture, language, and religion that it once held.

and evenings at the hospital, where the dead and wounded were brought. By week's end, church services had mostly resumed, and we could venture out, though few of the British dared to do so. Finally, our boys' schools and any shops that had somehow escaped arson opened again on Monday morning. The Arab schools remained closed as unrest still roiled some areas. No taxis dared be out on the streets and risk getting torched for picking up British passengers, known to use them frequently.

To hedge against suspicion, Harvey took to carrying his medical bag and stethoscope conspicuously as he walked the short distance to the hospital. It was generally understood that the Hippocratic Oath precluded medical personnel from taking political sides, and the availability of doctors might be the difference between life and death for the injured of all persuasions. Harvey performed the first laminectomy ever done at the hospital to remove a bullet in the spine.

All this trouble caused the mission to discuss sending us on to Oman after our two years of language study had finished; the hospital in Bahrain would need a veteran surgeon and director to replace the retiring missionary director.[13] Such demonstrations, as we had experienced up to that point, were not something a newcomer like Harvey should have to handle. The Arabs nicknamed him "the boy" because he looked so young, but he had already made a reputation for himself at the hospital. The Oman hospital would send Dr. Don Bosch, a well-seasoned missionary, to Bahrain.

We had been in Bahrain for one month and had a comfortable home, great fellowship, and had even learned some Arabic words and phrases. Eventually, we were able to move about on the main island, but we knew that disturbances were ongoing on Muharraq Island. The demand was for a representative government that would include more Shiites among the Sunni-dominated ruling class. The Arab primary schools opened again, but sporadic demonstrations continued.

One of the five pillars of Islam is the giving of alms to the poor. Harvey and I, newcomers to the Arab world, walked to the

---

[13] Dr. Harold Storm.

shops in Bahrain one evening. Along the sidewalks were numerous beggars who sat or stood all day to receive alms. A blind man held his hand out, and I dropped in a coin. Immediately, I was surrounded by street children, pulling at my arms and clothes, shouting for coins, and jostling me roughly. A shopkeeper saw the incident unfold and called us into his store. I was quite shaken, and we left only after the youths had gotten bored of waiting and dispersed, which seemed an eternity. My immediate reaction was "Never again!"

Upon reflection on the incident, I realized that I had experienced several distinct reactions: fear for my personal safety, which raised my need to put up "safety" measures to protect myself; overwhelming guilt about my riches in comparison to their poverty; a realization that I had shifted into a blind mode, which had blocked my vision and created an instant indifference to the poor; and a total misunderstanding of the situation. It took me a while to realize that my reactions were natural, and they became less pronounced as we gained experience.

In Bahrain we lived in a ground-level apartment on a street that led to a cinema. Every evening, our low front wall provided a back rest for beggars sitting on the sidewalk. They waited for returning moviegoers passing by after the evening's film, men who perhaps felt pangs of guilt because of the unwholesome dramas they had just watched. Their coins of atonement provided a decent income for many beggars.

One evening, I decided to give three Christmas oranges to a woman and her two children sitting nearest my gate. No sooner had I returned to the house than a man, presumably the head of that family, jumped up from his spot and snatched the oranges from all three of them. In anger, I went out and again gave the mother and her children some oranges. Casting a brief glare at the man, I stood by to watch them eat, which they did hurriedly on the spot. How does one learn to whom and when to give?

Two Arab brothers and their mother were the only Bahraini Christians in the congregation. The men's wives were both from Jordan. One brother was blind and inspired us with his preaching in the Arabic worship service from time to time. His oldest son read the Scripture and the liturgy passages for the sermon he preached. The other brother was our hospital administrator.

On Sunday evenings, Harvey's anesthetist, John Peter, from Katpadi, India, would join us for supper and then the English service afterward. Some of the single RAF men would come for afternoon tea, stay for supper, and then go to that service. They appreciated our hospitality and our home, with its comfort of little civilities and the warm familiarity of family life.

Work in Bahrain

We were in Bahrain to learn language skills, so we were not, ostensibly, to be assigned work. But with Dr. Storm retiring, Harvey was called in for surgery. He also filled in as the chief medical officer of the hospital, responsible for hospital meetings and for acting as head of the hospital at times of calling in the community for holidays and funerals.

Harvey was heavily involved with patients in surgery at the time of the riots. Most of the young men shot by police were brought to the American Mission Hospital by friends who had changed the rioters' names to hide their identity. The victim's friends stood by anxiously in the operating room, attentive and quietly menacing, to make sure the patient, in the throes of pain, did not inadvertently give away his real name or any other information.

Harvey also had to assist in a vaccination campaign to hold a cholera outbreak in check. The disease was apparently brought in by a traveler from Iran. The lack of enough vaccine made that project a great concern for the appointed team.

So, Harvey and our third Arabic-class member, Dr. Corine Overkamp, were deeply involved in hospital work and found it hard to find time for Arabic study. We were studying classical Arabic and learning local usage as well. We also had to learn to read and write the Arabic alphabet. The language is written from right to left, and books are read beginning from the back (as we describe it) to the front. On days of rioting, the boys and I stayed inside, so no classes took place for any of us.

The American Mission Hospital (AMH) in Bahrain, the first
hospital in the country, celebrating a century of service,
2003

Harvey's first case at the hospital was a baby with a
congenital abnormality. Harvey sent the baby to the government
hospital, where it died. The next case was advanced, inoperable
cancer. He also saw and treated a boy slashed across his chest; a
mother of seven who, he determined, had died from a botched
abortion; and an appendix patient, on whom he successfully
operated. Later, he assisted the newly employed Indian surgeon
with our son Keith's tonsillectomy.

I did not teach in Bahrain, but I enjoyed visits to the mission
girls' school when I found time. There were Jewish,[14] Arab, and
Indian children in that school; the youngest classes even allowed
some boys to attend. The medium of education was both Arabic
and English, from kindergarten to sixth grade. The standards of
the school were very high, and the pupils' results on national
exams were excellent.

---

[14] There was an ancient community of Jews in Bahrain (there were many
similar communities throughout the Arab World). Jews were accepted as
an integral, sectarian part of Arab society. As testament to this history, a
Jewish synagogue still stands in Manama, Bahrain. It was only
subsequent to the creation of Israel in 1948—and the expulsion of Arabs
from Palestine—that animosity between Arabs and Jews began.

Arab etiquette and customs

The Arab mindset is different from ours; their life ethics are from ancient times and less changeable than the ethics that we follow today and throw away tomorrow. They follow rigid ways of thinking and rules of etiquette. We learned not to make inexcusable mistakes, such as showing the soles of our feet (or shoes) to another's face, or mentioning a dog or a donkey without saying "excuse me" in the same breath, or even calling a child or an adult an animal name to characterize him or her.[15] The left hand is never used for handshakes, for passing an item to another, or for writing and eating purposes; it is the designated hand for personal hygiene after one's daily constitutional.[16] One may not leave a home visit without first having had coffee and sweets; to do so is tantamount to spurning the host's hospitality, a serious offense.

On the other hand, there are acceptable practices that would raise eyebrows in Western society, such as belching loudly after a meal to show one's satisfaction, the practice of men walking together hand-in-hand, and the habit of men going ahead of women or being attended to first. No proper adult male goes outside without covering his body from shoulders to knees or ankles. Males are very much out and about in public life, whereas mature females have stricter rules about staying inside and wearing the black cloak and veil when outside. This latter custom protects a young woman from being spoken to or approached in public, assuring her good reputation remains beyond reproach for marriage. Men and servants do the shopping and errands, while women stay at home.

Islamic law allows for up to four wives, which works well in rural areas, where labor is needed in the fields, but in the city, one needs a large home and much money for two or more wives and their offspring. It is not uncommon for an older man to take a

---

[15] There was one exception: "That woman is as slow as a mule."
[16] Islamic law punishment of thievery is cutting off the right hand, further adding to the punishment by forcing the offenders to use the unclean hand to do everything for the remainder of their lives and thus forever marking them as a thief.

teenage bride later in life and—contrary to the expectation of jealousy and struggle for supremacy—the previous wife or wives often appreciate the newcomer, who is expected to take over childbearing, field work, and housework, while the first wife relaxes and rules the harem.[17]

All children receive a given name at birth, plus their father's first name as their last name. Upon marriage, a girl does not assume her husband's family name as we do. In earlier years, very few children knew the date of their birth, but that changed with more schooling and as governmental censuses made documentation of citizens a requirement. Parents arrange for marriage, typically between first cousins or within the larger family circle. Children go to a school with their gender group, so promised teenage girls are seldom seen by prospective husbands.

Royal Arabian hospitality

The ruler of Bahrain, Sheikh Issa, invited all medical personnel on the island (mission, government, and oil company) to his palace to honor the soon-to-retire Dr. Storm. The whole mission group was invited for the occasion, but no Arabian women attended, not even the sheikh's wives.

At our arrival, we were greeted by one of the lesser sheikhs and ushered into a very large sitting room. Many guests were already seated on ornate banquettes lining both sides of the walls running the full length of the room, at the head of which Sheikh Issa and Dr. Storm were regally installed.

After all the guests had arrived and were seated, the signal was given for everyone to begin the procession forward to greet the sheikh and his guest of honor. We shook hands with them and then went to our seats. Servants came with huge coffee pots to fill our small, handleless cups with Arabian coffee. When the sheikh and Dr. Storm rose, guards and then guests followed them across the courtyard to the dining room. At the entrance, we washed our

---

[17] In Arab society, the part of the house reserved for wives, other women, and young children.

hands in the streams of water poured from golden pitchers into golden basins held by a line of servants with towels on their arms.

The dining tables extended one hundred feet down the center of the room. They were so loaded with food that the tablecloths barely showed. Down the center of the tables were eight circular silver platters with a whole lamb on each (including the head with eyes and teeth still intact). The sheikh gave the honored guest a lamb's eyeball, considered a great delicacy. The servants would just pull at the tender meat to put hunks on each person's plate.

To begin our meal, we were served individual bowls of soup with eggs stirred in. Before each guest were large platters of rice, one for each person. Half of the male guests ate with their fingers; the rest of us used forks. There were platters with whole chickens on them. Before I could protest, there were four kinds of meat on my plate. There were salads and highly spiced vegetable dishes and trays of watermelon slices, mangoes, pears, apricots, black cherries, and individual tapioca puddings and rice puddings in crystal dishes.

One worried more about how to politely leave the uneaten food than how to eat all of it. But no worry. When the sheikh was finished, the guests were also finished, like it or not. We stopped eating in the middle of a plateful and began dessert when he did. Then he rose to give a speech to the honored guest. In his speech, he mentioned that the mission had come to Bahrain not for its oil but for the welfare of its people.[18] A gift of gold was given to Dr. Storm, and then the sheikh left the room. We followed, washing our hands again in the water held by the line of servants outside the door.

In the courtyard were many lesser sheikhs waiting for their turn in the dining room. Women and children would then have their seating, followed at last by the servants. Generous amounts of food that remained went outside the compound walls, where beggars sat in anticipation of a good meal; nothing was wasted.

---

[18] The RCA missionaries came six decades before oil was discovered in the Arabian Peninsula. Virtually all other Westerners came after—and to gain from—the oil discoveries.

Once again, we sat in the large meeting hall to receive after-dinner coffee. Then we walked around greeting people, including the sheikh's uncles and male cousins who were his advisors. His rooms were cool, being air conditioned, so some of the foreign ladies brought stoles with them.

The sheikh was a very pleasant host. On Muslim holidays, the expected custom is that the men of the mission first greet the sheikh and his retinue at the palace before making other calls. Meanwhile, the women also go as a group to the favorite wife's palace first and then to visit lesser royal women. The whole day is spent calling.

Desert retreat

The Christians of Bahrain—Arab and Indian nationals, plus the missionary personnel—held a retreat along the shore of the Arabian Gulf at the lower part of the island. It was an overnight trip for the youth and the families of the church. We left after the noon meal in six cars and a large truck loaded with tents, cooking gear, sleeping gear, and other items for comfort. Taken along into the desert were dressed chickens and goats, rice, bread, and whatever else was needed to feed thirty-five adults and ten children three meals. Two tents were set up for women, two for men, and one extra for personal use a distance away and downwind.

Meals were prepared over an open fire, for which wood had been brought along. Being novices at Bedouin life, we let the potatoes for the evening meal burn instead of roast in the fire, the chicken was either charred to a crisp or raw (sometimes both), and all attempts to light the lanterns for the evening meeting were unsuccessful.

The purpose of the retreat was not purely for fun. The first group meditation was presented after the evening meal. When the children went to bed, the adults continued discussions into the morning hours. I had guard duty from midnight to 3:00 a.m. to keep a lookout for serious and potential enemies, namely, one tiny lizard who ignored my shout to halt as he approached the edge of our tent city.

After morning meditations and talks, individuals and small groups sought separate places to think through what they had heard and to meditate on God's Word. Earlier, the men had begun a fire in two pits and set two goats turning on spits over the fire. The men oversaw rotating the spits throughout the morning. Along with roasted goat, we ate Arabian-style rice with raisins, salad, and canned peas.

Rest, recreation, and singing followed the noon meal. There were volleyball games, and our boys gathered up many starfish from the beach. At four o'clock, the tents were rolled up and loaded onto the trucks for the trip back to our comfortable homes. We came home quite red from the sun and very thirsty after all our activity but delighted with the spiritual and social time together with our church family.

Visits to Bahraini homes

Join us now as Harvey and I visit two Arab homes. Our first call is at the home of Lateefa and Abdul Rahman. We will go by car to their village down the island a distance. Harvey must be attentive as he drives so as not to hit the goats wandering in the streets. Children gather at the well with the women; they enjoy saying, "Hello" to foreigners that seldom pass this way. The local women carefully cover their faces with their loose headcloths because there are men they do not know in our group. This village has recently received electricity, so the homes have lamps instead of lanterns.

Now we are standing at the third wooden door in a compound's long and high stone wall. No numbers or names are posted on the houses, but having been here before, we know which door we want. The family is expecting us; it is impolite not to give notice to the hosts when you are planning to call. Abdul Rahman, wearing a clean, white *dishdasha*[19] and checkered head cloth, greets us in good English. He was taught English by the oil company for which he works. His job enables him to afford such

[19] Also called a *thobe*, an ankle-length, long-sleeved garment, usually white, worn by men.

luxuries as a sofa and a bed in his sitting room, a radio, and even a car outside. He invites us in through a gate in the wall and leads us across a gravel courtyard to his small house. We women cannot follow the men to the sitting room; we follow a daughter to the women's quarters.

We remove our shoes, as our hosts have done, before entering the room. The interior is bare, except for hooks on the wall; some open shelves with bedrolls on them; straw mats on the floor, on which we sit cross-legged; and pillows—their nighttime pillows—placed against the wall for us to lean on.

Lateefa cannot speak English, so we speak slowly in Arabic so she will speak slowly for us. Her Arabic is colloquial, not classical, since she never went to school to learn to read or write. She says she is fine, her husband is fine, her children are fine, and she asks after our health. Then she mentions that she still coughs occasionally from the operation that Dr. Harvey did for her last month. He will take time to check her throat as we leave later. She is not wearing her black cloak—her *abaya*—but rather, a multicolored housedress, under which are white cotton trousers. A thin, mask-like veil (common among some Arab women), however, will remain on, for there are men present in the other room.

She sets before us a generous tray of oranges, mangoes, nuts, toffees, and dates. She has already sent the men a similar tray. We take care to use only our right hand to eat. Tiny, handleless china coffee cups are brought forth, along with a bowl of water, used as a finger bowl after we have eaten the fruit. Very hot and bitter coffee comes from the kitchen across the courtyard. Lateefa's stove consists of a metal plate across the top of three large stones that encircle the flames. Her pots and pans hang on several sticks pushed into the sandy floor. Since she lives near the sea, she has no need for a sink. She buys her daily bread from the local oven, which bakes for the whole area. Our hostess comes around to refill our coffee. If you do not care for more than those first sips, lightly waggle the cup back and forth to signal that no more is desired. This lets her know you are finished, and she can move on to another guest who has not had a coffee refill yet.

Now that coffee has been served, we may leave. When rising, be mindful not to frighten the goat that has been sleeping nearby or step on the chicken in the doorway. As Lateefa shakes our hands, her many bracelets jingle. They are gold and constitute the family's "bank." She pities those of us with only one ring on our hand and no holes in our ears for gold earrings.

All the little children who have been peeking in the open doorway now step forward to shake hands too. Our hosts have eight children in school and a fourteen-year-old daughter who will marry when all the parents' arrangements are agreed upon. Returning to the car while Harvey and Abdul Rahman check the wife's throat concern, we cannot help but comment on the happy, hospitable people we have just visited. We have honored their home, and they show us their appreciation by giving us their daily gathering of eggs to take with us. We leave behind us a typical Muslim family in an Arabian village.

Next, we shall call on our neighbors, Ahmed and Beszima, who live in our apartment building. Ahmed owns a large shop in the marketplace and speaks English well, for he attended a Lebanese secondary school and received his college training at the American University in Beirut. He wears a dishdasha to work but Western-style clothes at home. Beszima is with her husband at the door to greet us. She wears a short skirt and much make-up, looking like a typical American teenager, which, in fact, she is. They were married when she completed sixth grade in a Saudi Arabian village school, where English was not taught. She is, however, taking private lessons and beginning to understand much of our dialogue.

As we sit in their living room—a room like many in the United States—she serves a cold drink and joins us in conversation. She does not allow her servant woman to wash her Western dishes or to serve Western guests. Later, as she passes the chocolates, we know that coffee is coming. To the Arabs, sweets seem to be necessary before drinking a small cup of the bitter coffee. Bedouins often serve dates as a sweet, but in the city, store-bought desserts and sweets are considered the best.

Beszima has just finished fasting for a month during the daytime hours as the Muslims do, but Ahmed did not join her, for he has rejected both the Muslim and Christian teachings of his Lebanese schooling. The smell from the kitchen is spaghetti sauce with strong spices, a mixture of Western and Eastern tastes. Beszima spends much of her day shopping and visiting, always being careful to wear the black abaya in public, although she does not wear the veil. Aha! This coffee tastes weak! It is our Western, imported brand, rather than their strong, local beans. With the coffee served, she turns on the television, with its Arabic soundtrack, and we move toward the door to leave this home with its very Western-oriented lifestyle, which is replacing the Arab culture in many homes where there are young people.

These are just two of the many couples we have befriended. They are not Christians; in fact, the wives may never have heard the Gospel unless from the Beirut radio station. What they understand of our religion may be the "serious errors" they have been taught as children in their Muslim schools. As we continue our Arabic study, we pray for the day we can say, "The Lord God has given me the tongue of the learned that I may speak a word in season" (Isaiah 50:4).

A Bahrain wedding

At nine o'clock that evening, we went to a wedding. A man, who once was very active in the church but then returned to Islam, had previously married off two of his girls to Muslims. He had even trained one Christian man to return to Islam until he was ready to marry his oldest daughter. The other Christian daughter and son-in-law seldom attended the Muscat church, where the father-of-the-bride had moved from. This wedding was of the youngest daughter who was to marry a cousin of her own choosing, which is unusual since it is usually the parents that choose and not the bride.

The men sat with the groom, while we women went to the bride's house, decorated outside with strings of bright, Christmas-style lights. Meeting us at the door, the father led us to the second floor, where the bride sat in one of the rooms. We sat with the bride and her mother for an hour. Typically, the bride sits for three nights in a row in her beautiful, white, Western-style wedding dress and veil. She was heavily made-up and bejeweled; the palms of her hands and soles of her feet were painted with henna. We greeted her, but she did not smile because the bride must appear demure and pensive. She was very attractive and just fifteen.

Her sisters and sisters-in-law brought sweets, nuts, and drinks to us from time to time. Outside, the courtyard was filled with five drummers who would have also danced if space had allowed. The wedding contract had been signed at the time of engagement. We rose to leave at ten o'clock that evening when the bride began to prepare to go downstairs and be led to the groom's father's house, where more activities were occurring. This couple would not participate in them but would soon retire together for the first time. She had seen her husband before, but most brides have not until this third night of activities. Unless her husband had wealth of his own, they would make one room in his father's house their home.

In the city, contraceptives were known about and used by educated couples. When visiting the local women, we foreign women were frequently asked why we were not pregnant.

There is no such thing as privacy here. In their households of extended family members, privacy is not possible, except for the strict division of boys' and girls' areas.

Christian holy day observed in Bahrain

Our first Christmas in Arabia was in Bahrain, where our shipped household goods included decorations and gifts for the boys. We enjoyed the season quite as we would in America—minus the snow but with the cold. A north wind blew over the island, strong enough to put us into woolen suits and sweaters. Houses in Bahrain had no central heating—whatever the outside temperature, it was only slightly warmer inside. To warm a room, which might be only in the high fifties, a portable electric heater was moved from room to room to temporarily abate the chill.

Christmas was the same day as the birthday of Bahrain's ruler, Sheikh Issa, so many Muslim homes were strung with colored lights and decorations in honor of his birthday. We learned from our British neighbors that wreaths signify a death in the home, so the wreath on our front door was grim and unsettling to them—a spray of artificial greens would have been more befitting. Members of our Arabic-speaking congregation called on each other and brought gifts. I made homemade bread for each home we visited, later learning it was not highly appreciated. A store-bought present represents expensive giving, or maybe even a foreign item for the novelty, but handmade items were apparently considered "cheap" gifts. Besides, the recipients could check on the price of store-bought gifts.

Muslims called on Christians the day after Christmas (the British "Boxing Day") to honor their shared belief in Jesus' immaculate birth. Our menfolk sat together in one place, while the women joined together to receive visitors elsewhere. Sweets and coffee were served at every stop. Our Western practice of sending cards was not observed—it implied one did not intend to visit. On the other hand, the Arabs were caught up in our commercial habit of exchanging gifts with families and friends. Shops were decorated and busy before Christmas, but most of them closed on the holiday itself and on Boxing Day.

The Bahrain Petroleum Company (BAPCO) had a choir group that performed Handel's *Messiah* that year, and any other interested singers also joined the choir. The English-speaking congregation of many nationalities organized caroling groups for the hospital and the homes where Arab Christians lived. On Christmas Day, the church chimes rang for an hour.

We enjoyed Western cultural events, as well as diverse Asian cultural affairs in cosmopolitan Bahrain. At Easter the whole international Christian community from many language groups celebrated together at an outside sunrise service on the mission compound's tennis court. The cold winds of Christmas were now replaced by rising temperatures and high humidity. After the service, we had a breakfast together in the meeting hall. For Christians to call on each other was expected for Easter, but on this holiday, no Muslim took part in making or receiving a visit, for the cross and subsequent Easter events were not part of Muslim belief. Easter night we enjoyed an Easter cantata sung by our choir at the English-speaking service.

Visiting the Sultanate of Oman, October 1965

In October 1965, we took a three-week vacation from language study to visit Oman. Our first impression of Oman was the beauty of the country, with its dramatic seacoast and bare lava mountains. The women were dressed in brilliant colors, and everyone was so very hospitable. The mission family there was a closely knit group from several countries.

But soon, many frustrations began. The challenge of living in a very different culture cannot be ignored. It was very hot in Oman, although, mercifully, it was not the humid heat of Bahrain. We sweat profusely in the dry heat without even realizing it.

Drinking plenty of water was essential, but obtaining it presented its own frustration. The water came from a well, carried by a woman into the house in a large oil tin on her head. It needed to be strained, boiled, cooled, and refrigerated before drinking it was possible. The refrigerator was fueled by kerosene, which smelled and gave off smoke. Turning up the wick caused the walls to blacken from the smoke. Turning it down too much often meant snuffing out the wick entirely. In the summer, the refrigerator never got cold enough to make ice cubes. One morning, the kerosene ran out, and there was no extra in the house. Because women do not go out to do the shopping, I had to wait until Harvey came home from the hospital before new kerosene could be bought and the box refilled.

One of the missionaries brought an old tin box fashioned to fit over two of the stove's four kerosene burners as a makeshift stovetop oven so I could bake bread. But there was no white flour in the bazaar, and the Indian flour that was available would not rise with the yeast. The boys soon tired of eating the Arab bread that must be bought three times daily because it dried out between meals, and I came to understand why every foreign housewife had a helper in the kitchen.

In a letter home, I observed: "It's so hot that Dirk isn't very cooperative for his lessons, and Keith wants him to play. I can't expect the boys to be still all day, so we go walking. That means I must put on hot cotton trousers under my long skirt. Men stare if we go near the bazaar and merchants ask me where my cook is."

Since only men went to the bazaar, and it was assumed that all Westerners were wealthy, for a white woman to do the shopping instead of her cook was particularly confounding. Local women seldom went out in public and certainly never without donning their abaya and veil. But in their own neighborhoods, women went about wearing just a large colored shawl over their heads and shoulders, without the veil.

There was only one small Indian-run store with foreign canned goods. There were no frozen goods since electricity was erratic in the few places it was available. Fruits and vegetables on the stands dried out quickly in the sun and heat. Eggs were pullet size; butter and powdered milk came in tins. There were no tea bags, only loose tea leaves. Beef was butchered once a week according to Muslim ritual[20] and was very tough. And, oh, the flies! Returning from our walk, we almost ran into a man relieving himself[21] against the wall of our compound.

Some missionary families were happily preparing their homes for their children's return from boarding school in India. I could not imagine how they had managed the ten months of separation, yet they appeared to accept it. I prayed that I would be prepared for such a parting when it was time for Dirk and Keith to go.

Local children came to visit on the porch, bringing strong odors with them, as well as swarms of flies. Almost all the girls toted younger siblings. These girls had a hole in each nostril and each ear lobe for wearing gold when they were older. For now, the holes were kept open with strings. The children watched my boys playing soccer but did not join them since they did not understand what the boys were doing. We bought a ball for group activity with them.

One morning, I woke up to find the bar of soap I had put out our first night had disappeared. We had had visitors in the night— rats. Housekeeping with all the dust and sand was a challenge. Life in Oman was necessarily at a different pace. An afternoon nap

---

[20] Animals were butchered as prescribed by Islamic law: *Halal* is similar to kosher butchering practices.
[21] A common sight since there are no public bathrooms.

with a ceiling fan whirling overhead was a must. At night, we slept on cots on the flat roof inside a screened cage, hoping to catch a late-night breeze from the sea. We carried up a circulating table fan to use when the hospital did not need to use it for babies in incubators. Both boys developed heat rash, which made them restless. I kept repeating, "I have learned to be content in whatever state I am." But in reality, I was not learning it very quickly. I was, after all, a city girl not used to camp-style living. I was ready to go back to Bahrain on the next flight, but Harvey was truly enjoying the work in Oman.

The missionaries' weekly relaxation was a trip to Oman's spectacular beaches in the late afternoon, when the sun was low in the sky. We took a picnic with us to enjoy after swimming, while we relaxed and shared stories of the week. We women often swam with dresses over our bathing suits, unless we were inside the private grounds of Oman's Petroleum Development Company. The afternoon away from work offered an escape from the frustrations of daily life but never an escape from the heat. One missionary said, "It gets so hot, I'd just like to push aside the mountains!" The mountains surrounding Muscat absorbed the heat all day and then radiated it back onto the town through the night.

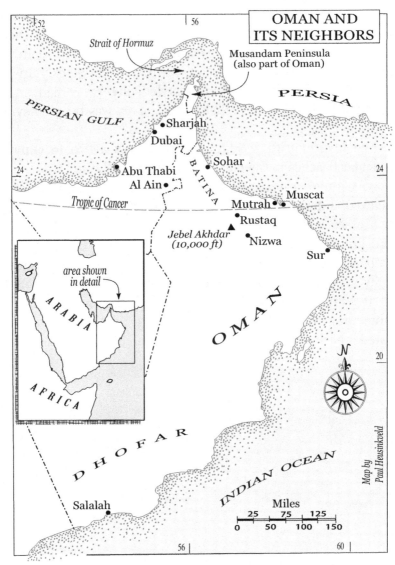

Oman, with inset map of the Arabian Peninsula

CHAPTER 2

Oman
1966-1974

In July 1966, we finished one-and-a-half years of language study; took a three-week vacation in Jerusalem with the Van Etten family; drove over sand dunes to visit the Blosser family in Buraimi, UAE;[22] and arrived in the Sultanate of Oman and our home in Mutrah.

Our hostel in Jerusalem was in the Arab section, enabling us to walk down a commercial street and practice our Arabic with the merchants—who wanted to speak only English. We limited our touring of the West Bank, and we could not go into the Israeli portion of Jerusalem.[23] Nonetheless, we visited Bethlehem, Jericho, the Dead Sea, and Petra. In 1966 this area was not busy with tourists; we thoroughly enjoyed walking where Jesus walked, and we reveled in the respite of a cooler climate for a few days. Being in the Holy Land was an inspiration and privilege. Our Jerusalem vacation remains a cherished memory.

After a brief return to Bahrain and a subsequent flight to the UAE, we drove five hours by truck over sand dunes, bringing us to Buraimi Oasis, where the Oasis Hospital stood tall amidst a village

---

[22] United Arab Emirates.
[23] Until 1967 a wall separated the West Bank (formally part of Jordan) and Israel. The wall ran through the middle of Jerusalem.

Margaret, Dirk, Keith, and Harvey
in Jerusalem, summer 1966

of mostly date-stick huts. The Evangelical Alliance Mission (TEAM) had established a clinic in Buraimi some twenty years earlier. It was staffed by two nurses, with the goal of providing safe maternity care to women in that remote part of Abu Dhabi. It grew steadily, and by the time of our visit, from forty to fifty general outpatients were being seen daily, and many deliveries were being assisted monthly. Some foreign workers there had studied Arabic with us at the mission language center in Bahrain. We developed a close relationship with the Blossers during our language studies and wanted to see them again. Because of the remoteness of Buraimi, they had little contact with native English speakers. Christian brothers and sisters are choice visitors in situations like that.

On our only full day with the Blosser family, we toured the hospital and the few shops that made up the town center. Because Buraimi was near the border with Oman, Harvey went to greet the sheikh of the nearest Omani village across that border. The next morning was our travel day again, but Harvey first tended a surgical case at three o'clock in the morning to remove a bullet from a man brought to the hospital. Retracing our sand-dune travel, we drove the twenty miles back to the airstrip at Abu Dhabi.

Abu Dhabi's "airport" consisted of a date-stick shelter with a Land Rover as an office. Boarding our small (10-seater), four-engine, Gulf Air airplane, the DeHavilland Heron, we flew low over sand dunes for about twenty minutes to arrive at a dirt airstrip near Dubai. Dubai's airport was more sophisticated, with an actual building for an office and a man selling dates and Coca Cola. The plane stopped in each of these villages for about thirty minutes to either offload or load mail, diplomatic pouches, and passengers. These flights—Bahrain to Muscat with stops in between—went twice weekly.

Arriving in Mutrah at five o'clock, we were warmly welcomed with a tea hosted by hospital workers, local Christians, and missionaries. That evening, we settled into our new home with our belongings, which had arrived with us and also by boat. Harvey again had a surgical case to remove a bullet, which made for two identical operations done in two different countries on the same day. His new work had begun.

Mutrah mission hospital

The American Mission Hospital in Mutrah was the only general hospital for the cities of Mutrah and Muscat[24] and for the people from the interior of the country. Muscat had a mission hospital for women's obstetrics, but cases for surgery were sent over the mountain road to Mutrah. The oil company built and staffed its own hospital for its expatriate people and its local employees. There were four doctors at that hospital; the mission hospital had two surgeons and two internists, with a female doctor, Dr. Alice Vanderzwaag, at the Muscat hospital. Development offers by outsiders to improve public health were rejected.

Harvey did surgical rounds on patients daily and sat in outpatient clinic two days per week, seeing any patients who came, and he performed surgeries three days per week and Saturday mornings. There was also occasional all-day duty or filling in for absent doctors. Harvey's work hours were usually from 6:30 a.m. to 12:30 p.m. and from 3:00 p.m. to 5:00 p.m., with sometimes an hour more or an hour less on each end of the day, depending on the season. Harvey said he was uncomfortable with what little he knew of treating tropical diseases, but he soon learned to recognize malaria due to its prevalence. Mercifully, malaria is one

---

[24] The twin cities of Muscat and Mutrah are separated by a mountain range. A winding road connected the cities, but its passages were often precarious due to all manner of traffic, from camels to handcarts to buses.

The mission compound in Mutrah—the hospital (*large building left of center*) was the first one in the country. The Doorenbos house is the large building to the right. The *burastis* (palm-frond houses) in the foreground were typical dwellings for Omanis. Between the mission compound and the *burastis* was a wadi (a dry riverbed that turned into a gushing river when it rains), used as a road.

tropical disease our family never had, probably thanks to taking a weekly prophylaxis pill throughout our time abroad.

The hospital was like a hotel: a family would bring a patient and stay with him or her for the duration of their treatment. There was an open room off the courtyard where women could prepare hot meals for the patients, though many just made their fires in the courtyard. A woman and her child or children would sleep under the patient's bed, while men liked to sleep on the flat, open concrete roof above the outpatient rooms. When beds in the hospital were full, new patients would be put on mats in the courtyard, their admission card reading "under tree one." Sometimes an IV bottle would be hung from the branch of a tree for the patient. One child awaiting a tonsillectomy was placed in the kitchen for lack of another spot.

The arrival of a sheikh with his entourage of servants, wives, siblings, guests, and children demanded that we hurriedly provide two private rooms for them. While they were in town, they would entertain visitors, do their shopping, and enjoy their "vacation" time.

Once, a couple brought a child who needed cleft-lip surgery. Harvey explained it would be a full week's stay after the repair. They rejected the surgery. The Omani Arab reasoning was that such a deformity would remain "if God wills it," not science.

Harvey watched as a patient in the wards wrote some words of the Koran on the inside of his water bowl. Adding water, he swirled it round the bowl until the ink dissolved into the water. Then he drank his self-made "medicine." It was his back-up remedy in case the hospital treatments did not work.

The polio panic of 1968

Polio struck in August 1968, and an immediate vaccination program became necessary to keep it from becoming an epidemic. One Wednesday, the hospital organized an afternoon of vaccinations with a vaccine ordered from Bahrain, London, and the local British oil camp. Very few people, however, came around. Then, on Thursday morning, four hundred inoculations were given. It took only one death on Wednesday evening, and the community panicked. We continued to have neighborhoods respond, so we had to cable London for more serum. All children under five were getting the vaccine, as well as anyone else who had not received it during a previous outbreak a few years back.

The oil camp realized the infection problem and was now keeping all town people away from their community. They called Harvey and admitted that his call to alert them earlier in the week must have been right. We had been to their camp's beach the day before to swim in the sea; that day, however, Rev. Jim Dunham was not allowed to have a planned afternoon church service at their camp. They did not want public gatherings or outside guests. Harvey hoped they would now help in getting more serum for our needs. It would have to come from London on one of their planes, for the regular Gulf plane was not due again until the next week, and the serum needed to be kept frozen.

By the end of the campaign to vaccinate everyone, over three thousand people had received the injection. But now, the struggle was to get those three thousand to return for the second and third shots, necessary to ensure immunity. The public did not understand why the first round was not sufficient.

Similarly, a blood-donation campaign was initiated to fill the hospital blood bank. The locals, however, believed that giving blood made a person impotent. Therefore, when the US Navy in Bahrain sent a ship to the Mutrah port, the hospital staff invited the sailors for an afternoon of games—pitching horseshoes, ping-pong, badminton, tennis, and indoor games—followed by tea and sweets. Before they left, we asked them each to give a pint of blood for the hospital's blood bank. Our children admired the young men and appreciated a tour of the ship, and the sailors enjoyed a break from their shipboard routine. As in Bahrain, some navy men attended the Sunday evening, English-language service at our mission church in Muscat.

Oman days and daze

Our family went on a trip to a village in the interior of Oman, far from the coastal cities. As our vehicle approached the place, we saw men sitting in the shade of a large tree outside the walled compound of the village. Harvey, our Arab guide, and our boys went to the tree, greeted the men, and asked permission of the sheikh to be on his land. Harvey had his medical kit in hand, for he knew he would be asked to treat any sick men and to leave medicine for the women based on their husbands' descriptions of their ailments.

During this greeting and treatment period, a woman wanted to see me, so she was called from behind the walls to see me while I was still in the car. She came to the car. Looking straight into the radiator grill, she declared, "She's not in there!" I opened my door, left the car, and introduced myself to the little old lady with the poor eyesight—as well as poor knowledge of cars.

I entered a home where several women sat, chatting over their coffee cups, while babies slept nearby with flies landing on their open mouths, sticky eyes, and hands. Despite the implication, the desert is not deserted of insects—especially flies. The women asked me about my family, as I did of theirs. They were surprised I was not wearing gold or silver, exclaiming, "Why! She doesn't even have holes in her ears to wear gold earrings. The poor thing!"

I asked if I could read from David's Psalms, and they readily agreed. When I asked to also read the Gospel, they poked each other, exclaiming loudly, "See! She's a woman of the Book." Together we enjoyed sweets, dates, coffee, and the fragrance of frankincense. When the car horn honked, I excused myself amidst their protests. But they all understood my hasty response to obey when my husband called.

The RCA had been at work in Oman for eighty years when we arrived in 1967. In 1939 they had established a girls' school—from first to sixth grades—to provide education for girls because the only government schooling Oman offered was for boys and only through the sixth grade. There was strong opposition to girls being educated since it was believed they "did not have minds or souls," nor were they allowed out in public as they matured. Obedient young girls had no voice in their futures, determined by their parents. Most villages had outdoor classes in Koran training led by an Imam. There, both boys and girls learned the Koran by rote. Very few learned to actually read the Koran, and fewer still learned to write Arabic, unless they went to Mutrah for regular school.

A different way of life

It was so good to be settled in our home in Oman. But how could I possibly say it was good after writing the negative notes from my visit in the springtime? Because I was now an Omani in my outlook and was content to make it my home. What caused this change in my attitude? I believe it was a renewed commitment and a new challenge that I did not have in the springtime. The challenge was to identify with the people, the work, and the Lord's kingdom here. Knowing their language and their ways helped build strong relationships.

When we first settled in, we identified with the missionary lifestyle and the thought patterns that prevailed in most mission stations at that time. These stations were run by old-school missionaries, in those days considered the unquestioned "experts" of local culture and language. We hoped we would also eventually become experts on the local people, culture, and language. These would be useful skills that would later become requirements of the new paradigm of missionary life. Over the years, however, reality set in, and some of my goals had to be modified.

Missionary life on the compound was reflective of the highest standards of American culture. The American-Christian work ethic prevailed. Church worship and structures were based on Western patterns.

I asked myself, "How did I ever get into such a culture?" It was surely not my choice to be in Oman. But it was my choice to serve the Lord as He led my husband to the mission field. Missionary wives were expected to work in the field alongside their husbands. The wives first learned the language, then we taught our own little ones and eventually sent them off to boarding school in India for an American education and social peer group.

The Arab woman had no choice. She simply lived with the philosophy, "If God wills it." The Christian woman has the choice to know and choose God's will for her life. She can make wise choices because, in trust, she turns to God's wisdom and guidance.

Learning to hear

It was a very hot day. I had scrubbed the floors before preparing the noon meal, and finally, I fed the boys at one o'clock. At two o'clock, Harvey still had not returned from the hospital, and I grew impatient and self-pitying. I was tired and just wanted to eat, shower, and rest.

I looked out our front door toward the hospital to see if he was coming—more honestly—to wish him to come just then. But nothing was stirring in the intense midday heat. Sweating and chafing, I was even more upset when a large transport truck arrived at the hospital entrance. Several men began rearranging the sacks on the back of the truck, then lifted a form, well wrapped in a blanket. Even her face was totally covered. A hospital employee brought out a stretcher to lay her on.

I did not have to wait for Harvey to come home to confirm it: she was a woman who had most likely traveled on the truck bed over rough roads for many hours from the interior of the country. She came because she had been in labor for more than two days, but the baby would not come, and now Harvey was fighting to save at least the mother's life. And she never once cried or moaned.

There I stood at my door with strength and health and the ability to clean my home and bake, and I was thinking, "Lord, what are you trying to say to me? Will I ever hear and learn?"

Muslim holy days

Though we have many holidays in America, two stand out as religious holy days: Christmas and Easter. Similarly, the countries of Arabia have multiple and diverse holidays, such as Mohammed's birthday. But there are also two holy days that are of great significance in the Islamic world: Eid al-Fitr and Eid al-Adha (pronounced "eed," which means "holy day" or "holiday"). In the Muslim lunar calendar, these days fall in different seasons each year. The Islamic calendar—based on the moon's rotation—is eleven days shorter than ours, so each succeeding year, the Muslim New Year's Day is eleven days earlier than the previous year.

Eid al-Fitr (break-fast in Arabic is *fitr*) ends the Muslim month of Ramadan, during which fasting from food and drink and abstaining from cigarettes and sexual pleasure are strictly observed during the daylight hours. In Bahrain a drummer goes through the city streets late each afternoon of the month to alert people that the day's fast has ended.[25] He knows the time to beat the drum according to the first sighting of the moon in the night

---

[25] The month of Ramadan begins and ends based on the first sighting of the new moon. Each day's fast begins and ends based on darkness or light (when white and black threads cannot be told apart). Moonrise is at a different time every day and sometimes at midday.

sky. In Oman the cannon at the old Portuguese fort is fired three times to ensure all people in the area have heard it. For towns and villages in the interior of Oman to know the night on which the moon had first been sighted—signaling that the month of fasting had begun—a man on a donkey would ride from the capital to each village to share the news.[26] The same was done to end the month of fasting. This resulted many times in the holy day feasts beginning earlier in the capital than in remote areas of the sultanate.

Because they fast all day and even spit out any saliva in their mouths rather than swallow it, the tired, thirsty observants are very happy to break the fast. In Oman the tradition was to eat a bowl of porridge with dates and coffee. The porridge came with a dollop of rancid butter and was shared by households in gathering places. This gave the women time to make whatever they could afford for the big family meal around ten o'clock in the evening. The fasters often made up for the lack of food in the daytime by gorging at night. Reportedly, more food is consumed in the evenings during the month of Ramadan than in any other period, despite public health service warnings against the practice. Even now, during Ramadan, hospital emergency rooms are often busy as people come in with gastric complaints.

The drummers were up an hour before sunrise to wake up households and get them eating before the fast began for the day. Little children, the sick, and pregnant women are not expected to fast, nor are menstruating women required to do so for that one week. The latter must make up missed fasting time later.

Eid al-Fitr, the holy days of feasting after Ramadan, typically lasts four days, which means not much work gets done during that time. Not surprisingly, little work gets accomplished throughout the entire month of fasting as people try to cope with low energy levels, lack of sleep, the beating sun, and extreme temperatures.

---

[26] The fasting month of Ramadan ends when the sliver of the new moon is seen. In this remote, mountainous spot, the probability of such a sighting is slim, so they depend on a donkey rider to come from Rustaq to inform them that a message had come from Muscat, declaring officially that the holiday had begun. Often the news came late, adding a day of fasting in the interior on the same day the coastal people began feasting.

The royal family sits to greet well-wishers on the first and second days of the Eid. Men go to those homes according to the host's rank in society and then on to the homes of their relatives, neighbors, and friends. Women visit women, sitting in the harem rooms of their homes. Coffee and dates or cookies are served, which assures that callers are well fed before the afternoon's tour is completed. Each call of the tour must be brief so as to visit as many homes as deemed appropriate.

The Eid is a time of joy and often of gift giving to children. Muslims look forward to it with anticipation and delight, and despite the hardships imposed by the month-long observance, they reminisce fondly when it is over.

Eid al-Adha ("*adha*" means sacrifice in Arabic) is a special ceremony during the Hajj (pilgrimage to Mecca) when each participant presents a sheep for slaughter as a sacrifice to Allah to atone for his or her sins. The ritual is also celebrated by Muslims in their home countries on the designated day of sacrifice— whether or not they were able to make the Hajj. They will make their sacrifice even before the pilgrims to Mecca have returned home. The pilgrims return to their home countries and assume the title "Hajji" before their names. The slaughtering of a lamb is a must by the pilgrims and their families throughout the Muslim world; it commemorates Abraham's willingness to sacrifice his son Ishmael[27] in obedience to God. The celebration is like the Eid celebrations at the end of Ramadan, with four days of calling, coffee and sweets, and family outings. The significance of this self-atonement kept some missionaries from calling on Muslims because the sacrificing of an animal does not equate with the sacrifice of Jesus.

Christians differ in opinion regarding how to participate with Muslims during the Eid. The Eid of the Hajj is theologically the highest religious festival for Muslims, similar in significance to Easter for Christians. Our missionaries continued to call on Muslim friends to wish them a happy celebration as a gesture of respect.

---

[27] Muslims believe Abraham was called to sacrifice Ishmael, not Isaac.

Muslims enthusiastically called on Christians during Christmas. They share not only the doctrine of the immaculate birth but also the joy of the occasion and its secular emphasis on gift giving. At Easter, however, it was not considered appropriate for Muslims to call on Christians because the death of Christ on the cross is anathema to Muslim religious doctrine. Next to Mohammed's tomb in Medina, Muslims have prepared an empty tomb for the burial of Jesus when, they believe, "he will come back to earth again to die."[28]

In Bahrain the Shiite holy day of Muharram was observed by an all-morning parade of Shiite men marching down the main streets of the city flogging their bare backs and chests with metal chains in which nails are embedded. The bare chests and backs of the marchers, delirious from the noon heat, were flayed and bloody. This practice was in remembrance of the death of Mohammed's grandson, Hussein, who had contested the acknowledged heir to replace Mohammed. Setting himself up as the new prophet, Hussein formed a sect, the Shiites, who to this day claim him as the designated heir of Mohammed. There was no calling by Christians following this holy day.

A typical day for Dr. Harvey

One morning during the Christmas season, Harvey left the house after an early breakfast. He first checked on the hospital maintenance crew. Since their manager had gone on pilgrimage to Mecca, Harvey had to sign checks and look over the day's business needs. He then began the surgery schedule, which included hernia repairs and Cesarean deliveries, the two most common surgical procedures. At midmorning, the police brought in victims of a bad road accident. All three surgeons (Harvey and the two Indian doctors) went to work, canceling the remainder of the morning surgery schedule.

---

[28] Muslims do not believe Jesus died but, rather, that He was miraculously snatched from the cross into heaven and someone else put in his place.

At noon, Harvey called the Ministry of Health to make an appointment for 1:30 p.m. with the minister of health to discuss personnel and other issues. At one o'clock, the mother of this very minister was brought to the hospital with a broken arm, so Harvey spent his Ministry of Health appointment setting her arm instead. At 2:30 that afternoon, he came home to eat, but the hospital called and said another important personage was in severe pain. Harvey left immediately, and I returned his lunch to the stove. At three o'clock, he came back to eat before doing more surgery. At five o'clock, he finished surgery and then attended to several patients waiting to be seen.

So we went late to the afternoon Christmas party at the American Embassy. There the children watched a film, but Harvey got called out to the Peace Corps camp where an American lad had been transferred a week earlier after Harvey had set his broken leg. The boy was in extreme belly pain, so Harvey had to order an ambulance (which never came), collect two pints of blood from volunteers at the party, and get to the hospital to prepare for possible surgery. He was concerned with the boy's low blood levels when he had set his broken leg and sent him back to the Peace Corps offices.

The boy had a delayed spleen rupture from the same car accident that had broken his leg, so surgery was required. Harvey came home to eat supper quickly while the boy was given blood. The boy had hoped to be home for Christmas since he was not able to work while on crutches, but he was not able to travel, so he and three other Peace Corps fellows joined our Christmas table.

The Peace Corps had arrived in Oman with twenty-five youth, eight of whom were nurses. The day after their arrival, the nurses were assigned to our hospital (where English was spoken and Arabic translated) for mornings of observing, teaching, and work. In the afternoons, the whole Peace Corps group met back at their camp to study Arabic, which would prepare them to be dispersed throughout Oman in schools and hospitals. Their supervisor requested that our hospital provide their medical care, and we were glad to do so.

Oman's weather patterns

We were in Oman for fourteen months before we had our first rainfall. In contrast to our arid coastal region and the interior's rugged, bare mountains, Oman has one high green mountain that experiences rain, hail, and occasional patches of snow. Roses, walnuts, apples, wheat, and other delicacies came to our bazaar once a year from this region. A complex system of underground tunnels[29] carries water from the mountain to numerous interior communities, providing spring water for their gardens.

Local people told us that the previous three years had not yielded an inch of water, causing it to be rationed in several areas. But the hot, dry air finally became heavy with humidity, making rashes and sweat appear on our skin. Soon the "windows of heaven" opened, and we had four days of rain, rain, and more rain. What a beautiful and muddy sight. Showers fell for two days, and real downpours followed, with a rainbow ending several hours of constant rain.

The washed mountains glistened with waterfalls and streams. Gardens absorbed the moisture and would produce luxuriantly. The thirsty land and its people were deeply quenched. In Oman the rains proved the statement: "that there shall not be room enough to receive it."[30] The roads became rushing rivers, channeled by narrow mountain passes. The flat concrete roofs held water instead of letting it run off, so inside rooms leaked and dripped. Fragile, date-stick homes were washed clean by the flow of streams through the hovels on their way to the sea.

Airplanes refused to land—the national airstrip and the oil company's airfield were rushing waterways. The dams built in the mountain passes for such rains could not hold back the water from

---

[29] Oman is famous for these ancient water tunnels (some over 2,000 years old and several miles long), called *falajs* in Arabic. The *falaj* system enabled vast increases in agricultural output.

[30] A reference to Malachi 3:10: Bring ye all the tithes into the storehouse that there may be meat in mine house, and prove me now herewith, saith the LORD of hosts, if I will not open you the windows of heaven and pour you out a blessing that there shall not be room enough to receive it.

flowing into the towns. Turbulent waters carried all the loose flotsam, gathered along the way, out to sea. Pots, clothing, brush and tree limbs, small animals, pieces of shops and their goods, garbage and refuse—all were swept up in the constricted widths of their channels and carried out to sea. Nevertheless, we were saturated not only with water but also with joy.

Another year, our rainfall was even greater and more unusual. Beginning on a weekend with a short downpour, including lightning and thunder, drops of rain turned into a deluge that measured over five inches and kept me from school and the market, moved some residents of cement houses into the only dry room in their homes, and reduced travel from interior towns, such that hospital attendance was very low. Patients were moved from dripping or open rooms to dry ones. To make matters worse, cold air moved in with the rain.

Once the rains ended, everyone laid out clothes to dry on mountainsides, rooftops, and tree branches. The new port construction was 75 percent ruined, causing six months to be added to its completion; the mountain road between Mutrah and Muscat was declared treacherous; mud houses collapsed; and date-stick houses, not well tied down, got swept to the sea. Rain came again the next month for two days; this time, we received a total of three inches.

Our vacation destination: Kodaikanal, India, 1968

Our 1966 vacation was to Jerusalem with the Van Etten family, who joined us again the next year for a vacation in northern India and Kashmir. We would be taking our 1968 holiday in Kodaikanal, South India, where an international school for missionary children is located. We were looking at the school as a likely place to send our boys. This was to be an adventure that our boys had heard about many times from the older mission children who came home every December and recounted endless tales of life (and mischief) at Kodaikanal International School.

To get there, we flew to Dubai, then took a night flight to Bombay (now called Mumbai). On this flight, there were seventy unaccompanied children of Indian workers in the Arab countries.

They were returning to their extended families and their Indian daytime or boarding schools. We spent Sunday in Bombay, attending church and taking an afternoon walk along the sea, as many Indian families liked to do.

Monday's flight took us to Madras (now Chennai), and we boarded the overnight train to Kodai Road. The next morning, an early bus took us up the winding, steep road to the high plateau where Kodaikanal sits. A cab took us to our assigned cottage, only a short walk from the school. Joyce Dunham, a fellow Oman missionary, had lit a fire in the fireplace to warm the cottage for us since the weather is typically cold and damp.

By afternoon, the sun came out, and we strolled around the nearby mountain lake and near the edge of the escarpment, overlooking the hot plains six thousand feet below. We marveled that we could see all the way down to the plains, to Madurai and farther.[31] Eucalyptus trees and many evergreens, pine trees, and blooming bushes, plus extensive green grass on the plateau, were salve for our weary Oman eyes.

Our boys were glad to be with the Dunham children once again. During our evening dinner with the Dunhams, the fog and chill returned, so we lit fires in our bedroom fireplaces to warm the rooms. The fires would die out slowly as we slept.

The next day, the boys went excitedly to their classes for the first day of "real" school. At noon we joined them in the school yard to eat our picnic lunch. This is a delightful, daily family tradition when parents are up at Kodai. Soon after we arrived, many parents left the hilltop to return to their jobs on the plains. Parents working in India can come up to Kodai throughout the school year, while we from the Arabian Gulf are farther away and have limited opportunities to travel to Kodai. Our boys excitedly brought home library books from the school "to be read immediately—after teatime!"

Harvey enjoyed golfing and long walks while the boys went to school. He also took the opportunity to visit Vellore Medical College, accompanying the missionaries who worked there when

---

[31] Kodaikanal is at seven thousand feet altitude; its cool weather and green hills are a welcome relief from the hot, dusty plains below.

they left Kodaikanal. I was asked to substitute teach in two sections of seventh grade math classes since the new teacher had yet to receive his visa for India. Over the course of those four weeks in Kodai, I enjoyed lunch with the family outdoors, two afternoon classes, and walking home with the boys after school. In the evenings, I prepared lessons and corrected homework papers, and yet, amid all this activity, we still found time for

Margaret, Dirk (age 8), Keith (6) and Harvey on the compound of Kodai International School in Kodaikanal, India, summer 1968. In 1970, Dirk and Keith entered the boarding school in sixth and fourth grades.

reading. Weekends found us hiking with the boys' classes. The school encouraged long hikes and the accumulation of hiking points to achieve awards.

Fellowship with other parents was rewarding for us, and in addition, we had sports, lunch together at the school, Bible study groups, and PTA meetings. We were impressed by the standards of education and the care of each child in boarding. We had two years to prepare ourselves mentally and emotionally for this expected separation. In the meantime, we were to return to the United States for our first furlough.[32]

On our way home to the United States in 1969, we stopped in Bahrain for three months to complete our formal requirement of two years of Arabic language study. Word came from Oman that

[32] Since its inception in 1891, the mission provided a year-long "furlough," a trip back to the United States every five years. The purpose was to speak to supporting churches, continue education, gain revitalized health from the strain of overseas living, and visit relatives.

Wadiya[33] had died after suffering six months from the pain of pancreatic cancer. His testimony was like that of the spirit of Job's. Hundreds of times each day, he would say over and over, "Praise God!" "Thank God!" "God is most merciful!" In the face of obvious suffering, this had a significant impact on his family and all who were privileged to hear him. His wife was not a Christian, but his older teenage son, Naim, was. Naim was doing well in a new technical training school in Muscat. The rebellious younger son, Yahya, refused to go to school and was deeply unhappy and a disappointment to his father.

In Bahrain we had a short memorial service as requested by Wadiya's wife's son from her previous marriage. That son worked at Bahrain's American Mission Hospital. Harvey gave a short eulogy in Arabic. I spoke of the occasion when Wadiya was given a new robe for the Easter service the previous year when his son Naim was to be received into the church fellowship. When Wadiya did not wear it to the service, the missionary who gave it to him asked why.

"Well, sir, my neighbor came to me for help and he had no robes," Wadiya replied. Wadiya was poor, never wore shoes, and his robe was seldom washed. I knew all that would change when he was greeted by his Father in heaven.

Another Omani friend interrupted our stay in Bahrain. Nasser, a blind man, helped the mission in exchange for love gifts (food, fellowship, gifts, etc.), and when possible, he helped Harvey with his building project by sifting gravel. He loved our boys and spent time sitting and talking with Harvey in the evenings. Though not a baptized Christian, he attended meetings frequently. His favorite hymn request was always "The Light of the World is Jesus." ("Once I was blind, but now, I can see.")

While we were in Bahrain, Harvey and I anxiously awaited Nasser's arrival. He had traveled to Dubai to visit a daughter and then planned to visit Bahrain with another daughter. But he did

---

[33] Wadiya Sulayman worked with the mission (beginning in the 1930s) as an evangelist, as a coleporter in the mission bookshop, attending prayer meetings, and leading Bible studies. Wadiya was an Omani, an indigenous Christian. His stepson worked at the Mission Hospital in Bahrain.

not plan on arriving with heart failure, so when he arrived, he wound up in the hospital, confused and weak. How he loved to hear Harvey's voice, for it was part of his former Muscat life, making him think he was there.

We visited him daily on our way to our Arabic lessons. As his condition allowed, we not only shared the Gospel with him but also sang songs he remembered from the church in Oman. We prayed in those days that we could bring him the joy of Christ in the midst of his family's needs and that he would truly see Him when he entered eternal life. His daughter in Bahrain had married a former church member who had turned against the church. Many years earlier, Nasser had shown great interest in the Gospel, but when he moved from Muscat to Bahrain, he removed his whole family from the church.

When Nasser died, Harvey was not able to go to the burial. Later he sat with the men as they read the Koran; I sat with the daughters and other women in a bedroom. I sat a few minutes without speaking, then was served coffee and dates, signifying I could leave. I stood, quoted some Bible verses, and promised God I would visit with the women again.

Changes in Oman

After home leave from May 1969 to June 1970, we returned to Oman via Kodaikanal, where our boys entered the international school: Dirk in sixth grade and Keith in fourth. On his entrance test, Keith got a 99 percent in music rhythm and the highest mark in reading. Dirk played the cornet and tuba, and Keith played the clarinet in the school band.

During our two weeks in Kodaikanal, a missionary doctor's baby had stopped breathing, and Harvey helped the parents keep the child breathing for four days and four nights until it finally could do so on its own. Returning to Oman, Harvey was soon very busy at the hospital, while I took up housekeeping and sewing work at the hospital.

July brought great changes in Oman when young Qaboos bin Said bin Tamur took over the leadership[34] of the country. A foreign radio announced, "The Sultan has abdicated his throne to his son!" The new sultan was to visit Mutrah and Muscat for official salutes and receptions, and he passed by the hospital on his first-ever visit to the northern capital. He had lived in the southern capital, Salalah,[35] where his father had also lived the past eleven years. Fearing just such an overthrow,[36] the father had kept Qaboos sequestered upon his return from England and his studies at Sandhurst Military Academy.[37]

The reception the Sultan received was colorful, with red cloth flags flapping gaily on date-stick huts, tall concrete buildings, shop keepers' stalls, trucks and bicycles, and at the hospital. A broad red banner and a joyous mood among the people welcomed the new sultan to town.

Harvey walked to the airport alongside hundreds of Omanis and was invited to be inside the enclosure of merchants, company heads, and the royal family. As a goodwill gesture, Sultan Qaboos released some three hundred political prisoners and inaugurated a radio station. On the first radio broadcast, the sultan spoke to his people and lifted many restrictions his father had placed upon them. Omani men could now wear Western clothes, smoke in public, and travel freely in and out of Oman.

Sultan Qaboos' uncle, exiled for ten years, returned to be named prime minister. Tariffs were lifted on all medicines and

---

[34] In a bloodless coup, Qaboos, the fourteenth sultan of Oman and Muscat, overthrew his father, Said Bin Tamur, who had strongly resisted modernizing his country. Said bin Taimur was exiled to London, where he died in 1972.

[35] Said bin Tamur preferred living in the southern capital, Salalah, because he felt more secure and distant from the political meddling in Muscat, his wife was from southern Oman, and the weather in Salalah was far more temperate than in Muscat.

[36] Successions of Sultans through fratricide was not uncommon.

[37] All British Army officers, as well as personnel from overseas, are trained at the Royal Military Academy Sandhurst, located near London. In addition to learning the necessary skills to lead an Army, Qaboos developed close relationships with British military officers who would command Oman's military and who would help facilitate Qaboos' coup against his father.

medical supplies so that they could be as cheap as possible. Customs were likely also lifted on food stuffs, and their prices went down very quickly. Drums and joyous chanting, a custom the former sultan forbade, lulled us to sleep nightly.

Harvey led the new sultan into the hospital and briefly explained our work. Qaboos sent a letter of appreciation to the hospital for the work of the mission and hope for future government and mission cooperation. The hospital was to begin a nursing school for sixth grade students, and the government opened a girls' school, to which many girls from the upper grades (4 through 6) transferred from our Christian school.

Christmas break

There was no snow or decorated evergreen trees, but there were, blessedly, two sons, back from school[38] in India, at home with us again in the winter of 1970. That made it a great Christmas time indeed.

There was plenty of Christmas activity, beginning with a dinner party for the missionaries and Indian hospital staff at the home of the Indian eye doctor on Friday night, December 18. Dinner, games, and songs made for a perfect evening, until we heard screams of "Fire!" The screams were coming from the reed homes of our nearby neighbors. We broke into groups, ran for extinguishers, and got them to the scene of the two date-stick homes in time to smother the flames at the back of the structures.

The next night, our English church choir sang at the Malayalam-language, Indian-congregation service. After the service, they served tea in the church hall and presented a short pageant. On Sunday afternoon, we drove to the oil company for their Sunday school program—presented in Dutch and English. That evening we had our English service at the mission church in Muscat. The choir sang; our teenagers and college youth sang with a guitar, and the Indian girls sang two numbers as well.

---

[38] Kodai School's annual "summer vacation" was in the winter, October to January, so that the children could enjoy the cooler months of the tropics.

Late on Monday and Wednesday afternoons of Christmas week, the missionaries and their children visited all the Christian Arabs' homes, one day in Muscat and the other in Mutrah. We sang a song, said a prayer, ate sweets, and drank tea in each home and felt very blessed by this warm custom.

Tuesday was the hospital program. Following a short service, we shared sweets with the employees, patients, and their families. After that, I went on to the leprosy compound for a similar service. All the patients wore new *disdashas*, with new turbans wrapped around their heads (every year, the American Leprosy Mission helps us provide new clothing for Christmas gifts), and each patient also received candies and fruit.

Wednesday night we hurried to church in Muscat for an Anglican service of nine lessons, conducted by the padre of the British armed forces in Bahrain. The British people of Oman read the lessons and led us in singing carols. The lovely service never varied from year to year.

On Christmas Eve day, the girls' school pageant was presented with our own children included in it. The boys were soldiers with no speaking parts, and the guard of Herod's palace was our schoolgirl, who was deaf and mute. She was delighted to be included.

Christmas Day, we opened our presents early. The rug we had bought in Kashmir in 1967 had been found and finally arrived exactly in time for our celebration. In the morning, we gathered with the Arab Christians in the hospital chapel and then had coffee and sweets at the home of Dr. Don and Eloise Bosch. For lunch, I invited two single ladies and an Englishman for the noon meal.

The next day, Arab men from town visited the men of the mission at our house while we women received Arab women at another home. After brief congratulations, the visitors ate sweets and drank coffee before leaving to visit the homes of Arab Christians.

Family camping

Coinciding with Dirk and Keith's return home from school in November 1970 was the arrival of our barrels, shipped via sea freight from the United States. Among the contents was a tent for camping. Though Harvey could not get away from the hospital easily, we managed some wonderful trips to the seashore and into the sandy, mountainous areas of the interior.

For our first such trip, we engaged a boat to take us to an isolated cove by the sea, south of Muscat. We swam and gathered shells at low tide, as well as caught fish for our aquarium. We watched fishermen checking their nets out at sea; we saw a few *dhows* (large sailboats) and an oil tanker pass by. A full moon that night meant we had no need for lanterns. At noon we sang songs, played board games, and read books in the tent, keeping us out of the intense midday sunlight. Keith taught us several songs he had learned at school.

On another trip, it took two hours to drive the twenty miles to our camping site, where we set up a tent in a *wadi*.[39] A stream pooled enough water for a little swimming hole, and the tall mountains on either side of the wadi kept the sun off us, except during the noon hours. Two cars, a camel with a rider, and a few goats were the only interruption to our solitude that weekend.

To camp in the interior, it was necessary to stop and ask the local sheikh's permission to be on his territory. Therefore, the sheikh had a group of male patients awaiting our return trip so that Dr. Harvey could see them. Having known this was likely to happen, Harvey had placed his medical bag in the car. He got out to treat the men, as well as to address the problems which they told him concerning their female family members. The boys got out to stretch their legs and play, while I stayed in the car, as women are expected to do.

On the day we broke camp and returned home, the government had changed the flow of road traffic to driving on the right side of the road, as in most of the world, instead of the left side, as the British had established. The change went smoothly; it had been well prepared and timed to take place at midnight on December 31. This was part of the modernization plan of Sultan Qaboos. Part of the success of the transition was attributed to

---

[39] A *wadi* is a dry riverbed—often used as a road—that, when it rains, can turn into a violent and dangerous gushing river.

there being relatively few vehicles in the country, and most of them were military and oil company vehicles. A public education campaign of radio advertisements and road signs gave citizens plenty of advance warning. All traffic stopped at noon, December 31. During the night, new traffic signs were unveiled. By 8:00 a.m., January 1, 1971, the switch had quietly occurred. There were no reported accidents due to the change, and our return home was without event.

A memorable trip to Oman's interior

Our car was packed. Saeed,[40] with his wife and son, sat in the middle seats; Harvey, Dirk, and I were in the front seats; Keith was squashed gamely into one seat in the back of the car amidst luggage, camping gear, and food stuff. Our scenery changed from the straight coastal road to small dunes and then to low hills covered with more and more pebbles and rocks. At Rustaq, a fertile garden area, the road became a wadi, and we were soon driving between rocky hills and low mountains. We entered a narrower canyon with large boulders in the wadi. Making our way around the last boulder, we began to see green on the mountainsides and in the valley. The wide valley ahead displayed green, terraced gardens of fruit, sorghum, and alfalfa, with mud-brick homes lining the hillsides.

Arriving midafternoon on the last days of the fasting month, we were greeted and stared at by just about everyone in the village. Saeed, the village sheikh, had returned to his people and was greeted as such, despite his double "stigma" of Christianity and leprosy. No one declined to shake his hand (withered by leprosy) or shrunk from his presence. He was the leader and judge—respected greatly in all the area. He said he never had to prepare meals while there since his people had brought gifts of food to him.

---

[40] Saeed, the chief of a small mountain village, had contracted leprosy and come to the mission leprosarium for treatment. While there, he had become a Christian. This excursion was to return him to his village.

In the time we were there as his guests, all the villagers came to greet him. His son's wife served us tea as more villagers arrived to greet Saeed. We persuaded Saeed that we should pitch our tent and be alone these final days of fasting since our family would not need to fast all day or wait to feast at a long night's party.

We pitched our tent in a dry wadi, so there was no water for the boys to swim in, but they could climb the nearby mountains, and after lunch in the tent the next day, Harvey and the boys went exploring. While they were gone, several men came to call for medicine and found Harvey not in, so they politely and apologetically backed off a distance (from this female's tent) to sit under a tree and await his return when he could treat them.

The next morning, we went to see the extensive gardens of Saeed's family, returned to the tent for lunch, then helped his son's family move to the house they would be in through the cool and rainy months of winter.

As dusk fell, we pulled up stakes and returned to the son's house, where he prepared dinner for all of us—a tray full of rice, over which he had spread goat meat and its broth. After coffee, we were informed that a neighbor had also prepared an evening meal for us. With lantern in hand, we climbed up a mountainside to eat with them. They served bowls of the traditional wheatberry soup, known popularly as *freekeh*, served each night when the fast is broken, before the big meal is ready.

Back at Saeed's house, we prepared our sleeping bags in his sitting-cum-sleeping room. We played a game while Saeed and his guests and family ate their big meal in the hall, which would later become the family's sleeping room. Harvey and the boys went out to relieve themselves; a very young grandson led me to a garden farther away.[41]

Throughout the night, we heard mortar and pestle pounding coffee beans and onions and the swish-swish of the goatskin bag being pummeled to make butter from goats' milk, all in preparation for the feast day. In the darkness before dawn, everyone snuck out to the gardens before dressing for the day.

---

[41] When living among Arabs, personal hygiene was a significant challenge.

Putting away our clothing and sleeping bags in the shelves of the room, we were ready to celebrate the first day of the holiday with guests that Saeed would host in this room.

We had devotions with Saeed and then breakfast, after which many men came to visit. I left the room and sat where the women gathered. Breakfast was cold, cooked cereal, much like the wheat soup from the night before, only now with melted butter, into which one dipped balls of cereal formed in the hand. Our boys had gone off with village boys and must have found food elsewhere. Every new guest brought her own container of cereal, and we had to taste from them all, as did the men. Harvey distributed medicine throughout the morning. Before noon, the men stood shoulder to shoulder in lines and did shuffling dances. The women, who were watching, imitated the dances, but only out of the men's sight. At noon we were fed kebabs with two types of flat bread.

In the afternoon, Saeed's wife wanted to go to her family's village to greet them, so we all clambered into the car. Along the way, men from another village stopped the car to ask Harvey to lunch there the following day and see the sick. He said we would stop on our return to Saeed's village. Upon arrival at our destination, everyone came out to see the car and its strange white occupants. The women gave me sweets in an upper room and led me to the garden swing where I would be their guest and swing and sing. The women were returning from using the stream for bathing purposes.

Back in the upper room, bejeweled women gathered around "poor" me, with only one ring and a strange bracelet—my watch. Their fingers and wrists had silver, plastic, and beaded bangles on them; their feet were heavy with thick silver anklets; their nostrils were pierced with a gold stud on each side. In Mutrah the jewelry of preference was pure gold.[42] A tin of peaches was opened and served with very sticky dates and then coffee.

---

[42] Under Islamic law, husbands could divorce their wives suddenly and without warning by simply stating "I divorce you" three times. Thus, women wore all their jewelry so that, if they were quickly divorced, their valuable resources could be taken with them.

Once Harvey had treated all the men needing medical care, they allowed women into an area for him to see. A baby had a cleft palette; a four year old walked on weak, spindly legs; and another baby had congenital syphilis. A woman needed surgery and said she would come with us to the hospital later. Lots of headache pills were passed out, but for many illnesses, there was no help in such a remote area.

On the return trip, Harvey passed out his last medicines from the back of the car: eye ointment, ear drops, cold tablets, and stomach soothers. He successfully pulled one tooth. Meanwhile, village women gaped through the windows of the car and asked Saeed's wife, "Aren't you afraid to ride there?" "How do you know where to go or what to do?" She proudly said it was quite easy but then got very confused about how to get out of the car to greet those women.

After spending one more night with Saeed's family, we packed and left the next day amid many goodbyes and large amounts of food. We left them all of our sweets and treats from the coast. The patient that was to return with us to go to the hospital never showed up.

Saeed's family decided to stay on another week with their relatives and neighbors. The rest of us drove to Rustaq, with its magnificent gardens, from where we headed out across the desert scrub land on unknown trails. Stopping occasionally for directions, we eventually reached our destination, the village of Effe.

Wells and Beth Thoms[43] had taken us here some years ago to visit Saif, a tailor who also peddled medicines. He read the Gospels frequently and sang hymns he loved, yet he never committed himself to Christ. Hearing of Wells' death, Saif had hurried to Mutrah to sit and mourn with the hospital men. More recently, he had written to Jeanette Boersma, a mission colleague, requesting

---

[43] Wells Thoms, MD, was the son of Drs. Sharon and Marion Thoms, who were among the original members of the Arabian Mission, having joined in 1898. Wells joined the mission in 1930 and retired in 1970, serving most of his career in Mutrah, Oman. For more on Wells Thoms, see David G. Dickason's *Faith, Hope and Love: The Hakeem's Journey* (Van Raalte Press, forthcoming, 2021).

us to stop for a visit at Eid time. We promised him we would try to do so.

Saif's nephew invited us to share the noonday feast with him and then led us to Saif's home. Upon our arrival, an elderly man informed us that Saif had died the morning of Eid. Harvey sat with the men, and I was led to an upstairs room to mourn alone since Saif had no immediate family. The nephew wept upon opening the room that Saif had asked him to prepare for his friends from Mutrah. Being sick, Saif had told his kinfolk that we were coming and that he would go with us to the hospital. His Bible and hymnbooks were set out for our use. The nephew was sure his uncle had died of a broken heart from the news of Wells' death.

It was a sad ending to our tour as we drove back to tell the news to our church friends. The trip to Saeed's village had taken four hours to cover 115 miles, and the eight hours of travel home over bumpy roads compounded our low spirits. But we had kept our promise to visit with Saif.

Dirk joined an Arab family and then an English family on two other trips to oasis gardens. Keith was happier at home with us. They both enjoyed mission playmates who were also home from school. And they played with the Arab boys. We, and sometimes our mission families, were invited to attend films at the British army base outside of town.

The night before the boys returned to India, we were invited to dine with an Arab family. Our boys gave their outgrown bicycle to their playmates from that family.

That night the realization that family time was over for them began to quiet and sober them. Keith kept his feelings and thoughts to himself, but Dirk spoke of not wanting to go back to India—not because of the school there but because of the fun they had had at home. Keith would return to his same dorm, and Dirk would move on to the sixth-grade dorm for boys. Both would have new teachers.

Hospital changes

There were many "straws in the wind" in Oman concerning the mission hospital's future relationship with the government medical services. A team from our RCA offices came to review and consider the problem. The team had previously visited the Kuwait and Bahrain mission hospitals for evaluation and consultation.[44]

The proposed relationship was important, and my personal inclination was that the time had come to hand over our work to the government and offer our assistance to them under their management. There was absolutely no hope of our remaining a totally private hospital amid expanding free government medical services. Our missionaries went on record in favor of turning over our work to the government.

Despite our resolve, we were yet to hear the opinions of the visiting RCA medical team. The government had already told us that they wanted to subsidize our whole program so that free treatment could be given to all Omanis starting the following January. The government made clear their desire for our cooperation and that we would remain as managers.

Increasingly, we felt that, in view of the many potential problems ahead, it made sense for the government to take over and reap all the responsibility as well as the criticism. The government did not want us to pull out; they needed our skilled staff and everything that made our hospital function—at least for a few years.

Government contracts were awarded to build six major centers around the country—each with a forty-bed hospital, a boys' school, a girls' school, a post office, a power station, and a police station. Each center would have satellite clinics and schools, and each satellite would, in turn, have village medical units. Assistance was given to farmers to buy equipment and market their products, and to facilitate this, new roads were needed. The first hotels were built, and a deep-water port was under construction at Mutrah's seashore, the financing of which would come from the

---

[44] The RCA team was concerned about hospital funding. The Arabian Gulf countries, with their newfound oil wealth, were building modern hospitals and providing free medical care. While the missionaries were funded by the RCA, day-to-day mission hospital operations required payment from patients. With free government medical care available, fewer could afford to pay the mission fees, and the RCA could not pick up the shortfall.

accumulated, unused oil revenue of the past four years, with future expenses to be paid from substantial, though limited, oil income.

Our mission hospital had 120 beds, several departments, and a smoothly functioning staff. It delivered good-quality medical care. Our facilities were stretched to the limit, so we were struggling to find ways to finance a much-needed expansion and update of our buildings and equipment. How could we possibly do it?

Enter Sultan Qaboos and a new government ready to help the poor, which constituted most of Oman's 750,000 people. Food and medical expenses consumed most people's budgets, so food prices could be lowered by reducing import customs. But the government had little infrastructure on which to build a healthcare system. Could the government reduce the cost of medicine? Would it even be feasible to make medical services free?

Candid and friendly discussions began between government officials, an expert RCA medical team, and members of our hospital staff. Realistically, we could not see more than a few years of existence as a private, good-quality hospital in light of the government's soon-to-come free medical care. Could our ministry in Christ's love to the needy be done under government sponsorship?

In the end, the government invited us to continue ministering with our own staff and to choose additional staff as needed. Our hospital would be the major referral hospital for the entire country, and thus, we would be integrated into the national medical scheme. Our staff would be placed on the government salary scale, almost double what we had been paying them. Major policies for our hospital would now be determined by the government. It was significant that our experience and advice was carefully regarded in those early months.

What about our Christian witness? I believed our Christian presence was more important than the presence of an institution. Missionaries are sent to be God's disciples, sensitively sharing the Gospel of forgiveness and reconciliation while living and working in another culture. Did I need to work in a Christian institution to do this? Did any of us? I am convinced that mission institutions accomplished much in Oman in Christian ministry.

But to be candid, mission institutions had not been conspicuously successful in establishing large churches in Arabia. I continued to believe the Holy Spirit was calling for more Christians to work here in secular, as well as Christian, institutions. I would not change my values, my goals, or my dedication to Christ because the institution in which I worked was now under government supervision.

In December 1970, in a momentous speech, Omani radio broadcast Sultan Qaboos addressing the hospital agreements that had been reached:

> As of the first of January, all Mission medical facilities are to be leased to the government so as to become a part of our total medical development program. This is not a government take-over but a generous cooperation of the Mission, whom we appreciate for their years of service among us. A team from the RCA came to Oman to approve this action. We ask the expatriate staff to stay in Oman and continue to build the "new Oman" with us.

In his English letter to the mission, the sultan stated his appreciation once again but asked that we do no evangelizing outside the hospital walls or publicly.

As of that January, the government began leasing the hospital and subsidizing our total budget, with the exception of missionary salaries. That change doubled our $225,000 budget to $500,000, with an additional $200,000 set aside for capital improvements in that year alone. All citizens of Oman were now eligible for free treatment and services. The hospital's name was changed from the American Mission Hospital to Ar-Rhama [Mercy] Hospital. We rejoiced for the people and were grateful to be able to remain a part of their medical system.

The first large government hospital would open later in 1974, and long-time missionary Dr. Don Bosch was chosen to be the chief medical officer there. That hospital would eventually absorb all our surgery and obstetrics cases—our two strong points. The Muscat women's hospital would close its medical work, and the mission would be allowed to continue to use all the buildings and land of their compound: church, hospital, school, mission housing, and the small cemetery.

The Mutrah hospital would close temporarily for remodeling, and the staff—Omani, foreign, and mission—would be dispersed to hospitals and clinics throughout the country. The mission compound would be restructured completely, so that the mission would then comprise one pastor's house and the small church in Mutrah. All other Mutrah property the government would use for medical work and to house personnel, as was the original intent of the mission for Oman medical work.

The Muscat church building sat adjacent to the school rooms, and so the growing congregation of several language groups would begin building outside Mutrah on land the sultan gave for that purpose. Also, the Danish bookseller in charge of the bookshop situated in Muscat's crowded marketplace wanted to move to the new land and, thus, larger quarters as soon as possible.

Our girls' mission school in transition

Providing education for all Omani citizens challenged the sultan's new government. As with hospital work, the mission was eager to cooperate with programs that the minister of education presented. The first major change was the school schedule. The government had a Sunday-to-Thursday school week; Friday was for Muslim prayers at the mosque, and Saturday was free from work or school. The mission adapted the government schedule to Monday through Thursday for regular school. Special-needs classes, when necessary, were held on Saturday morning, and Sunday was reserved for Arabic church in the morning and English church in the evening.

Our school became full, with an abundance of children wanting to attend the lower grades; enrollment totaled seventy, representing a mixture of Muslims and a few Christians. We enrolled most of the Omani students returning from Zanzibar;[45] they spoke Swahili and English and now needed to learn Arabic. In one of my classes were four Omani-born girls, with covered hair and ankles hidden by lace-trimmed pantaloons under long skirts (in later years replaced by pantsuits), who needed lessons in Arabic and English. On the other side of the class sat three Omani girls from Africa, with short, covered hair and ankles showing below calf-length skirts, who spoke either French or English fluently—learned from mission schools on Africa's mainland—but had no knowledge of Arabic. Before me sat a microcosm of the tensions in Oman in this mixture with "new" Omanis. One group would necessarily have to change, and it would be the newcomers who would quickly adopt the traditions of their new homes.

We also added into our second grade class two deaf and partially mute children, a seventeen-year-old disabled child, a partially paralyzed child, and an albino child. These last five children required extra individual lessons, especially on Saturday mornings. In many cases, lessons were taught in two languages in order to be understood. Our former students moved on to the government schools.

The government decided to coordinate all lessons in the curriculum; thus, we had to include Islamic history. We were not entrusted with Quranic (also spelled Koranic) teaching,[46] but neither were we forbidden to teach our Bible lessons. The government had books necessary for Islamic history, but we were short of English books and had to order them.

When our mission teachers decided to invite the government teachers to tea, five young women came. All of them were refugees from occupied territories of the Middle East[47] and spoke the Arabic dialects of Lebanon, Jordan, Egypt, and Palestine. The Arabic dialect of Oman was difficult for them to understand, but

---

[45] Zanzibar had been a province of Oman, but a 1964 revolution ousted the Omanis from Zanzibar; their return caused considerable disruption to Omani society.
[46] A Muslim teacher was brought in to teach those classes.
[47] These were Palestinians who were refugees in other Arab countries (after Palestine was occupied by Israel in 1948) and now spoke the dialects of those countries, and who then came to Oman as refugees.

classical Arabic, as required in the classroom, helped them converse with students. They arrived in dresses below the knees but no trousers or black cloaks. In school they wore pant suits. The Muslim teachers wore head scarves to differentiate themselves from the Christians with uncovered heads. The government teachers were also frustrated by "medieval Oman"; their living quarters were locked nightly at eight o'clock to "protect" them. They enjoyed speaking English and Arabic with us, but we detected bad feelings against us who, as Christian Americans, were suspected of supporting Israel.

After school on Mondays and Wednesdays, I ran a two-hour class at the hospital's nursing school, teaching eleven boys and three girls who needed help with arithmetic. These students were all good English speakers, so that made teaching easier.

Government leads the way

Change came rapidly from the time Sultan Qaboos' reign began in 1970 up to March 1974. We were amazed at the progress of the institutions built, commercial contracts signed, and new laws and regulations. In less than four years, the country opened its doors to returning Omanis expelled from Zanzibar, foreigners of every trade or interest, and even tourists. Its swelling population lived in newly constructed neighborhoods of small brick houses, complete with air conditioning. Narrow streets were jammed with cars, trucks, motorcycles, and buses. A larger airport to meet the cargo and passenger influx was opened.

This new Oman saw a discernible affluence that began with the exploitation of the country's oil resources. Increasing materialism vied with traditional values and religion for people's attention and worship. The progressive government initiated development of schools, roads, healthcare, and social services. Education introduced youth to global ideas. Change occurred in the Arab lifestyle, work habits, and cultural patterns. An influx of foreign tourists, business entrepreneurs, and low-paid workers changed the social fabric. Yet vast pockets of villagers throughout Oman remained unaffected by such change, remaining innocent of the capital region's new lifestyle.

During the Israeli-Palestinian war of 1973, the sultan could not spare troops because of the longstanding military conflict on Oman's western border with Yemen. So Qaboos ordered one Omani nurse from every hospital to go to the war effort in Palestine. He also decreed that every Omani's salary would be deducted a quarter its normal amount for the war in Egypt.

When Ramadan started in March 1974, once again nothing was to be consumed between the first rays of dawn and the last light of dusk. But the new, large foreign population, not required to fast, often unknowingly offended Omanis by eating publicly during the daytime. But for that matter, not all city Omanis fasted since their businesses kept them occupied. The ruler, however, decreed that working hours would be shortened in all institutions —including schools—for the month, and any necessary overtime would be doubly compensated.

Our second furlough from the Muscat assignment began at the end of June 1974. Not all of the planned new arrangements for the medical program mentioned above were fully in place before we left for furlough. Harvey intended to return to Butterworth Hospital in Grand Rapids to study as a fellow in orthopedic surgery. Oman's rapid development of highways was bringing road accident victims to hospitals, so he wanted to be better prepared in orthopedic trauma care when returning to Oman.

We were leaving a vastly different Oman than the one we had entered a few years earlier. The change the average Omani had witnessed during Qaboos' first five years of reign is hard to comprehend. Omanis stepped out of a noncommercial, nonelectric, uneducated, isolated, medieval society and into the twentieth century. What did a Muslim, whose only textbook was the Holy Koran (with all its answers for living life), think of jet airplanes, bookstores, boys' and girls' schools in every village, and television? What would become of their self-identity? Would instability ensue?

We saw all around us a falling away of ancient, traditional religious practices and concerns in pursuit of materialism and its many seeming benefits. Even the Omanis returning from Zanzibar, stricter in their practices and ideas because of their years living among African religions, appeared to adjust comfortably to the new Omani lifestyle.

But we were mainly interested in the challenges confronting another kind of Omani, the Christian Omani who continued to live in a Muslim society that was developing a new identity. We wondered, in this new context, how would a convert identify with Christianity? The male convert faced the pragmatic question of making his livelihood and engaging in work. Too often his mentor had been the missionary, and he had subconsciously assimilated American culture into his Christian lifestyle. The few Christians in Oman were employed by the mission. That made them dependent on the mission for money and placed them in debt to the mission for newly acquired prestige. The female Christian convert was not of great concern to her Omani family and friends because of the traditional Omani attitude toward women. They were believed to have no souls and thus had no voice in society. Yet, as converts from Islam, they faced ostracism, stoning, and divorce from husbands and families. A male child born to a converted wife was sent to his grandparents for upbringing, lest he be persuaded into Christian faith.

In Oman the RCA had established a women's hospital, a general hospital, and a medical compound for contagious diseases, principally tuberculosis and leprosy. The patients stayed there for longterm care until their disease was "arrested." The leprosy patients were mostly men who came from far-off Bedouin villages. The medicine they took made their eyes water, but the disease made their eyebrows and beards fall off. It also damaged their nervous systems so that they lost fingers and toes after unfelt and untreated cuts and sores caused those digits to erode.

Two or three afternoons each week, about ten of the recovering lepers gathered under a shade tree to learn how to read and write their Arabic language. These Muslims, both men and women, prayed together and sang hymns before their reading of lessons from the Bible. When they were asked to choose hymns to sing, their favorite hymn was "Count Your Many Blessings." The lesson would begin slowly as each person, turn by turn, struggled to hold his Bible while wiping their eyes as they dripped tears onto the book.

Sick with disease and far from home, these lonely scholars still could name their blessings. Their goal was to return to their villages with the prized document which stipulated that they were no longer outcasts. Moreover, they would then be able to teach the children to read and write, a very exalted position in Bedouin society.

One member of the leprosy colony, a judge from a remote village, became a "nuisance" for his acceptance of Christianity and was asked by political authorities to leave the capital and the hospital compound. We pitied him for his loss of the church fellowship as he was banished to a village where no other Christian lived. His response was one of joy: "Don't talk that way! I'll be the first missionary to take the Gospel to my village." His identity was not with the mission or the church but with his Lord and Savior Jesus Christ.

Every Omani Christian faced anew the challenge of identity. Hospital work was on Sunday; Friday was the day off. Nurses educated informally by the missionaries were unable to get government salaries if they worked elsewhere. Some were assigned to remote villages, and their families were not always happy to leave the advantages and affluence of life in the capital. The missionaries were no longer their bosses, and they felt lost in the Muslim crowds that prayed five times daily in public, fasted during daylight for a month, and spoke the name of Allah throughout common conversation. Faced with the challenge of identification as a Christian, few were likely to be strong enough to remain in the Christian faith.

When we returned to Oman twenty years later, in 1995, we scarcely recognized the neighborhoods and towns we had known. Our former home had been razed, making way for modern buildings. The mission hospital, now one of the national medical facilities, was soon to be razed. Electricity now reached even the remotest Bedouin villages, as did satellite dishes.

The people as well had changed. Miriam, a former teaching colleague told us: "Dr. Doorenbos, you couldn't practice medicine here now for we have diseases which we didn't have when you were here: diverticulitis, high blood pressure, appendicitis, gall bladder complaints, and hypertension."

"Why do you have these diseases now?" Harvey asked.

"There are two causes: (1) the supermarkets that have an abundance of food, and (2) the television, which creates hours of inactivity," she responded wisely.

As we observed these tremendous societal and economic changes for ourselves, it was apparent Oman had moved from its sixteenth-century lifestyle to that of the coming twenty-first century in only twenty-five years. Yet, remnants of centuries-old culture remained. The family was still the basic structure of Arab society, with each member working for the good of all. Any disgrace on the family's reputation by one of its members is severely punished, assuring that security and social esteem are maintained for all.

Some early reflections still applied to the new Oman. The more we saw, the more we understood, and the more we heard and knew of the Arab world and peoples, the more our hearts ached to share a new way of life in Christ with them. It dismayed us to see how quickly they accepted our Western ideas via television and cinema. How often the forbidden liquor flowed into mouths of the youth who left Islam, except for a show of piety on holidays. How often the people cried for Western freedoms and rights while denouncing the decadent social patterns of the West. How seldom they listened to the Gospel, much less asked for it.

What fantastic changes money can make to a secluded culture and its people, educating them overnight in the lessons of materialism. Even in the desert, what Arabs knew of America came via imported TV programs. Yet, they recognized the mission people had "different hearts." They often said this of the Christians who worked in hospitals and schools and on development projects.

CHAPTER 3

Ethiopia
1975-1999

During our 1974-75 furlough in Grand Rapids, Dirk picked up band and swimming in his sophomore year; Keith enjoyed guitar lessons, skiing, and football in eighth grade. As planned, Harvey undertook training in orthopedic surgery at Butterworth Hospital.

By April 1975, we were preparing to return to the Arabian Mission. Boxes littered the living room: empty boxes, boxes stuffed with clothing and treats for the boys going back to Kodaikanal, and boxes of clothes and household items for us in Oman.

Then the message came: the minister of health of Oman had a good supply of surgeons but a short supply of housing, and therefore, our return visa was denied. That evening, our mealtime devotional reading was "God's Appointed Detours," with the text from Hebrews 11:8: "By faith Abraham . . . went out, not knowing where he was going." How timely God's Word was for us.

We began to consider our alternative options: join the TEAM hospital in Abu Dhabi, return to an RCA hospital in Bahrain, find another hospital in an Arab-speaking country, or look farther afield to one of the two RCA hospitals in Ethiopia that needed a surgeon at that time. It was a lot to consider.

By June the decision was made to respond to the RCA's call to go to Ethiopia for however long the Communist regime in power at the time would allow us American "capitalists" to remain there.[48]

Regarding paperwork, we found ourselves overwhelmed. We four needed visitors' visas for three weeks in Oman to sell our stored household goods and personal items there. We would be taking little with us to Africa. The boys needed Indian re-entry visas for school in Kodaikanal. We also required Ethiopian visas and documents for government work permits. There would be more shots specific to Ethiopia to be entered into our health books. Harvey planned the travel tickets in all directions.

In July 1975, we traveled from Grand Rapids, Michigan, to London, Bahrain, and then Oman. There the family split again as the boys traveled eastward to school in India, while Harvey and I went westward to Ethiopia, on the eastern edge of Africa. Although a continent away, Ethiopia is a mere stone's throw from the western tip of the Arabian Peninsula.

Arriving in Ethiopia

We had visited Ethiopia on our way home to the United States in 1974 when missionaries there urged Harvey to fill in for a surgeon shortage at two mission hospitals. Now, free from the work in Arabia, we accepted work at the Dembi Dolo Hospital. We were welcomed to the American Mission guest house in Addis Ababa,[49] the capital of Ethiopia, and henceforth often our temporary lodging over the course of more than two decades.

We spent a week obtaining papers for residency in Ethiopia, applying for Harvey's work permit, and stocking up on food items and goods available only in the capital. Then Harvey boarded a small Ethiopian Airlines (EAL) airplane and flew to Dembi Dolo, roughly four hundred miles due west of Addis, near the border with Sudan.

---

[48] The long-time emperor Haile Selassie had been overthrown by a Marxist regime in September 1974 and died in August 1975.
[49] Addis Ababa was commonly called "Addis," as it will be in this chronicle.

Keith, Harvey, Margaret, and Dirk in Dembi
Dolo, Ethiopia, December 1975

Harvey went to Dembi Dolo to replace the mission's only
doctor so she could go home to care for her ailing mother. Dembi
Dolo had now been a whole year with no other doctor. Harvey
worked alone for fourteen months before Dr. John Knowles of
Scotland came to join him. Marci and Paul Leemkuil also arrived.
Marci, a registered nurse, took charge of nursing at the hospital.

Patients were brought in from distant clinics and places—
either by an EAL government plane landing at the airport outside
the town or by the Missionary Aviation Fellowship (MAF) plane,
which could land on an airstrip close to the hospital. In the rainy
season, transporting anyone by truck or car was difficult because
of rutted, muddy roads. Patient care involved performing
caesarean section deliveries, treating bullet wounds and bowel
obstructions, and curing tropical infections, internal and external
worms, and eyesight problems. The tsetse fly caused sleeping
sickness; Kenya beetles blistered the skin as they crawled over
victims at night; chiggers in the dust and dirt planted eggs under
toenails; fleas and mosquitoes carried malaria; snails in streams
and rivers carried schistosomiasis; and bedbugs under wooden
seats and in upholstered furniture left angry welts on the legs.

In order to accompany a Sudanese refugee who was
returning to her home near the Sudanese border, I took the next
plane to Dembi Dolo after Harvey's. As a woman, she could not

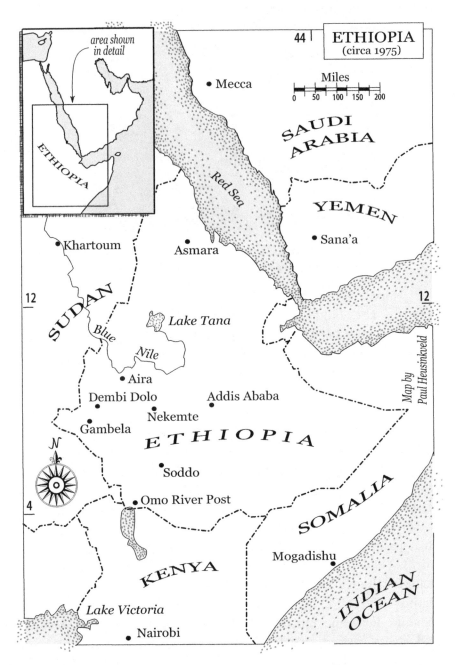

Ethiopia, with inset map of Eastern Africa

travel without a companion. I was also her translator since she spoke only Arabic and her tribal tongue. Our purchased items would come later by truck to Dembi Dolo because the rainy season had started, and roads were muddy and had developed potholes.

The road from the Dembi Dolo airport into town was not much more than a path, so driving was difficult. But what a delight it was to experience rain daily after ten parched years in Arabia where rain came briefly once a year, if at all. Our living room faced the valley to the east, so we saw beautiful rainbows most afternoons. Ethiopia has two seasons: the rainy season and the dry season. A day in the rainy season is often half rainy and half sunny.

Everything flourished in our garden except celery and sweet corn. Field corn was the farmers' staple food. Local bread was made of ground corn or of ground teff, a very small grain like millet. The dough of this bread, called *injera*, is fermented for two days and then baked over a wood fire on a large circular clay surface. It resembles a pancake when baked and serves as an edible plate for stews, vegetables, or whatever else one wants to put on it.

Our kitchen had a two-burner, countertop gas stove, seldom used because of the irregularity of getting gas tanks from the capital. A large, iron, wood-burning stove continually boiled water for drinking, washing clothes and dishes, and bathing. Most cooking and baking was done on that ancient wood stove. Wheat had to be cleaned and ground before bread could be made, and when put to soak overnight, wheat made our morning porridge. Garden produce needed cleaning, and we shelled, sorted, and roasted peanuts; squeezed limes and lemons for lemonade; ground tough local beef; and killed and dressed chickens. We hired a schoolgirl and a housekeeping girl for the chores at home so I could teach at the school.

I was asked to teach at the secondary school in Dembi Dolo where five other Americans were teaching alongside the Ethiopian staff. English and math were the subjects given to me, but conducting school was an off-again, on-again affair. The students at the government high school refused to attend classes to show empathy with Addis students striking against the military government in favor of a democratic one.

At our church's Bethel Evangelical Secondary School, the teachers came every day to ready their classrooms, but our students, when called to come, were reluctant to do so because the protesting government students harassed them on their walk to school. Just when we were finally able to fill up the classrooms with students in the seventh through tenth grades, the Marxist government closed all schools until a new curriculum could be cobbled together. East Germans had moved into the Ministry of Education, and textbooks would eventually be printed with the Communist ideology. The students who came to our school were sent home, including the boarding students who packed up and left until further notice.

For one week, the Ethiopian government ordered all idle men (meaning the teachers) to work on the roads that rain and heavy trucks had destroyed. Four of our teachers and our school's director, Dr. Solomon, had studied at college in the United States, but all our men answered the call to work on the roads in order to protect our school from scrutiny and criticism.

I was assigned library work, so with the help of a student, I put books into shelf order and typed catalog cards. My teaching schedule was to be seventh grade English, eighth grade math, tenth grade literature, and library. Dr. Solomon also wanted me to teach Arabic class for tenth graders after school. The boys and some male teachers came to Arabic class, but the girls chose the French lessons given by another American teacher. Teaching Arabic came to a halt when Ethiopia and Sudan fell out; it was prudent not to be heard speaking the enemy's language.

I also taught elementary English classes twice a week for the fifth and sixth graders at the church's primary school. During the summer break, I taught a refresher course to the church's primary school teachers. Most of those teachers were not more than eighth grade graduates themselves, but they were not interested in English lessons. They repeatedly asked for help reading the philosophies of Marx and Lenin. They expected certificates of graduation, no less, to their next English class level. The English class was soon eliminated from the program. It was a confrontational summer and, when it was over, the church gave these small schools to the farmers' associations to run. These were farmers without budgets or education.

Through one of my students, I met a grandmother who was an invalid in very fragile health. Her grandson cared for her as she lovingly cooked their meals and washed their clothes from the limits of her wheelchair. However capable she was at home, she did not have the capability to traverse Ethiopia's dirt and stone roads. But her grandson was an attentive, clever boy and came up with a solution: every Sunday morning, he came early to the missionary compound to borrow a wheelbarrow. Into that, he gently lifted his tiny grandmother and then pushed off for church, settling her into a chair once there. What a sight that was.

One particularly bright boy in my mathematics class informed me he would soon be quitting school because he could no longer afford the tuition. Harvey and I made a point of helping the brighter students who needed money, so we included him as well. To earn money for school supplies, he came every afternoon after class and cut the grass around our house. Bent low at the waist, he worked his way steadily across the yard, rhythmically shearing with a small sickle in one hand and a tuft of grass in the other. He also kept an eye on the vegetable and flower gardens. By this work, he earned approximately five cents per hour, a goodly sum for a local—and a child no less. He had worked hard for his pay and beamed with pride as he walked away, coins in hand.

Foreigners often traveled through our area, so we frequently had expected and unexpected guests. Greek merchants set up shops with goods that foreigners might buy. Arab merchants set up shops with the kinds of items that local farmers and villagers needed. A Saturday market held predictable garden produce and wares spread out on cloths on the ground where women sat, watching passersby, and calling out their goods. Some surprises might be available, and there were always hens, sheep, goats, and occasionally mules, for sale.

Churches of Ethiopia

Christianity came to Ethiopia in the fourth century when two Egyptian slave boys survived a shipwreck on Ethiopian shores. Taken to the king, they witnessed to their Orthodox faith, and he sent them back to Egypt to train for future priesthood in Ethiopia. For all these centuries, the Orthodox (Coptic) Church has been Ethiopia's leading religion. Services are led by priests who read or chant the whole liturgy in the ancient priestly language of Ge'ez, a language known only to priests and their families.[50] The service includes many Judaic rituals, such as burning incense, displaying the replica of the ark in the Holy of Holies, following dietary laws among church members, and reserving an outer hall for women to enter for a short worship time to light a candle and kiss the feet of Mary in a large painting on the wall and then leave.

January 6 (Western Epiphany Day) is the Ethiopian Orthodox Christmas Day. From its foundation in the fourth century, very little has been made of the season of Christmas, so there are few traditions Ethiopians can call their own. Orthodox Christians the world over, particularly in Greece, Russia, Syria, and Egypt, usually celebrate Christmas on January 6. That is true also in Ethiopia. Our Ethiopian evangelical churches follow the Orthodox calendar for Christmas, Lent, and Easter.

City folks began adopting Western Christmas culture. Exchanging Christmas cards and decorating store windows became vogue in the capital. Most Christmas cards were reproductions of the beautiful ceiling and wall paintings in the ancient churches of Ethiopia. The only hint of new customs in our town was a pine tree in the front of the church with one or two discarded baubles on it. There were also shiny paper cutouts—probably emulating the missionaries' homes. Gift giving was avoided because of Ethiopia's poverty and the dearth of trinkets and toys; new clothes were given at the New Year time in September, if a family could afford it.

---

[50] Ge'ez, an ancient South Semitic language, is the liturgical language of the Ethiopian and Eritrean priesthood and is difficult to understand by anyone outside the priesthood.

January 20 is Epiphany (Timket) Day for Ethiopians. Priests carry a small replica of the Ark of the Covenant, kept in every Orthodox Church. The colorful procession of priests moves from the church to the river, where they camp overnight in a tent. On Timket Day, the crowds come to the river's edge to be sprinkled with water by the priests in commemoration of Christ's baptism. A procession of priests, chanters, and a crowd return to the churchyard where the priests put the little ark back in its place in the Holy of Holies and then sit down with the crowd to enjoy bread and tea.

During the forty days of Lent, no meat is eaten. Weddings, therefore, where meat is served, do not occur during Lent.

As European missionaries came, the emperors allocated tribal areas for their work in hopes of winning tribal loyalty to the throne and bringing peace among the contentious tribes. Missionaries also brought medical and educational advantages to the local communities, often neglected of those services by the central government. Evangelical churches grew in great numbers, incorporating the Orthodox Church's Gregorian calendar and its dietary rules but using the emperor's language of government, Amharic, for services.

In recent centuries, when missionaries entered Ethiopia, they brought with them contrasting Catholic and diverse Protestant doctrines. Catholicism established churches during the Italian occupation of Ethiopia (1936-43). Protestant missionaries were given sections of the country for their work after the Swedes had earlier established the first Protestant work in the north and west of the country. Scandinavian and German work made for a strong Lutheran persuasion. Most small sects and denominations were closed by the Communist government that took power in 1975. It was only this Lutheran group that the Communist government recognized and accepted.[51]

When missionaries working in neighboring southeastern Sudan were ejected, Emperor Haile Selassie gave them permission

---

[51] It was a common practice of Communist regimes to recognize denominations of nonindigenous churches in order to undermine the historic ecclesiastical hierarchies, in this case, the Ethiopian Orthodox Church.

to work in southwestern Ethiopia with the same tribal and language groups they had known in Sudan. The Presbyterian-Reformed church work had been centered in Sudan. It was now known as Bethel Churches and operated under the umbrella of the Lutheran Church, recognized regionally as the Evangelical Ethiopian Church or Mekane Yesus (Amharic for the "Place of Jesus").

Qes[52] Gidada's story: "The other side of darkness"

Early Presbyterian missionaries in Dembi Dolo shared the Gospel with a number of blind beggars and taught them skills to earn income. One such young man was Gidada Solon, blinded by a smallpox epidemic that took the lives of his seven older siblings. He was twenty when he accepted Christ, and he studied to become a pastor. The missionaries taught him to read Braille in their school for the blind. He became Qes [Reverend] Gidada, the second ordained pastor in the area. Qes Gidada's son, Solomon, was his companion and guide; he was also my school director.

Qes Gidada Solon ventured over hills and into far valleys to witness to whatever tribes he met. He had a remarkable memory of God's Word. He usually rode a donkey while Solomon walked beside him. Solomon's brothers also accompanied their father on his travels and received schooling when they were not needed by their father.

Qes Gidada was incarcerated for the five years Italy occupied Ethiopia and forced Protestant churches to close prior to World War II. Orthodox priests also had him imprisoned when he preached in "their" territory. He was tortured while in prison, but he never failed to use the opportunities to spread the Word among his fellow inmates and guards.

Some Sunday afternoons, Qes Gidada invited Harvey to preach at the jail. It was a ministry dear to Qes Gidada's heart. He also was a spiritual leader of the Dembi Dolo region of the church. He was even invited to visit the palace of Emperor Haile Selassie.

---

[52] Also sometimes spelled "Kees," pronounced "case."

Qes Gidada (the blind pastor) and his son,
Solomon, PhD, in Dembi Dolo, 1976

But his prison experience exposed him to tuberculosis, and in late December 1976, he died. His son Solomon was in Addis at that time because his American wife had severe gall bladder disease and desperately needed surgery. The Communist government had given them exit permission papers, and the Presbyterian Hospital in New York City was awaiting their arrival. Solomon had chosen to tend to his wife rather than to be in Dembi Dolo for the funeral—an unheard-of choice, based on local custom.

When someone has died, before the burial of the body, no one eats in the home, but the family receives visitors, and everyone sits in silence. No talking is done until the body is buried, usually within twenty-four hours of death. After the burial, groups of visitors bring food for the family since the fire in the home is not to be lit for a week. Every family member's head is shaved to show respect for the dead elder.

With much wailing, a huge crowd carried Qes Gidada's coffin to the church service and later to the churchyard cemetery to lay him to rest. Later, the grave was razed when the Communists desecrated the stones, and the cemetery was made into a new market area with the vendors sitting on the flat bases to sell their goods.

Solomon went on to Rochester, New York, to get a PhD in education. While he was gone, the missionary wives sent food daily to the school compound for the six children and three young female workers in his home. When Dr. Solomon returned to Ethiopia in January of 1977, neighbors and church members asked him why he returned. They thought he most likely would be imprisoned along with the other American-educated young teachers at the school. His response was. "My wife and I have six small, precious reasons to return to our home in Dembi Dolo, prison or not." Dr. Solomon became the principal of the Dembi Dolo's Bethel Evangelical Secondary School (grades 7-12) where I taught.

Ruphael

At nine months of age, Ruphael was brought to the Dembi Dolo Mission hospital by his mother. He was born with club feet, turned ninety degrees inward at the ankles. While Harvey was doing the corrective surgery on the baby's feet, his mother disappeared. It is likely she thought nothing could be done, and the boy would be unable to farm when he grew up. That left Rufi—as we called him—an orphan to live at the hospital; Ethiopians are not easily persuaded to foster others who are not their own kin.

A bond grew between the doctor and his little patient. After a time, the child learned to get out of his crib and toddle after Harvey in his casts, even when Harvey took his coffee break every morning at home. Rufi's first English word, learned in our home, may have been "cookie!" With only a few pieces of baby clothes and a hospital gown, Rufi needed clothes as he grew. As often as I went to the capital and when the boys and I went to Nairobi for their visas, I would buy outfits for Rufi. When Harvey blew up a balloon one day, the little boy's eyes shone with amazement and delight. Rufi appeared fearless when our sons gave him rides on their motorcycle.

Dirk and Keith

Our boys came to Dembi Dolo and our new home from school in India for Christmas 1975. Along the way, they visited the missionary school in Addis to see if they might want to transfer there.

There was not much for them to do in Dembi Dolo. They helped keep the grass airstrip near the hospital in good shape and enjoyed greeting the planes that flew in. They even took turns relaying and receiving messages on the morning mission network radio when the usual person was absent. Over that radio, we responded to an offer to buy a motorcycle from a missionary who was leaving his work. Meanwhile, generous colleagues let the boys enjoy their motorcycles during their Christmas vacation.

Their experience in Dembi Dolo over Christmas break was so positive that they left us in January to return to Kodaikanal, having decided for themselves that they would leave India at the end of the school year and register at Good Shepherd School in Addis.

In May of 1976, the boys left Kodai School, returned to Ethiopia, and enrolled at Good Shepherd School in Addis for the school year beginning in the fall. Keith would enter tenth grade and Dirk twelfth grade. They spent the summer with us in Dembi Dolo, and Dirk helped with the construction work team. Several times he went with the team to a remote site where they were building a new clinic. Again, the boys helped with radio messages and airstrip upkeep.

Harvey found free time from hospital work to continue the boys' driving lessons. When the boys walked with me to the secondary school, they enjoyed the chattering colobus and vervet monkeys up in the trees along the path.

In the final weeks of summer vacation, the boys and I went to Addis. The boys needed permanent Ethiopian resident visas to stay in the country, and that requirement necessitated a short exit out of Ethiopia—in this case, a trip to Nairobi, Kenya. The day we flew out of Dembi Dolo, the boys' motorcycle arrived on a truck. Harvey enjoyed trying it out during breaks from the hospital.

Harvey had now worked for a whole year with no other doctor. He not only did surgery of every specialty but also sat through the morning outpatient clinic. Often he answered medical questions on the radio from other mission stations and from the hospital's remote clinics. How grateful he was that there was a landing strip for the MAF airplanes close to the hospital.

The boys and I spent plenty of money in Nairobi on clothes, food, hotel, and visas. We also enjoyed the National Wildlife Park at the city's edge where Dirk took many photos of the abundant wildlife: big cats, elephants, giraffes, ostriches, and so much more.

After returning to Ethiopia and settling the boys into their respective Addis dorm rooms for the new school year, I returned to Dembi Dolo and Harvey.

Fourteen months after we arrived in Dembi Dolo, Dr. Knowles and family arrived to help relieve the work at the hospital. After turning over the outpatient department to Dr. Knowles, Harvey took his first break to Addis to buy supplies and see our sons. I went along because I was now on the Good Shepherd school board, and a meeting happened to coincide with his trip. The boys were doing well, and both were on the honor roll. It being Thanksgiving weekend, another family invited our family to join them for a camping weekend at Lake Langano.

Unexpected adventure

After being in Addis with the boys and for a school board meeting, it was time to return to Harvey at Dembi Dolo, but the plane was full. The Presbyterian Mission director, Harold Kurtz, had a ticket on the next EAL plane and suggested I go to the airport with him and try to get on that plane. I did get a seat and got off in Jimma, about two hundred miles southwest of Addis. We boarded an MAF plane the next day, heading toward Dembi Dolo. Harold was going to discuss with Harvey the political concerns arising at the hospital, and I got the remarkable privilege of an MAF flight to four mission stations before arriving home.

Stop 1: Omo River Post, where Bob and Morrie Swart and Lillian Huisken[53] (who had been a nurse with us in Oman) were working. Bob built windmills with local men and placed them along the riverbank. From the air, one can see miles of brown

---

[53] Rev. Robert and Morrell (a nurse) Swart and Lillian Huisken (a nurse) were RCA missionaries with the Joint Reformed Presbyterian Mission.

brush and sand—except along the fertile riverbanks, green with crops because of the windmills' water supply.

The mission houses were two concrete and metal Quonset hut-style buildings with a long cement slab between them covered by a screen to serve as a living-dining area. The local people had igloo-type mounds covered with skins and grass, into which one entered on hands and knees through a low entrance. The houses were intended for sleeping only, so did not require height for standing. Beside the skin-and-grass domes, there stood a platform on poles for grain and food storage, built higher than the house to protect the food from scavenging animals.

Stop 2: A quick delivery of mail and freight at a station near Omo.

Stop 3: The Ghimeera airstrip ran right down the middle of a flat mountain plateau with a steep escarpment on each side. On one side of the airstrip were the clinic and mission homes; on the other side were the primary school and the mission workers' homes where we left a local teacher who had flown with us.

Stop 4: Teppi was a mission station troubled by radicalized local youths and party leaders long before communism's arrival. We found the Schreuder family and Leatta Wiedenbach[54] sitting around a card table with little else left in their homes. They had sold most everything and were ready to leave at a moment's notice as they feared for their lives. Because of ongoing property disputes with community leaders, they were subjected to continual harassment and could not endure much more, but Harold Kurtz and our Finnish pilot, Seppo, assured them that MAF's last flights would be for evacuating the stations the following week, before MAF was officially nationalized. A week later, Lillian left the station at Omo, but the Swarts chose to stay with their truck and boat, ready to evacuate in those. MAF left the country and, unsurprisingly, both of Swart's vehicles of escape were confiscated. They ended up leaving their post on a small, expensive, private plane.

---

[54] Rev. Al and Sue (a nurse) Schreuder were RCA missionaries. Nurse Leattta Weidenbach was a Presbyterian missionary.

Stop 5: Finally, Dembi Dolo, where Harvey and Ruphael were waiting for me at the airstrip. I was happy to be home but grateful for the tour of other mission outposts.

Motorcycle brigade, January 1977

Our boys again came home for Christmas 1976. They loved riding the motorcycle and frequently rode it into the countryside. One of them would come to school at noon to bring me home for lunch, while the other took me back for afternoon classes. Before returning to Addis for the second semester, they made a joyful and unforgettable motorcycle trip with other motorcyclists to Gambela.

We were seventeen adventurers with precious government travel permits in hand. That is, there were three American high school boys, four Ethiopian mission employees, and six American missionaries on twelve motorcycles, plus two American and two Ethiopian passengers in a back-up vehicle. The Land Rover pick-up was loaded with motorcycle parts, tools, food, sleeping bags, gas, and a spare tire. We occupants kept up the rear of the brigade like morale cheerleaders. The three boys took off first, and others fell into line for the long, rough descent from Dembi Dolo at over six thousand feet, down the escarpment to Gambela at one thousand feet. The two older teens were in Gambela in six hours, impatiently awaiting the rest of the brigade just outside the town.

The winding, downhill road was muddy and potholed from rain, trucks, and cow hooves and was either pure rock or stony bed in several stretches. But all things considered, it was not in too bad of a condition. For the fifty-six miles down, we older and wiser ones made the descent slowly—never going over fifteen miles per hour. That meant we arrived in ten hours.

We stopped at one village where an Ethiopian teacher had left to visit his in-laws, and two students got into our vehicles, hoping for a ride to Gambela. Another stop was at a police station to report our presence and show our papers. The break for lunch was a good time to review our progress. One missionary teacher on her small "putt-putt" was shaking from fatigue and gave up. An older missionary wife had fallen several times, so she gave her bike to Harvey and rode with me in the car. Another missionary teacher drove the car on to Gambela, where she would join a nurse on a downriver canoe trip to visit church clinics, share medicines, and tell Bible stories.

Along the way, we saw forests, fields of coffee, grain, sorghum and corn, and many fruit trees. The autumnal forests had dropped yellow and brown leaves. We often had to maneuver around people, donkeys, and mules, and at one point, baboons were sunning in the road and stubbornly made passing very difficult for humans.

From the escarpment, we finally entered the plains of sand and red clay soil, burnt fields and forests with charred trees, and everywhere towering anthills, higher than a person. The land was mostly nonarable, except in places where it had been burned for planting. There, grass alongside the paths was so tall it blocked the endless cornfields beyond. Local villagers subsisted on corn mush, so little else was grown there.

With our passports and permits, we reported to the police again. We found large, abandoned warehouses along the riverfront and temporarily settled in a partially demolished one in which a missionary nurse lived. Most of the group went to a hotel in town. The river was low, so no boats from Sudan were transporting goods either to or from the port anymore. Most of the people spoke Sudanese languages because Gambela was once a part of Sudan. The mission doctor took us all to a Greek restaurant for a spaghetti supper then to his home for homemade ice cream. Our tired group had a good sleep and spent most of the next day repairing and cleaning our motorcycles.

Our motive for bringing the pick-up truck with us was to fetch a grinding stone for our school kitchen. With that objective accomplished, we drove two hours to the Pokwo clinic, situated only nineteen miles from Gambela but on a very poor road. Former missionaries had constructed a boulevard from their homes to the water's edge using fruit trees. A hospital, a school, and homes for workers, missionaries, leprosy patients, and patients' families lined the boulevard.

The Anuak men of Pokwo wore shirts and shorts; girls wore only skirts, and women covered their bodies with draped cloths.

Children wore nothing. The women stuck toothpicks in the flesh below their lower lips to stretch them, and they wore lots of beads on their foreheads and necks. They all smeared ashes on their bodies to ward off mosquitoes. We put a spearing victim into the cab for our return to Gambela and brought him onward up to the hospital in Dembi Dolo for Harvey to do surgery on.

Back in Gambela, we retired early after the supper we had brought. Next morning, after a late breakfast, we shook ashes, sand, and grass from our sleeping bags, helped pack the truck, and prepared to leave.

Once again, the three boys took off first on their motorcycles, with Dirk leading the way. Having arrived home in just four hours, Dirk prepared supper and heated bath water for our arrival. The heavy grinding stone on the back of the truck made for slow progress, especially where the roads became ditches or gullies. After stopping for several motorcycle repairs and lunch, we came upon a cold and glum Keith, whose bike had a flat tire. He had waited a long time for us, only to be disappointed when he and his bike rode the rest of the way home on the back of the truck. We arrived at eight o'clock in the evening, after eleven hours of driving.

Expelled, 1977

Jealousy of the hospital workers' salaries and privileges at Dembi Dolo fueled discontent in town, and talk of action against the hospital had to be squelched by the local governor (a Hope College graduate, as were we), the chief of police, and the farmers' association leader. But the hospital workers were eventually led to believe they could take over the hospital, control the revenue, and acquire their pension funds. The chief leader promoting this misinformed notion was the local government health officer, whereas the Ministry of Health in Addis had neither a plan nor the money to run this remote hospital.

One morning, Harvey was asked by Qes Gidada Solon to give a Christian message to the prisoners. Harvey recognized one unhappily jailed man because, just the week before, he had been made to testify in court regarding the cause of death of the prisoner's wife. The man was already in jail, and his wife's body was decaying, but court minds were set: "She has been beaten." And Harvey, their ostensible expert, was expected to agree with their forgone conclusion, but he knew better and could not. Thus, they questioned this new and young Doctor Harvey: "Don't you know beaten bodies when you see them?" He was lectured and berated at great length, accused of being ignorant of his profession.

The radio message from President Mengistu Haile-Miriam was loud and clear: "Ethiopia now has a Permanent Military Government, following Marxist-Lenin lines." In Dembi Dolo, the voices of the young people were louder still, and clearer: "The missionaries and all American-educated Ethiopians are exploiting the nationals."

We heard of war in the north of Ethiopia with Eritrea, a province longing to secede from Ethiopia. There were, as well, troubles in southeastern Ethiopia with Somali insurgents. The Nuer and Anuak tribes in southwest Ethiopia were engaged in ongoing harassment and war. In the capital, youth were incited by professors to promote antigovernment actions, while the government searched for and eliminated youth of the four other Communist parties that opposed the party of the reigning regime, the Derg.[55]

The government declared it would take over all schools, especially foreign ones. Our sons wrote of hearing shooting in Addis nightly, the expelling of US diplomatic personnel in the country within four days, and watching prisoners digging huge holes outside their school fence daily—only to find them filled (to cover bodies) the following morning. Students were confined to the school compound most of their last two months.

In Dembi Dolo, two of the invited speakers to our school's chapel program touted Communist teachings, and soon, ninth graders were asking to speak much along the same lines. One student speaker was not so much anti-American as he was anti-Christian and quoted Communist texts instead of the Bible. That

---

[55] Derg: the Coordinating Committee of the Armed Forces, Police, and Territorial Army, ruling Ethiopia from 1974 to 1987.

day the students applauded their classmate loudly; I responded by dismissing the student workers at my house for a week. To quiet the fomenting anti-American sentiments, the Presbyterian Church wisely put the school under the control of the Ethiopian Evangelical Church, Mekane Yesus.

In March a trade school run by the German mission in our province was taken over by local forces. It had excellent, up-to-date machinery. A month later, another mission trade school was nationalized, with the government declaring, "We cannot allow private schools to continue with their subversive teachings." Radio Voice of the Gospel's Addis program property, building, audiovisual department, and publishing department were nationalized. The *Radio Voice of Revolutionary Ethiopia* was soon on the air.

The Heli-Mission helicopters were nationalized. News came over the church radio that one family after another had been evacuated by their mission and left the country. At the Dembi Dolo government secondary school, an impromptu "inquisition" was held one afternoon, and thirty students were found to have "antigovernment sentiments." They and one teacher were whipped by the inquisitors. When the Derg heard of it, they stepped in and declared the ambitions of the youth inquisitors both illegal and premature.

In May government conscription took many men and then later boys to the northern war with Eritrea. I went to Addis to attend a board meeting at my sons' school and to enjoy a play they were both in. They came from their school across town to be with me at the guest house the Friday night I arrived. On Saturday the government announced a curfew of all cars for the weekend. My boys walked the length of the city to get back to their school compound. They were stopped by soldiers on street corners twenty times to show their ID cards. But they were not searched by every soldier they met, as Ethiopian people were. There was no shopping nor board meeting nor Sunday church for me, and the school's play was cancelled both nights due to the curfew.

In May EAL seldom sent planes to Dembi Dolo, so we waited for three planes to take us to Dirk's Baccalaureate in Addis, but we were unable to get there in time. On May 30, MAF flew all six of its planes safely out to Kenya. Those pilots returned to close their families' homes and leave for MAF work in new countries.

On June 2, a government plane arrived in Dembi Dolo, allowing us to fly to Addis for Dirk's graduation. The trip to the airport took us past the police station. They were waiting to stop us and directed the men into the station for questioning. They slowly searched Harvey's luggage, also packed for our upcoming July flight to America. Marci Leemkuil's husband, Paul—an agricultural specialist—was not allowed to continue on to the airport. The police did not want us to catch the plane—thus, they took their time questioning—so Marci strutted into the station, stuck out her very pregnant tummy, and said she did not want to deliver her baby there. That moved the police. "Oh, No! No! Go!"

Before leaving the station, our school principal had to sign his name for responsibility to assure that all four of his teachers (including me) would return to their work until the school year ended in June. Otherwise, he would be imprisoned. It seemed no harm was really intended, but they nonetheless felt compelled to harass us.

Paul Leemkuil was not allowed to leave Dembi Dolo; moreover, he was no longer allowed to teach. The students did not like agriculture lessons and spoke against Paul. An edict was issued that all the land around the church and mission buildings belonged to the revolutionaries. All Ethiopians were allowed to own just five hundred square meters of land and only one house. Stores in Addis owned by Greeks, Italians, and other foreigners were nationalized, including the buildings and the goods within. We stored our personal goods in a locked room in hopes of returning, and on July 2, we left for a brief furlough.

We felt at peace in the countryside as turmoil prevailed in Addis. The number of people shot in the street increased. The war with Eritrea and its demand for secession continued. The CMS mission and the Swiss mission evacuated all personnel. The German mission school in the capital was closed by the government, and rumors of a government takeover of Good Shepherd School became real. Keith chose not to go to yet another new school but to return to his former school in India, where he had spent his primary and middle school years.

In Addis many people awaited exit from Ethiopia since most expatriate work was hindered throughout the country. Some missionaries sold everything and others took two suitcases, but later groups were not allowed any personal items to be removed from their homes, including the children's toys. Believing we might return, Harvey and I decided to store our personal items. We were advised to have a small bag of essentials packed and ready should a plane arrive without warning.

We had come to Ethiopia assuming a two- or three-month tenure under communism but instead enjoyed two rewarding years of fellowship and work.

After we left Ethiopia, reports from Dembi Dolo came to us in America that all remaining RCA and PCUSA[56] mission personnel had joined the mass evacuation of all foreigners. At Dembi Dolo hospital, hostility toward Dr. Knowles was fomented by four young ringleaders. The local revolutionary council demanded payments from the hospital come from the employees' retirement benefits, while the Ethiopian government demanded a payment from the mission, the equivalent of one year's running budget, and the government would not grant exit visas to Dr. Knowles, Paul Leemkuil, or the Presbyterian representatives for Ethiopia unless more than one year of total running cost of the Dembi Dolo hospital was paid to the government. The Presbyterian mission did not have any funds to settle this demand. After two weeks of keeping these missionaries hostage, an agreement was reached by the mission, paying a minimal symbolic amount, and exit visas were finally granted.

The ramifications of the Communist takeover of the mission programs in Dembi Dolo were made clear in the aftermath. The stories of two of the young people with whom we worked is instructive.

Letters from Aberash

I was in my second year of teaching at the church's secondary school, Bethel Evangelical Secondary School in Dembi

---

[56] PCUSA, Presbyterian Church of the USA.

Dolo, when I met Aberash. As a young Christian girl, she spent much time searching for truth in the midst of Communist "truths" being taught to her and her classmates. She was confused by the contrast between the teachings of the Bible and of the Communist regime. She often quoted King David's words: "The fool says in his heart, 'There is no God'" (Ps. 53:1). One question was often raised: "Why do they [her Communist peer group] hate me?" Being in the school choir, she ran into many scheduling conflicts; the political meetings for youth were set at the same time as choir practice. We discussed the issues and prayed together for her future growth as a Christian.

Harvey and I left Dembi Dolo, soon followed by all the missionaries expelled by the local Communist government. The hospital was soon staffed by Cuban medical personnel, but the school was staffed by Ethiopian teachers and a missionary teacher.

In 1978, upon my return to Ethiopia in a different mission field, I was again in touch with Aberash, this time by letters. She responded to me from Dembi Dolo:

Bethel Evangelical Secondary School
Dembi Dolo, Ethiopia
February 9, 1978

Dear Mrs. Doorenbos,

How excited I was when I received your letter last week! I thank you very much for your thoughtfulness. I have no words to express how God loves us and He cares for us. It always leads me to say God really loves me to bring you back to Ethiopia.

Everything in this compound of ours is going well after vacation. We even got light from the town. The evening study hours are changed until 11 p.m., but twelfth graders can study even to 2 a.m. I really would like to go to university if it is God's plan. Before that, I would like to have a job for one year to support the nineteen people in my family. I even want to have a job toward the end of May, but I don't even know where I would apply to. Pray for me please just to solve these simple problems.

Read Job ch. 4 and especially vs. 4-5.[57] Convey
my greetings to Dr. Doorenbos. Write when you can.
God bless you, Aberash

Aberash passed the exam into the university in Addis but
failed in her first semester studies there. Unwilling to return to her
village, she "saved face" by accepting the government's offer of an
education in Russia.[58] That was an awesome step for a village
child, yet many were taking the opportunity offered to them. I
received several letters from Russia, one of which read:

The U.S.S.R.
November 24, 1980
Dear Mrs. and Dr. Doorenbos,
How do you do since we met the last time? I am
very fine thanks to our Lord Jesus Christ. When you
were in Addis, I was having trouble at the Office of
Foreign Affairs because of my passport. I came to see
you on Saturday but was informed that you had gone
back to Aira. I was very sad but nothing to do.
For me the flight was on October 12. We had a
nice journey to Moscow. Our educational attache was
at the airport, so we didn't face any problem. We
didn't stay long in Moscow because we were very late
to start our lessons. So we had to move to other areas
for preparatory program.
Now I am about 1,500 kilometers away from
Moscow. Because we were late to begin our program,
we really faced great problem in knowing Russian
language. I didn't have a single minute for relaxing or
writing letters to friends like you. Thanks to our Lord,
now I am well. I understand and speak this language,
if not very fluently.
We take five subjects, four of them completely in
this new language, but our history lesson we have in
both the English and the Russian language. During my

---

57 "Your words have supported those who were stumbling, and you have
made firm the feeble knees. But now it has come to you, and you are
impatient; it touches you, and you are dismayed" (NRSV).
58 About twenty-four thousand Ethiopian students received scholarships
to study in the Soviet Union (Gabrielle Tetrault-Farber, "Ethiopian
Ambassador seeks to Upgrade Dialogue with Russia," *The Moscow
Times*, 16 June 2015).

arrival of the first three weeks, I was almost tempted to go back to Ethiopia. But now God is with me; I am always joyful.

Anyway, I enjoy my life in this country now; after this the plan is not my own but God's plan. For me to be here is something better than nothing. If God is with a person, one can live even in jungle. I always cheer up myself and make myself joyful. But for many students, it became impossible, so they are always sad. Many of them are homesick. For me to stay in Ethiopia without education or job is nothing. Anyway, life is not expensive; especially food is very cheap. For our winter clothes, the Russian government is responsible.

Drop me a letter when you can, Aberash

I was awed by all she had experienced. She spoke four languages: her mother tongue, Oromo; Amharic, Ethiopia's official language; English, the secondary school's medium in Ethiopia; and Russian. Everything was reportedly provided, so what could she repay? It was her mind and soul they wanted to capture. "I am to stay until I understand Marxism," she once wrote.

Her strong faith, however, sustained her. Her faith provided comfort when she was imprisoned upon returning from Moscow to Ethiopia. The government had changed once again, and she, like so many youth, was arrested as a subversive against the government.

In later years, she and her husband would work for an international company. She was typical of the second generation of Ethiopian Christians attending mission schools and churches. Deep faith was their strength throughout the Marxist regime.

Ruphael's story continued

When we took our departure from Dembi Dolo, I believe Rufi was crushed in spirit. Since we were suspected of being among those distrusted "American Imperialists," we were not allowed to adopt him. The government did not look favorably upon adoption, especially when there was a biological parent somewhere. But a little girl left at the hospital would be rather quickly adopted by local parents—girls can make good housemaids.[59]

After leaving Dembi Dolo in July 1977, we were invited by the church to work at a hospital in Aira, some distance northeast of Dembi Dolo. When Keith came home from school in India for Christmas, the three of us went back to the house in Dembi Dolo to retrieve our stored goods. We also brought little Rufi new clothes. He and the hospital staff could not understand why we did not take him with us to our new assignment.

When the Cubans[60] took over the work at the now nationalized government hospital, Ruphael remained under their care. An older boy joined Ruphael at the hospital; he would later teach him the ways of the "street" and the bad habits of such a life. Discipline was not structured, and Ruphael's school attendance was poor.

Ruphael's legs began to turn inward again as screws in the braces and casts broke down. The Cuban staff could not repair the damage, so they sent him to Harvey in Aira for more corrective surgery. He would not stay off his feet until they healed, so he developed a permanent limp. He came twice to try the school in Aira and was received into a family home. The government did not allow local adoptions, and the villagers did not trust Rufi, so he eventually returned to Dembi Dolo.

From there he went to Addis and got into political and police trouble, so he fled to Nairobi, Kenya. With so many young Ethiopian refugees in Nairobi, the police often rounded up a group and imprisoned them—Ruphael included. He did not communicate with us for a very long time. After our retirement in America, Ruphael called us from Australia. He had found not only training and work in exile but also a female Ethiopian refugee to marry him. They were now settled in Australia. Over the years, we had prayed that he would settle down and become a parent who would raise a good family, the kind he had never known.

---

[59] Knowing the difficulty of adoption, we were careful to never let any orphan child stay for meals or overnight in our home.
[60] In addition to Cuban doctors, when Somalia invaded Ethiopia in July 1977, Cuba sent sixteen thousand troops to assist Ethiopia in what became the Ogaden War.

CHAPTER 4

Aira, Ethiopia

Back in America, we deliberated not only where we were needed but also where we could use our Arabic. The general secretary of the Ethiopian Evangelical Church sent us a message via the Presbyterian Church USA, saying, "As you know, we are anxious that some of the work interrupted last spring can begin again. Specifically, we believe that Dr. and Mrs. Doorenbos are needed, not only at their particular hospital but also as a sign of hope for the whole Church, the dove returning to the ark with a twig." We heard God call us to return to Ethiopia via that letter.

Our assignment was to the German Mission Station in Aira, Ethiopia, where the German Hermannsburg Mission had established work many years earlier. We had served there briefly after we left Dembi Dolo in 1977. En route to Ethiopia, we stopped in Hermannsburg, Germany, to meet the home board of their Ethiopian mission work. Their medical team in Aira had left when the government sent drafted boys to the hospital for their physical exams before they entered the army. The doctors, who were pacifists, could not conscientiously do those exams, and so they left.

Arriving in Addis, we stayed at the American Mission guest house, where we met the Presbyterian representative of the American Mission. He was clearing out his home since he had finally been released from house arrest by the Communist government. He could now go home to his family in America. We became acquainted with the staff of the German Mission headquarters, conveniently situated in the next block from our guest house.

The 525 kilometers (330 miles) from Addis to Aira can be traversed in fourteen hours or so. The trip can also be lengthened indefinitely. Of course, whether it is the rainy season or the dry season makes a great difference. In the rainy season, one deals with slippery mud, potholes, and the need for chains; in the dry season, clouds of dust obscure one's vision.

On this occasion, we were lent an old Land Rover with a canvas-covered back that the Presbyterian mission did not want to keep sitting in the compound lest the military confiscate it. This vehicle would bring us to our new home after an exhausting trek.

Bringing all we needed for our home, we packed the Land Rover in drizzling rain. We carried two hundred pounds of flour, sixty pounds of sugar, a sixty-pound battery for the clinic, and one hundred liters of gasoline. The cargo pushed the Land Rover down onto its springs. On top of the cab were three suitcases, fruit and vegetables in a plastic tub, mail for all the missionaries in our area, and a spare tire. We put on new front tires in anticipation of a rugged road ahead—mostly stones and sharp rocks.

On Friday we set off from the Presbyterian guest house and went two doors up the street to the German Mission guest house to pick up our guide, the Aira Hospital administrator. The sun was bright and warm; our spirits were high, and happily, no complications occurred at the various military inspection points we encountered along the way.

The car's motor, however, began to die shortly after we set out. Harvey stopped and worked to get it going again. He did not succeed, so the administrator and I got onto a bus going back into the city.

A missionary offered to return to the marooned car with the mechanic who had previously "fixed" the car for $2,000. The mechanic claimed he had only fixed the front shimmying and the rear transmission; he had never looked under the hood. Hearing our description of the Land Rover's troubles, he said he doubted that a new carburetor would be needed. Our missionary friend drove the mechanic, our guide (the hospital administrator), and me to where Harvey had stayed with the broken-down car.

The mechanic worked on the distributor wires and other parts, and the car started—as it always did when things got jiggled around. The mechanic and our missionary friend returned to the capital while the rest of us went on, content to know that all was well.

Suddenly, we heard a "Bang!" and found that the rear right tire had blown out and was torn to pieces. The spare, formerly one of the front tires, quickly replaced it, and we set out again on our odyssey. Before too much longer, however, the engine gave us more trouble. It had no difficulty going downhill, but going up the next hill, it stopped halfway. Once again, we jiggled and fiddled with the engine, but we gave up when the starter button no longer turned the engine over. We sat, we slept, and finally we heard a truck coming our way, which towed us into the next town.

Ambo, an Italian-built town—still very Western in some sections—did not have a single garage. It did not have even a Greek or Italian mechanic left in town, but people said there was an Ethiopian one available. Harvey got some youths to push our car into the courtyard of a hotel. The new mechanic took out the distributor parts and really worked on the wiring until rain forced him to quit until morning. We had a large, Western-style meal since we were very hungry. An Englishman from the medical school was there for a seminar and recognized Harvey as the doctor from Wollega Province who had sent pathological specimens from the hospital's lab to the medical school for examination.

We had a great night's sleep and felt refreshed in the morning. Harvey's breakfast was interrupted by the mechanic, and they set out for the wretched vehicle. The Englishman joined me for conversation and asked how we would ever get to such a remote place as Aira in the rain. I shrugged and assured him that we would keep at it.

At eleven o'clock that morning, we were back in the car but went down the road only to a tire shop. It was filled with more people than tires. Because it was market day in Ambo, we drew a good-sized crowd of curious onlookers. Harvey found one used tire good enough to be a spare, and he had a tube inserted into it.

The afternoon was clear, and our travel was great. Throughout our trip, several military inspections took place, although they were generally brief and amiable because we were foreigners.

On the outskirts of Nekemte, the car stopped once more. But Harvey fiddled under the hood, and it got us to the Swedish mission station where we spent the night. Although the government had taken over the hospital and several buildings, the Swedes still had the church, Central Synod church offices, and several private houses. Nekemte was our region's capital, where we renewed our resident and work permits annually.

A young Swedish mechanic was finishing a turbine project when Harvey brought our car to him. The two worked all afternoon to tune it up to carry us the rest of the trip. After dinner with his family, we went to the guest rooms for another night of good sleep. Sunday morning was dark, but we attended church at seven o'clock in the morning and reflected on God's provision throughout our travels.

Declining breakfast, we set out at eight-thirty that morning to reach Bodji by nightfall. It was raining steadily when another blowout on the fixed spare tire stopped us; a new tire had to be put on in the rain. Harvey's jack was not high enough, so a passing truck driver used his. The driver and his partner spoke Arabic, which helped Harvey, but we were ever grateful to have our own Ethiopian hospital administrator with us to translate the local languages along the way. Farther on was a fine breakfast stop, where we had a great meal, including white bread.

About noon we entered the town of Gimbi and took the tire to be fixed. While a local mechanic worked on it, inserting another tube and putting on an external boot, we had tea in a nearby cafe. The rain stopped, and the sun came out as we drove on. Eventually, we left the main road for a dirt road covered by stones, but our Land Rover did well going around and over them. Once more the rear tire went flat, and we had to fix it since we no longer had a spare. We were very anxious to be at our destination, the Western Synod church compound in Bodji.

When we drove into the church compound at Bodji, the whole mission group—six German and Scandinavian families—happened to be in the yard. Greatly surprised, they warmly welcomed us. Since we had left Addis on Friday, no one along our route had radioed ahead that they had seen us. The Western Synod folks had wondered where we were. They were thankful for the mail and cargo we had brought for them and graciously provided lunch and housed us overnight before we continued on to Aira.

Anxious to be on our way the next morning, we borrowed a new spare tire instead of fixing our flat one. Being unfamiliar with the unpaved back roads, Harvey decided to convoy with a car going partly our way. In a light drizzle, we set out with the motor running smoothly. To negotiate the mud and hills, Harvey put chains on the rear wheels. He looked a mess of mud, but we went steadily on. The sunshine alternated with light rain.

When the driver from the Bodji group turned off our route, we continued without any knowledgeable companion to help. We were on a new road to Aira, and Harvey was unsure of the terrain. Almost inevitably, he drove into deep water standing in the middle of the road, not realizing it was a swamp or that we had lost a chain. The car settled into the mud, and we were good and thoroughly stuck.

Six boys watched us grind to a halt. They soon helped bail water with a plastic mixing bowl, and I assisted, using a shovel. Harvey and our Ethiopian hospital administrator left on foot, looking for help. Before long they returned with five men to help dig, bail, and push. Soon the young boys grew tired of helping and went swimming in the river. After two hours of getting nowhere, we unloaded the car, placing all our belongings on dry land. Fortunately, the sun came out, so our goods did not become rain soaked, and I sat guarding them while the men tackled the job.

After four hours of digging, everyone was splattered from head to toe. Eventually, using a tow chain, the men pulled as Harvey steered, and the car finally eased onto solid ground. I wept tears of joy, which amused the little boys standing by me. No matter, the car was free, and we could get underway again. Harvey commented that he did not think we were going to get out of the muck that day.

Reloading the car and reinstalling the old chain, we drove into the nearby town to take a familiar route we knew. Dark skies made us nervous; nonetheless, we confidently set off, determined to motor through the endless daunting mud holes, and we were initially rewarded with no flat tires or motor troubles. The hospital workers, who had heard by radio that we would be arriving about eleven o'clock that evening, realized they would now be getting out of work before we arrived.

As fate would have it, we would not have a victorious homecoming of man overcoming machine. The vehicle won. We maneuvered the worst sections along the hills, stopping twice to check the back chain, which was prone to break. On the ascent to one final hilltop, I saw Aira spread out on the next hilltop. Leaving the main road, as all other tracks had done, we climbed a grass route parallel to the impassable road. But halfway up the hill, the rear tire began to spin. No matter what we tried, we could not reach the top.

We decided to walk the final stretch to Aira. Leaving Harvey behind to fuss with the auto, the rest of us set out up the muddy hill, each with a shoulder bag of essentials, an umbrella, and a feeling of defeat. But we should have also had walking sticks because the same slippery mud that made the going difficult for cars also made it a struggle on foot. It was a slow and messy walk; we slipped and slid and even fell but finally managed to walk into the very quiet hospital compound. The hospital matron, Sister Tine, in her crisp white uniform, was the first to greet us mud-covered vagabonds.

Harvey had stayed with the car trying to start it, but later, when it began to rain, he gave up. So close to home, he finally left the car, walking to Aira without it. Our administrator-guide was very disappointed, but there was no other option. As the rain increased, he employed a boy to stay in the car for the night with a blanket, Keith's sleeping bag, a flashlight, and oranges to keep him company as he guarded our goods until morning.

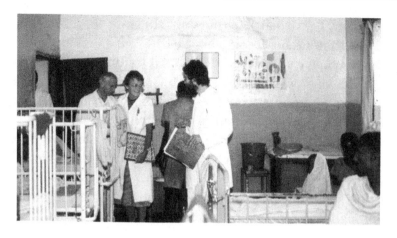

Harvey Doorenbos, nurse Monica (Swedish), and Dr.
Scherbaum (German) doing patient rounds in the
pediatric ward of Aira Hospital in 1982

Almost unbelievably, we were home. Soon, we were
showering and enjoying a late-evening meal with Sister Tine. Later
still, we had coffee at another home.

In the following days, we learned that it had taken a month
for twenty coffee trucks to drive to Bodji—and they were preceded
by a tractor-bulldozer. It is only a day's drive in the dry season.
Over two hundred coffee trucks had gone south to load the coffee
to take to Addis, and then they went through the same long ordeal
on their return to Addis. The trucks gouged deep troughs into the
roads, spoiling them for all who came later. When they got stuck,
they literally dug deep, leaving a rut that was hard to avoid later.

I had been calmer on this trip than previous ones. When
traveling, I delighted in the scenery, but on this trip, it seems the
scenery was one scene in one place too many. The hopelessness of
making any progress out of the swamp raised my alarm system,
and I was especially anxious for Harvey since he worked so hard.
In reviewing the trip, we regularly exclaimed over the
thoughtfulness and generosity of so many friends and strangers
along the road. Despite the challenges, we were again convicted
that God wanted us to be at work in Aira, and He guided us daily
to that end.

The Aira mission compound was spread atop a hillside with a
hospital, nursing and secondary schools, a boys' hostel, and

housing for the expatriate nursing students and teachers—all located within a fenced complex. Nearby, out the main gate, was the Bible school compound and the road leading up the hill to the market area in the village center.

This remote area would be our home for the next twenty-three years. We rarely saw our sons. Keith visited us twice during his Christmas vacations from school in India. He then entered Hope College in Holland, Michigan, where Dirk was enrolled. Both boys visited us again in later years. Keith brought his wife and their first son on his last visit to Aira, and Dirk came alone twice, then brought a girlfriend on a later visit. These were always special occasions.

Keith comes home for Christmas, November 1977

Keith's first trip home from Kodai School in India was in November 1977, shortly after we had returned from our brief stateside furlough. He was at ease in Addis but did not know anything about Aira. Friends met him at the airport in the capital, housed him, and helped him get his permission papers to travel west to us on a bus. He got off the bus at a town where he had to divert to an all-weather, unpaved road. As we had arranged by phone, he stayed overnight in that town at the church's school for the blind. Our hospital car fetched him home one week after he had departed from Kodai School.

It was on this occasion that the three of us went to retrieve the goods we had left in Dembi Dolo and had a chance to see the little orphan Rufi once again. What a warm reception we received from church leaders, hospital workers, and school staff. Dr. Solomon now had no one to teach math at the school. We attended church on Sunday morning with Rufi sitting on our laps. It was not easy to leave again.

One day, shortly after Christmas, our Aira compound experienced a fight between a drunk teacher, some health students, and the farmers' police—the only ones allowed to carry guns. The ruckus took place just outside our house, so we stayed inside away from the windows. We harbored one frantic student who was passing by and got caught in the melee. The local court had previously jailed the teacher for attacking a student, thus beginning all the trouble.

Two days later, the hospital staff were called from their afternoon tea to prepare for injured victims of an overturned truck. Keith joined the men who went to help at the scene of the tragedy while Harvey went over to the hospital to receive the injured. Two local men had jumped on the back of a truck to help unload it, and both got crushed when it rolled over. The driver was brought to Aira with a smashed chest; sadly, he died the next day.

Ethiopian Christmas is celebrated on January 6, so we prepared a feast for the hospital workers. Keith helped slaughter two sheep. The blood was drained and the intestines blown clean and chopped for boiling in the blood with many onions. Fortunately, the boiling of this popular dish was on a wood stove in its own shed, so the stench did not permeate the house. The butcher was paid with the sheep's skin, feet, and head. To have meat was a rare treat; to sit in fellowship was a privilege.

The meal consisted of large, thin circles of injera layered onto circular trays and ladled atop with mounds of thick meat and vegetable stews. One pulls off pieces of the bread base to pinch up morsels of food. Bones are served at the end of the meal for any meat still clinging to them and for the marrow inside. Except for these few trays and drinking glasses for juice, there are no dishes to be washed. Before and after the meal, hands are washed in water poured from a pitcher into a basin. Coffee and tea are served after the hand washing.

Addis in time of crisis

One day Keith and I were sitting in the emigration office in the capital to obtain his proper exit papers to return to his school in India when we heard many gunshots coming from the large prison across the road. The guns were used to "clean out" the prison cells to make room for the next group of prisoners. I glanced at Keith. The young Marxist cadre saw that and said, "You don't like that, do you?" I replied, "Some mother has lost her son this day." He shouted, "Mothers must realize that in a revolution the enemy must be eliminated." I kept still to be sure that Keith received the papers he needed.

An Addis taxi ride

I took the front seat in a taxi going to the city center of Addis. At a stop, a young woman ran frantically up to the taxi, threw open the door, and clambered in next to two elderly matrons in the back, imploring the driver to go. Our taxi was quickly surrounded by soldiers with guns aimed at us. They wanted to arrest the girl, and now they had her cornered. She cried hysterically against leaving the taxi, saying she had already lost a family member to "them," but the old women shouted and pushed at her to get out.

My mind could not grasp the drama unfolding before my eyes; the harrowing scene seemed to play out in slow motion. She was a university student; perhaps her crime was holding the wrong Communist party membership card. Originally, there were five Communist parties. Now, all members of four parties were being "eliminated" to secure the supremacy of one, the Derg party. She did not want to go with the soldiers—she knew her fate. She probably also knew they would fire on the taxi and perhaps kill all of us to get her.

But the soldiers did not shoot. Too many times previously, in their zeal to arrest someone, they had fired at random into cars, harming innocent Ethiopians and sometimes foreigners. Because of the latter, the government had ordered that the soldiers could not shoot if a foreigner was in the car. They spoke angrily, but their guns were silent as they reminded each other of my presence in the car. *"Ferengi"* ("foreigner") they kept repeating. Finally, the girl made the agonizing choice to do as commanded. She got out and was marched away, pushed along at gun point, almost certainly to torture and perhaps execution.[61] Our car proceeded on its way.

---

[61] During the dictatorial rule of the Communist Military Junta (known as the Derg) in Ethiopia (1974-91), there were from an estimated five hundred thousand to two million casualties. Tens of thousands were imprisoned and executed without trial.

Eventually, the two visibly shaken old women in the back seat arrived at their stop and got out. When the taxi reached my stop, the driver turned to me and said quietly, "You saved our lives."

"No, God was our protector!" I protested, but I understood his meaning. He told me his taxi had been in the garage eight times the previous year for repairs from bullet holes—repairs paid for by him each time. When I think of that day, I recall a young girl giving up her safety—and perhaps her life—to protect the four of us with her in that taxi.

Keith's summer and Christmas vacations, 1978

May 1978 in Ethiopia was a season of rain, mud, and shortages of food and other goods. For Keith, it was the occasion for a long trip from India to Aira. It was extended due to Ethiopia's shortage of fuel for airlines and vehicles, as well as a shortage of truck drivers willing to brave mud-soaked roads. We went to Addis to greet him, help him acquire needed travel permissions, and bring him home to Aira. Keith spent three weeks traveling from India to Aira and back again—and only four weeks actually in Aira.

The limited availability of foreign foods and other goods was due to the government's refusal to allow merchants to engage in foreign exchange. Shortages of cement for building was due to demands made for the rebuilding of war-torn Eritrea and northern Ethiopia. Due to a dearth of imported bottled gas, we used wood stoves in our homes and carefully rationed gas stove usage.

Arriving in Aira, Keith had no sooner settled in than a visiting British dentist arrived for ten weeks. She came to train the health assistant students to use anesthetics when extracting teeth. She insisted on living with us and stayed in Keith's room, so he moved to a smaller room. For ten weeks, she cooked her own vegetable meals and occasionally ate with us at our table.

December 1978, Keith's last stay with us before heading off to college, began with him being stuck in Addis for a week. He kept our friends there busy helping him get permission to leave the capital, as well as additional permissions from the governor of our region to ride the bus in our area. Once again, he stayed overnight at the mission's school for blind folks. He then found a ride on the main road to a crossroad village where we met him for the last leg of the journey home. His delay cancelled a weekend camping trip that Harvey had planned for the two of them. Since Harvey had no other doctors to spell him at hospital during Christmastime, those plans were no longer possible.

Keith helped inventory medical supplies in the storerooms and on the pharmacy shelves for the end-of-year report and for ordering new supplies. Because he had only a twenty-day visitor's visa, we had to send him back to Addis on New Year's Day to begin his return to India. The government had asked Harvey to fill in for a Russian surgeon at the large government hospital in the provincial capital of Nekemte for two weeks, so Keith stopped there to say goodbye to him on the trip back to Addis.

Our next time together, May 1979, was a wonderful experience. We attended Keith's graduation in India—with Dirk joining us from the United States—followed by the eastward trip home via Malaysia, the Philippines, Hong Kong, Taiwan, Hawaii, and Washington State.

Keith's eight boarding school years meant he had spent sixty-four months away from family and home. But it was going to college—separated from us by the Atlantic Ocean and then some—that was the most painful because it divided our family members for longer periods.

Education is a right

At the beginning of their reign in 1974, the Communist government decreed that education should be available for everyone. They were adamant that all could and would read the writings of Marx, Engels, and Lenin. Since their works were not available in Ethiopia's Amharic language, English became the medium of secondary education.

At Lalo Aira Secondary School in western Ethiopia, we limited grades seven through twelve to seven hundred students, which meant turning away three hundred. School staff urged smaller class sizes, so our classes were always limited to seventy at the entrance date. But they soon swelled to seventy-five or more as new students appeared on the first month.

One year the nation's seventy-five thousand twelfth graders took the university entrance examination, but only four thousand were accepted into university, and four thousand more entered special technical schools. The exams were very difficult, but the passing grade was lowered to 40 percent in order to find the eight thousand for higher education. It was lowered further to 35 percent for girls to get into university. Girls had little time to study after school for they had to gather firewood and water and help prepare for the evening meal. After the meal was over, the candle was snuffed out, and all family members went to sleep; these patterns left no time for study.

The seventh and eighth graders had no desks or textbooks; they squeezed together on long benches, never complaining. Some rooms put three students onto two chairs. The daily lesson was lecture, which was then written on a chalkboard by the Ethiopian teachers. The students wrote the teachers' notes verbatim into their small notebooks. The library had few books, and the laboratory had no equipment. The mission sent boxes of books to the library, and I classified and catalogued them. We also sent a modest order of glassware and chemicals to the laboratory, so teachers could demonstrate experiments for the students.

Harvey and I chose to give scholarships for tuition or travel to needy students of mine who excelled academically. But how to choose? I asked the teachers with whom I worked: "Is giving money to promising students reasonable in this culture? Is the need truly there? Is there potential in the student?" Although teachers knew the potential of their students, some could be biased and give special marks to their favorites. All Ethiopians seemed eager for the foreigner to give, if not to their relatives, at least to their friends' children. Knowing my students by name and their abilities helped us to give over one hundred scholarships and to watch the encouraging results over the years.

Direct payment—in this case putting the money literally in the hands of the intended recipient—was necessary. Adults did not always give children the gift meant for them because of what the parents decided were greater family needs. Most parents, however, encouraged higher education for their children, with the expectation that the educated children would then take care of their parents in the future. Gifts from foreign aid workers and agencies did not always come with a guarantee of delivery if they did not pass directly from the benefactor's hand to the beneficiary.

Besides giving at school, we also contributed to a fund for poor patients at the hospital and to a general fund for the poor at church. Both offered anonymity and allowed us to tell beggars who came to our door to go to the institution for help. The church and hospital funds relieved us of the decision-making process of whom should receive support. It also discouraged recipients from becoming dependent on us foreigners.

The Communists saw to it that literacy classes for adult villagers and farmers were held after school, using young students from secondary school as their teachers. As the lessons progressed, and the adults needed simple reading material to practice with, it became clear that the Communists had not prepared any simple readers for these basic classes. Ostensibly, they were preoccupied with writing new propaganda texts for the upperclassmen in order to communicate their principles. As a result of this lack of preparation, newly literate farmers were given the only readers available: children's Sunday school primers, just recently off the church press.

Part of the school curriculum for day students was political education—replacing forbidden religious education—and labor education. The latter included digging water ditches, building outdoor toilets, planting trees, terracing fields on hillsides, and repairing roads and bridges. These "classes" were not voluntary. University entrance not only included the previously mentioned difficult exam but also depended on participation in political education and meetings and labor education and work. I was obliged to oversee a group of students after school each week. One day a secondary student looked up from his intense ditch digging to ask "What do your students in America do for labor education?" I did not have a wise answer.

Mandatory political meetings absorbed everyone's time, especially on Sundays. Young people (called "cadres") searched villages, beat the bushes for absentees, and reported offenders. In an area above the Blue Nile Valley, boys were sent down into the valley to collect a quota of bamboo shoots on Sundays. If a special youth meeting was called by the church at 9:00 a.m., those boys gladly left home at 2:00 a.m. and collected their amount of bamboo so as to be in church on time.

No card-carrying Communists were allowed to attend church services. This applied to all educated adult workers in the school and in the hospital. When a child was to be baptized, however, the mother and usually the father were in attendance on that Sunday.

A Swedish pastor and two German pastors took three Ethiopian pastors in their car to Sunday preaching assignments in the countryside, a forbidden action under the Communists. All six were imprisoned, and their car was confiscated. Two nights later, we missionaries held an evening prayer meeting for the imprisoned men in our home. Before we even began praying, two Catholic nurses from Dembi Dolo showed up in their small Volkswagen and knocked on our door. They needed a place to sleep for the night. Offering them our guest room, I also explained the meeting and its purpose. I was delighted when they said, "Oh, we met the two released German pastors sitting by the roadside, waiting for someone here to fetch them." Quickly the meeting broke up as Harvey went to retrieve the pastors, and I passed on the good news to the men's wives.

After the early years of Communist rule, almost all the missionaries, their schools, and airplane supports were closed throughout the country. Travel anywhere outside Addis was greatly restricted by the need for travel papers. Outside that area, most churches were closed, but services continued to be held on the lawn of the churchyard.

Funerals were important occasions for evangelism since they were important to all cultures in Ethiopia. Youth choirs would sing together on the open back of a pick-up truck, preachers would shout out the message of Christian love in long sermons, and everyone could pray, sing, and share together. Even the deceased's relatives who had embraced the ideals of the Communists and held Communist Party cards attended funerals of a family member. We heard more than one "Party Member" confess that the preacher seemed to be speaking directly to them at the funeral.

Faithful Dure

Dure (pronounced "du-ray") was a well-educated student from the church secondary school in Dembi Dolo. She joined the school staff as a secretary, receiving a good salary. She was taunted and threatened by the young local cadres to join their ranks in the Communist Party which had no respect for intellectuals who did not adhere to Marxist ideology. So Dure left her church and school job in Dembi Dolo for less visibility. She moved into a small house next to our home and became the secretary at the church hospital where Harvey worked. She shared her strong faith in the morning meetings at the hospital chapel, as well as among staff and patients throughout the working hours.

We were chatting at her place one evening when we were interrupted by a knock on the door. She opened it and faced one of her former tormentors with his rifle in hand. My appearance behind her dismayed him—but not enough to shorten his lengthy speech of intimidation, ordering her arrest and return to Dembi Dolo with him. When he finally paused, he seemed confused by her silence and lack of fear while she spoke fearlessly:

> You have a powerful position in the Communist Party of Dembi Dolo. It is your work, but, you see, I no longer live under your jurisdiction. You have no authority here where I have found peace in Christian work and fellowship.

Speechless, he turned and left us to join his colleagues waiting in the car. Later, he encouraged cadres in Aira to agitate her.

As she calmly discussed the altercation with me, she recited Matthew 10:19-20: "But when they arrest you, do not worry about what to say or how to say it. At that time, you will be given what to say, for it will not be you speaking, but the Spirit of your Father speaking through you."

The local cadres in Aira began to pressure her again, so she moved on. Having relocated in Addis, she was found again and imprisoned. We later heard that she paid a high bribe for her release. She married soon after that and emigrated with her husband to Japan where he had work. I am sure that she prized her freedom every day.

Troubled Diriba

Diriba was a young student in our secondary school. I taught some of his beautiful sisters and even attended one sister's church wedding. But I had met Diriba only once in the classroom at the end of his senior year, my first year of teaching. I had been asked to help the twelfth grade teacher supervise the national Leaving School Certificate English exam. From the time I was in the room, Diriba smoked cigarettes and turned around in his seat to copy answers. No one corrected Diriba, clearly the spoiled darling in a family of mostly girls. He graduated, but with very poor results.

He returned to our school after the compulsory two-year intensive theoretical and practical Marxist training for all Ethiopian youth who were studying in eleventh or twelfth grade or in the university. They became the cadres to promote Communist ideals. He had not passed the university entrance exams, yet he still held community favor and so was assigned as a sports teacher at our mission secondary school. He was a hero on the field, an untrained teacher in the classroom, and an unrelenting enemy of the church, his actual employer. Soon realizing the profit which spying and reporting for the Communist leaders would bring him, Diriba became a "hatchet man" for the party's devious designs on the church.

The church began Sunday services at 9:00 a.m. so the party could use the building and its captive audience after service for its lengthy and hot afternoon meetings. Diriba scheduled the youths' mandatory sports matches for nine in the morning. Subsequently, the church changed its start time to 8:00 a.m., and Diriba changed his program accordingly. And so it went until eventually church start time was changed to 6:00 a.m. Fortunately, Diriba refused to get up that early. So the youth came to church before sports began. Comrade Diriba spied on everyone, often getting his fellow teachers drunk to make them chatty. We learned that he got paid for such spy work. One Sunday, Harvey and I stood nearby and looked on as he openly and brazenly paid off young boys for some work they had done for him.

A turnover of the school director and several staff members brought some outstanding Christian teachers to replace some of our more committed party members. But not Diriba. The new teachers were afraid of Diriba's power in the party but stayed with us for at least that one year. It was that year in which Diriba went to arrest a farmer falsely accused of an offense. Imprisoning him, Diriba had two schoolboys hold the farmer while he beat him to extract information. Instead, the man died from internal bleeding, and Diriba was put in prison himself. Much later, we learned that during his long prison term, he reportedly turned his life around and searched for Christ.

After six years away, Diriba returned to his family. Looking gaunt and tired, he had lost the malevolent "twinkle" in his eye. He acquired a bar woman for a wife, and they had two children. He earned some money by going from town to town, buying and selling goods. At home, he spent almost a month in hospital, being too weak to rally to his former athletic self, and he soon died at his parents' home. He had potential, but he made foolish choices. He shone in sports, but he chose to serve the Communist regime.

A family's losses

Harvey and the district superintendent for our church synod held frequent meetings concerning the needs of Aira's hospital and satellite clinics. The family members were close friends of ours. Harvey often treated the pastor's first wife in the outpatient clinic for her headaches and illnesses. I taught the pastor in night school classes and their seven children in the secondary school system. Their firstborn children were twins: a boy and a girl. The son graduated from high school and went on to college to study mechanics. The daughter enrolled in seminary and married a seminary student. She became a teacher because women were not yet ordained in the Ethiopian Evangelical Church.

When his first wife died, the pastor married a young woman, and they added yet another set of twins (again, a boy and a girl) and another child. One day the pastor sent a notice to Harvey that he could not meet as planned due to personal reasons. His firstborn son had reportedly "come home to die"—a code phrase for having contracted AIDS. The son died and was buried as soon as his twin sister arrived.

We joined the funeral procession from the home to the church, falling in behind the pick-up truck carrying the coffin (a carved-out tree trunk—not brass and satin), the male mourners, the wailing community women, and finally the rest of the men. I was amazed at the crowd who joined us; it even included Muslims. At the church, women entered and sat inside while men stood outside. Some younger men and boys picked up heavy stones to take to the grave to heap on the fresh mound, thus thwarting hyenas from digging up the body.

Harvey and I sat outside on sheltered benches, and after the service, we walked over to the gravesite where, except for the men carrying the coffin, only women stood close to the grave. The boy was not buried near his mother's grave because the cemetery had no planned lots for families.

After the burial, we filed past the family seated on the grass away from the gravesite. This way the family could receive condolences and still maintain the required graveside silence before the burial. Youth and women continued their high-pitched wailing at intervals throughout the whole procession and after the burial. The family could then eat the meals their neighbors and friends had prepared for them.

Harvey's work

Harvey, the only surgeon at Aira Hospital, was also the hospital's medical director and maintenance supervisor, a teacher for classes at the Health Assistants' School, the church synod's chief medical officer, and the supervisor of the synod's twelve outlying clinics. That said, he enjoyed every day of his many years at Aira as a missionary physician.

Believing that an ounce of prevention is worth a pound of cure, Harvey kept promoting public health programs through the two other doctors and health assistants. One doctor took responsibility to oversee the work of the clinics in the countryside, and the other doctor focused on mother-child care and nutrition, especially among expectant mothers. The farmers' associations also wanted public health instruction from the doctors. In addition, Harvey continued to train the health assistants in the outpatient department so they would recognize what cases they could handle.

In one rainy season, Harvey's work included standing in at a government hospital for a Russian surgeon during his two-week home leave, traveling to a northern clinic for two days of surgery there, compiling a medical report for the previous year, and coordinating the work of a British dentist who spent ten weeks at Aira Hospital. With the government either taking over or closing most mission hospitals, Harvey eventually became the only American doctor working in Communist Ethiopia.

Harvey kept his US medical license up to date by listening to surgical audio tapes from the United States, reading US and British medical journals, and attending a two-week continuing medical education conference sponsored by the US Christian Medical Association every other year in Kenya. These, plus his surgical cases, gave him the credit hours he needed to be licensed continually by the State of Michigan Licensing Department.

Harvey experienced some endemic diseases himself, yet he never contracted malaria due to the small prophylaxis tablet we all took weekly throughout our years abroad. Harvey did suffer two bouts of hepatitis, first type A, and then a year later, type B. These struck our family hard when we lived and worked in Oman, but hepatitis never recurred. Harvey did endure typhus, typhoid, schistosomiasis, and frequent parasite infestations over the years in Africa.

Although Harvey was trained as a general surgeon, he became experienced in all branches of surgery since there were no specialists in the rural areas. He accepted patients with cleft palates, did surgery for orthopedic problems, performed hysterectomies for cancer patients, and did caesarian sections for women who could not deliver. He also learned eye surgery when he helped visiting ophthalmologists during eye clinics; these yearly clinics drew numerous people for care. He showed patience and gentleness with burn cases when they took a long time to heal, and he helped many HIV patients when the disease found its way to our remote community.

Once, he removed an ovarian cyst of 22 kilograms (48 pounds) from a teenage girl. Another time, he tried to diplomatically convince a couple to accept a tubal ligation after their eighth child's birth. But it was girl number eight for the family, so no tubal ligation was allowed in case a future pregnancy might result in a boy. Another time, Harvey removed a tumor as big as a basketball from a man's forehead.

One year, there was an epidemic of a severe strain of meningitis. The hospital beds were filled with patients, then when the outpatient waiting area filled up, still more of the afflicted spilled over into grassy areas of the hospital courtyard—many of them needing nasogastric feeding tubes to get nourishment into their bodies.

For twenty-three years, Harvey served Aira Hospital in medical work, teaching, and maintenance and building concerns, as well as in fellowship with staff and patients alike. He committed himself to the work of the church and its synod, which oversaw the medical work. When he retired in 1999, Harvey knew many faithful hospital colleagues would carry on the responsibilities at Aira Hospital.

Trip to Agelu Metti

Having decided to inspect the hospital's clinic in Agelu Metti during a holiday break, Harvey asked two nurses, Sisters Leena and Elisabeth, and me to accompany him on that trip. We three women sat in back, where normally only two can sit, and took turns sitting over the metal tire covers. We set off for Nedgo Clinic, traveling west from Aira to the only road going west from Addis to the border. The next morning, a man of the Gumuz tribe, the storied ebony-black people of the Nile Valley, met us along the way. He had been sent by the Agelu Metti Clinic to act as our guide down the steep escarpment. In our small Suzuki car, our Gumuz guide sat up in front with Harvey. We continued toward the clinic, where we would be greeted by the Norwegian nurse who ran it.

In some stretches of the road down the escarpment, it felt like we were going down almost vertically; in other places, the narrow dirt road seemed like it was cleaved out of the mountainside. There were horseshoe turns and many ruts, rocks, boulders, and mudholes to avoid; in the back of the truck, we were tossed around like salad. The mountain views, however, were spectacular. The valley was a continuous forest, except where trees had been cut to provide room for farmland. The Gumuz people did not plough but simply scratched the ground and dropped in seeds regardless of the rocks and tree stumps that shared what passed for a field. The trees surprised us because the valley was mostly savannah.

The people are not tall and lanky like the Sudanese across the border but short and heavy. We got out of the car at a village where it was market day and were met with greetings and hugs by many people. The few males in trousers and shorts were Oromos from the highlands; the rest were Gumuz who wore shorts or miniskirts and little else. The girls there braided their hair and then patted on a paste of butter and red clay to keep it neat for a long time; this was also effective against lice. They wrapped greased strings of leather or rope around their arms below and above the elbow. Most girls had beads around their necks and a loose wrap for market days or evening warmth. A woman named Sister Ingrid lived here alone in a large brick house. A car battery powered her two electric light bulbs.

We toured the clinic building and a village that had been mostly Christian at one time. We greeted the women and were soon surrounded by children—all naked but well nourished. The men and youth were at the market on Saturdays and in their fields all day Sunday. They grew cotton for the Oromo traders to transport to markets in the highlands. The village stood on the banks of the wide, unhurried Nile River.

In the evening, there was a feast to honor a heroic young man who had killed a crocodile. The croc was skinned and its hide stretched out to dry on the grass roof of a hut. There was dancing in the moonlight by the males and singing and clapping by the girls following them. We sat around a fire while a goat was slaughtered and roasted in strips placed on sticks above the fire.

We sang for them and the men sang for us.

Sunday morning, the only known Christian left in the area asked us to hold a Palm Sunday worship service in his home. He had gathered a group of children for the service, and we brought along some more. The children all sang choruses for us, and Harvey preached, with a translator repeating each sentence.

The local witch doctor was a powerful leader in the village. Through a translator, the Christian man spoke of his fear of the witch doctor and of his dream that Satan had called to him. "I don't know how to read or how to

Typical Aira market scene of mother holding a child wrapped to her back and a basket of food to sell on her head, leaving her hands free

pray. I'm afraid I'll leave Christ as all the others have. Please help us here." We were in tears as we assured him that we would ask many Christian friends to pray for him and the Gumuz tribe.

The attitude of the highland people toward these Nilotic people was akin to their attitude toward animals. Even our church leaders did not care to help them; the Oromo health assistant's wife refused to come and live with her husband there. The church pastor assigned to work there did not come either. But the people loved Sister Ingrid and praised her kindness and devoted care of them.

The life of women in rural Ethiopia

Reading Proverbs 31:10-31 makes me tired, especially verse 27: "She does not eat the bread of idleness." Verse 15 mentions that the noble woman had servants, so she did not do all the work alone. But she was not idle "for the sake of the welfare of the family." In the time of Proverbs, it was expected of all females to be married and not idle.

The same was surely true in rural Ethiopia. For example, Prov. 31:15 tells us, "She rises while it is still dark." We could often hear the women pounding coffee beans or grain or spices before dawn. They would dry the coffee beans in the sun so they could remove the shells. Then they would roast the beans and pound them into coffee grounds to add to boiling water. The very poor would pound the discarded shells gathered from their neighbors' kitchens to make their coffee.

Proverbs 31:17 says, "Her arms are strong for her tasks." Several times a day, local women would walk either to the river or to a well for water, carried in large, heavy clay pots on their backs. They also had to fetch wood for the evening fire. Only females prepared food; males were not allowed in the cooking area. As little boys, they were taught to stay away. A young couple or a family without girls to help the wife would often ask to have a niece from a poorer relative live in their home to help with kitchen work.

In this traditional culture, males owned all property, land, wealth, livestock, and family members. The patriarch would make all of the decisions and was the disciplinarian of wife and children for the sake of the family's reputation. He permitted the death of a disobedient child caught in a crime. He would "beat" his wife weekly to ensure her behavior was good in public and private. One day, in class, I asked the students to use "as if" in a sentence, and I received the sentence: "He beats his wife as if she were a donkey."

When males returned home at dusk, the females washed their hands and feet, then served them the evening meal so they could eat first. Later, the females would eat with the children, making sure to leave enough for any servants. Older girls attending school had little time to study since they had to help at home. Thus, they often had poor grades, failed classes, and had to repeat the year. In one class of twelfth graders, only six of the ninety-six students were females.

Parents could withdraw their girls from school when they reached maturity out of concern for their safety on the long walk to or from school. An old Ethiopian proverb says, "You [males] cannot pass by a girl on the road or a field of sugar cane without acting or tasting." It is the responsibility of males to protect their own females. If the father or older son left home for a few nights, a male relative would be asked to stay in the home and look after the family. Women without men to protect them were very vulnerable and a great social problem. Widows were seldom married again and had to return, if possible, to a father's or brother's house for protection.

At puberty, girls were prepared to be married, unless they continued in school. Parents arranged the marriage between the families involved. There would be no hand holding, no dating, no kissing—even after marriage—between the couple. The mate would be chosen for his or her character, not for looks or education. The bride-to-be would be "bought" at engagement time with gifts of gold for her and cattle and clothes for her parents. She would be considered the groom's wife from that point forward. The bride would belong in the husband's home after the wedding; she would not, however, change her name to the husband's family name.

Women tended the gardens, cultivated the fields, and raised poultry. They never plowed fields with oxen, sowed seeds, or tended livestock in pastures. Males were travelers—especially those who could afford bus and inn fares. Every wayside inn in Ethiopia offered a traveler food, drink, and women's services. Thus, men brought home HIV and shared it with their wives who could not refuse their husbands' marital privileges.

Africa's mortality rate is high, hurting families and leaving orphans. Death in Africa also comes from malaria, wars, tribal battles and atrocities, drought and famine, and wild animal bites—especially snakes. For females, another factor leading to early death is childbirth, due to the girls being married off very young or getting to the hospital too late after an extended labor of two or more days at home. It has been said of Africa: "One generation in the West is two generations in Africa where (1) teenagers are already parents, and (2) thirty year olds already have one foot in the grave."

My American reaction to a death notice was often, "What did she die of? How long was she sick? What treatment did she get?" The African response was short and simple: "She's dead." When a wife died, the husband would be left with children he could not manage. He frequently remarried a young teenage virgin. She would want her own children, with the result that both parents often neglected the former wife's offspring.

When teaching a unit on punctuation, I used the following sentence to illustrate how punctuation marks can make two entirely different meanings of one sentence. "A woman without her man is nothing." That sentence and the notion behind it, considered unacceptable by Western women, was highly acceptable and appreciated by the boys in my class. The girls' clapping and glee, however, silenced the male majority when I would rewrite the sentence punctuated: "A woman—without her, man is nothing."

Abebe

At the time of the widely publicized famine in Ethiopia in 1984, the government enforced a mass movement of people from the northern areas of chronic food scarcity. They were moved to our western region, forced onto large trucks or buses without any reference to family relationships or any goodbyes. Many died on the trip westward from starvation or sickness.

The older children of our school were told to make shelters of sticks with grass roofs for the newcomers in an out-of-town settlement area until they could make their own homes. None of them spoke the local language, but some communicated in the country's common Amharic language.

On a hillside near us, the Lutheran World Federation sponsored a food-for-work project to build an earthen dam and employ the many starving refugees. Hundreds of these newcomers, as well as many poor local people, were conscripted for the six-month project. The dirt was dug out from a hillside by men, then women carried it in sacks to the dam's site in a continuous, circular procession from hillside to dam site. At the end of each week, they received a sack full of corn as payment.

One day, an accidental cave-in of the digging site occurred, and both men and women were injured; one woman died. Abebe, who was brought to the hospital, suffered paraplegia and used a wheelchair. The teenager had no idea where his parents or siblings were. An orphan among a different tribal group, he could not be discharged to a home and became a permanent resident at the hospital.

He was an intelligent lad who quickly picked up the local Oromo language and a smattering of English. Nurses and patients' relatives took time to teach him to knit socks and sweaters, as well as to sew. He eventually joined the sewing group in the hospital's laundry room. He wanted to go to the primary school to continue what he had learned in his northern homeland, but the rocky roads ruined his wheelchair tires. As his "substitute" teacher, I taught him three times weekly in math, English, geography, Bible, and other subjects as needed.

Through the care given, the preaching of the Gospel, and his reading of the Bible, Abebe became a disciple of Jesus. Abebe soon was wheeling himself into other rooms of the hospital to enthusiastically share his new faith in Amharic with the patients. As missionaries went to Addis, they brought back pamphlets and Bibles and books for Abebe to sell to patients and their families. The money he earned went to buy more books and yarn. Only God could have planned such a combination of tragedy and joy to bless our hospital with this effective evangelist.

As our retirement date drew near, Harvey wanted Abebe to have his own house, so he arranged to build one at the edge of the hospital compound. This way, Abebe could be close for the care he needed and for his missionary calling among the patients. A young boy lived with him as his helper. Abebe said he was grateful for his accident because it brought him to the Lord. He continued to share his faith with joy in his little home and among the hospital patients and visitors.

Deredje

When a poor farmer's son passed his eighth grade exams, his father would naturally assume the boy would work the family farm with him in their isolated village. But Deredje's desire was to go to secondary school at the mission compound, an hour-and-a-half walk. The father finally agreed to Deredje's attendance, but the boy was expected to help with the herd when he came home on the weekends. To be closer to the school, Deredje found a place on a merchant's front porch to sleep on school nights. His mother sent him off to school every Monday morning with a sack of dried corn kernels for nourishment throughout the week. The merchant's wife kindly cooked the kernels every day for him over her fire.

At the mission school, I taught Deredje English and math, in which he excelled. He seemed eager to learn but was frequently absent. The absences concerned me so much that one afternoon I asked him about them. He explained that he had elephantiasis of the leg and feet. The swelling is caused by a chemical in the soil, and often, as he walked the path to school, his swollen feet would crack open and bleed. He was embarrassed to enter the classroom.

Harvey and I suggested Deredje ask his father's permission to be in the school dorm on school nights at our expense and to spend the weekend with his family. His father consented, and Harvey taught him how to keep his feet clean, dry, and always in socks and shoes, which we bought for him. He had regular meals in the dining hall of the dormitory, plus three hours of steady electricity in the evening to study by. He excelled in every class. To show his gratitude for our help, after school, he would cut grass in our yard, all with just a small hand sickle. On weekends, he dutifully went home to assist his father with farm work. He was a gentle, conscientious, grateful boy.

Deredje's diligent study habits paid off, and he passed into the government university with no need to pay tuition. We provided his bus fare to Addis, some pocket money, and a warm jacket. His science studies led him into beekeeping upon graduation. His capabilities and integrity were noticed by his supervisors who eventually sent him to Germany for a master's degree in beekeeping and later to China for a doctorate in beekeeping.

Deredje would go on to find himself a lovely wife and have two sons who would, themselves, become excellent students at a private school in Addis. He built the family a house and bought his own car. Over the years, he has been in frequent contact with us, always expressing gentleness and gratitude. His education made such a great difference in his life.

Etienne

Every morning at the secondary school where I taught, the students lined up at the flagpole before classes began. They worshipped God with music presented by a student choir, heard Bible readings, and prayed. Sometimes students led the gathering; most often, the staff led. Then one day, the local Ethiopian rulers sent the school a warning.

"Praying among youth in our Communist country is forbidden, and singing hymns is not allowed. Students must work and not pray," the letter commanded.

So, what should we do? Our school director said, "We'll obey, of course!" And every school day until the Communist regime fell, we met before class at the flagpole to salute the new flag, sing the new national anthem, and obey the new decree by reading only from Scripture, sometimes adding a related homily. Their edict had forbidden only singing and praying; they did not realize that those exercises were only two parts of the morning worship. To save face and not have to admit being caught off guard, they never came back to correct their mistake of omission.

During many of these morning sessions, we might end our prayer with "in the name of our Lord Jesus." One of our seventh grade girls, Etienne, would pass out and writhe on the ground whenever she heard those words. First the teachers thought she had epilepsy, but she tested negative for it. The medical staff did not know what to make of it.

We learned Etienne belonged to a family with many witch doctors. Harvey said some of the cases that looked like epilepsy were in reality demonic possession. When they came to the hospital, church leaders were called to counsel them. Demon possession was part of the belief system of African countries and differentiating it from epilepsy was difficult. I asked the teacher who knew the family if he would counsel her in their language and promised that I would pray for Etienne and for his counseling time with her.

Etienne soon desired to be whole in mind and spirit, so breaking away from her family's ways, she was baptized and later received into church fellowship. She grew up to be an excellent nurse at the hospital, marry a Christian man, and become a healthy, loving mother. She is an example of the work being done by the church through its Christian school and hospital.

A visit to Boka Sirba

On the international May Day holiday in 1986, we drove from Aira to the Nedjo Clinic for an overnight stay, then farther west to Mendi Clinic, where Harvey and I and Sisters Leena and Eva stayed with a Norwegian doctor. The next morning, the doctor joined us as we descended to the Blue Nile Valley. An hour later, we arrived in Dallati, where there was also a synod clinic, so we stopped to visit the Norwegian nurse and his family. Dallati has extensive, high-quality, pink marble deposits that the government workers carve out of the earth in huge slabs for export to Italy.

After Dallati, the roads got rougher and the air hotter as our truck wound downward to the valley floor. We sheltered temporarily in a hut set up for wayfarers who go down to that area for work. The next day, we drove on to the Abbaya River, which flows into the Blue Nile. We crossed the Abbaya River in a rowboat, leaving our truck behind. Once across, a wind came up, and the local people were scared to return to the home shore. But after a brief stay on that side, we all returned safely.

Life is timeless for the Gumuz people; they do not burden themselves with agendas as we do. There is no school in Boka Sirba since they do not want the highlanders imposing their ideas and culture on them. The men carry guns, which is something the Communists permitted none of the highlanders to do. Gold mines are important to both the Gumuz and the highland tribes, but neither group trusts or pays any deference to the other.

The temperature, above 105 degrees, became even hotter when the breeze died down and we got a cooking fire going inside the hut. Harvey, the two sisters, and one Ethiopian slept outside in hopes of catching a coolish breeze in the early morning hours. I slept in the house.

In the morning, we had coffee with a local family, then Dr. Torvik and Harvey saw patients at the clinic. By ten o'clock, we were eager to head back up to the cooler highlands. We drank a lot of water on the short trip and stopped our ascent midway so some of us could swim in the cleaner-looking river halfway up the mountain.

Special days

Market day was always on Saturday, despite the Communists' desire to change it to school days. They wanted to force youth and farmers to attend their political meetings. Families came long distances, with fathers in the lead, mothers behind them carrying goods for sale, daughters carrying babies, and sons guiding the donkeys loaded with more items to sell.

Women sat next to their cloth where their goods for sale— salt bricks, spices, maize, sorghum, coffee beans, tobacco, fruit, and blocks of soft butter wrapped in banana leaves—were all displayed. Potters placed clay vessels in one area, chickens were tied up in another, and weavers set out a variety of baskets. The scene made a delightful collage of colors, sounds, scents, and humanity.

Men stood by the animals, chatting, while keeping an eye on their wives, ready to swoop in and take any money made from sales. It was pocketed for later in the afternoon when the wives had gone home to prepare supper. The men meandered home, stopping at intervals to buy a shot of home-brewed liquor outside kitchen windows on their way. No man drank his own wife's liquor—nor would he take from her the money she made from her liquor sales. She devoted part of every night to tending her home distillery, preparing liquor for sale at market or for folks passing by her own window.

Whereas Ethiopians celebrated Christmas on January 6, according to their calendar,[62] we foreigners celebrated Christmas together on December 25, when our cooks and gardeners were available to prepare the feasts for us while we needed to be at the hospital or school until the afternoon. Then, on January 6, we were responsible for our own kitchens and housework while the Ethiopians were with their families for their Christmas festivities—a convenient arrangement for all. Ethiopian neighbors often prepared a sheep for their feast, sharing meat and cost with other households. The poorest households might have some chicken parts or maybe no meat at all.

Lent in Ethiopia is based on the Ethiopian calendar and can start during the muddy, rainy season or later, during the dusty time. As in the West, Lent lasts forty days, during which no meat is sold or eaten. With Lenten season looming, weddings would take place soon after Timket so meat could be served.

Weddings

After the groom's men—not the groom himself—present the family of the bride with the groom's gift—clothes, money, oxen or sheep, and especially gold—the bride's family bargains until they receive an acceptable amount and then the engagement period begins. The bride immediately dons the gold and is then understood to be "chosen." The bride's family plans the date for the wedding. In the weeks before the wedding, female relatives help buy and store barrels of drink to ferment, cows to slaughter, and as the date gets closer, they prepare vegetables and other delectables.

After a late-morning breakfast at the groom's house on the wedding day, the groom's party either rides on mules or in the back of pickup trucks or walks to the bride's house. Singing and dancing crowds join in ahead and behind the procession. Dinner is at the bride's house with relatives, the groom and his entourage, and special guests, such as the drivers and other foreigners.

---

[62] The Ethiopian calendar has thirteen months: twelve months of thirty days each and a final month of five days (or six days in leap years).

Outside the house, long tables await neighbors from the community and friends from afar.

A choir of mostly girls stands at the gate to greet incoming groups. Before they can enter, tradition requires the best man and a spokesperson of the gatekeepers to step forward and discuss how much it will cost to permit the newcomers into the compound. Meanwhile, behind the best man, men are busy beating the dust off their trousers and coats with handkerchiefs and wiping their heads and faces of evidence of their journey, raising a dusty cloud that comes to settle again on their shoulders.

Once inside, everyone crowds into the large front room at tables covered with borrowed tablecloths and drinking glasses. Hands are washed before and after the meal by girls circulating the room with water pitchers and basins to catch the dirty run-off. The couple drinks and eats certain bits of traditional foods thought to ensure fertility, and then they receive the blessing of the girl's parents and important elders. Trays of injera, ladled over with cooked vegetables and hunks of raw meat, accompanied by small bowls of spices for dipping the meat into, are put down on tables for guests to share.

Once the groom is ready to leave, his party—now increased by the bride and her attendants—departs for the church, taking as long as they can on the roads so as to create an appropriate spectacle and show off their group.

The bride's parents and helpers will not go to the ceremony; they must continue to feed and entertain all the guests that continue to arrive for up to a week afterward. Nor may they see their daughter again for a while since she now belongs to the groom's family.

After the church service ends with blessings on the couple (but no kissing), the wedding party and important guests will go somewhere chosen for its picturesque backdrop—hopefully with many flowers and much greenery—for photos of the couple and their party. Then it is off to the groom's family home for the evening meal, similar to the noon meal. As the guests, who are almost all men, remain eating, the groom and bride and her attendant and his best man retire to another room for the newlyweds to consummate their marriage. Only the groom and best man will return to their guests to bid everyone goodbye.

Young people who have attended university have dropped some of these traditional customs and replaced them with modern ones. Before we left Aira, some wealthier homes had buffet-style wedding dinners with a great variety of food, including salads, drinks, and bottled beer—the latter two offerings recently introduced in Aira by merchants.

A traditional wedding

I once attended a more traditional wedding than the town weddings of our salaried workers. The groom, an orphan, had a small salary at the hospital as a technician in the operating theatre. The construction of his small house and some wedding expenses were covered by a German nurse for whom he had worked. The bride was a school dropout of not more than eighth grade level.

After church, Harvey and I decorated our car and Sister Leena's car with bougainvillea branches and crepe-paper streamers. A taxi was pressed into service to carry the men in its pickup bed. Another doctor's wife and I were the only females. Due to the delay finding a driver for our car, we arrived at the groom's house late for breakfast.

First, salted and roasted wheat kernels were spooned into our hands for munching. They came with a beaker of local honey beer with bits of leaves and stems floating in it. We sipped the beer through tight lips to filter out the debris. Some guests preferred a drink like Kool-Aid, so we were given a choice. The servers were the groom's best man and two attendants. They wore green suits and red shirts.

Once the groom sat down, trays with five or six layers of injera were brought out. On each tray were four hunks of raw meat and four knives (hammered from penny nails) for cutting away bite-size pieces. For guests avoiding raw meat, there were chunks of cooked meat. A serving girl came around spooning a mixture of salt, chili pepper, and plenty of melted butter onto the injera. The guests dipped bits of meat into this mixture before popping the glistening morsels into their mouths.

Following the meal, an evangelist gave a short meditation. Because the groom had no living parents, other relatives had to bless him before he left to get his bride. These were hands-on, verbal blessings. We then drove out a country road a long way before reaching the bride's spacious courtyard and home.

Wherever he and his party walked, the groom was preceded by both a little girl and a little boy, each holding lit white candles. They led the party from car to house then vice versa and even throughout the house. No outdoor movement of our groom was made without the men's choir singing and shouting and dancing in front of him. Entrance into either the bride's house or the groom's house was greeted by a local girls' choir. Custom demanded that the best man pay the leader of the female singers to let the groom's party enter, and dickering for the amount kept us standing out in the sun for some time. Fortunately, the bride was not "wilting" in the sunlight as we were.

Upon entering the bride's home, we received more drink and corn. Then the groom's party went into another room to fetch the bride to the table. She wore a traditional Ethiopian white dress and had no attendants. Her girlfriends and relatives were occupied serving the meal, with the girls serving the food and boys serving the drink. Outside in the doorway, the girls' choir was still singing loudly.

For lunch they served trays of injera with several types of stews and dishes spooned onto it. Meat dishes included chicken and beef. The groom paid for most of the feasting that day. The bride's parents still had a week of well-wishers to feed when they arrived to congratulate them. The beer was dumped out and exchanged for sweet honey wine, not yet fermented. Raw meat was again served on a fresh layer of injera, laid on top of any leftovers on the trays. Stewed tripe was served at this time; undesirable food found its way to the floor for the chickens and cat.

The guests went out to wash their hands while the family of the bride and the groom's party had a special blessing together for the couple. Young male relatives of the bride loaded her dowry items into our cars since she would not be returning to her home for at least a week—maybe longer.

The party came out and overloaded the pickup cars. Harvey had to wait until the little boys got off. We arrived at the church at four o'clock for the two o'clock service. It was very hot in the church. None of the bride's family attended the service, with guests arriving at their home.

The bride carried a white umbrella, which would have been useful if she had been on horseback, but it was not necessary in this instance because she rode in a car. She had a white purse and white sneakers but no jewelry other than a watch the groom had purchased for her. All the items she wore were part of the dowry he had paid for her. Her dowry also included outfits for her family members.

After a simple ceremony at the church, we drove off at 6:30 p.m. for photos. Because it was dusk and late, not all of us got out of the cars to be in the photos. We drove back to the groom's house at seven. When we went home after the meal, the bride and groom retired to the bedroom to consummate their vows. She probably had a girlfriend to be with her, and he had his best man.

Christians among Communists

Ethiopian culture, Christian since the fourth century, did not adjust easily to Communist rule. Juniors and seniors in high school and university students were indoctrinated in camps for two years and then armed with guns and sent back to their villages to teach communism to their elders and to uncover subversives. Despite these extreme measures, devout youth and elders met secretly in homes at night for prayer. Anyone arrested could expect torture in prison, or worse.

One day our high school classes were interrupted so students could attend a political meeting on the football field. I sat with the teachers who nervously insisted that I, as a foreigner, did not need to stay. But I wanted to. The meeting opened with the slogan "Etiopia *tikidem*" (Ethiopia first). The meeting's purpose was to flush out students who were "Pente," young people labeled Pentecostals for their enthusiastic witness and worship.

An hour in the hot sun passed, and no one came forward. The leaders had an informer's list and knew full well who they were after, but they needed to show their power. During the second hour, a fine Christian lad walked—nearly rushed—to the leaders' table. Coming forward, he shouted loudly, "I am a Christian! I believe in the Lord Jesus Christ as my Lord and Savior!" Everyone was stunned as two waiting guards took him roughly aside and marched him to prison. I left, not wanting to witness another minute of the horror. By leaving, I missed seeing eleven more students on the list bravely follow his example, coming forward and being led to off prison.

The county prison was crowded with people imprisoned for political suspicions or disobedience, including Christian students and older folks for their religious beliefs and practices. The twelve arrested students, once released, told us they had prayed and sung songs in prison, read the Bible, and spoke boldly of their faith. In time, a worried guard went to the county governor to inform him: "While these Pente youth are in our prison, other prisoners are being won over to their faith."

The threat of conversion of other prisoners forced officials to release the Christian youth to their homes. Such instances of intimidation and imprisonment of our church people would continue regularly during the seventeen-year rule of the Communists.

CHAPTER 5

Rebirth of Ethiopia
1991

In early 1991, the civil war intensified, forcing the government to close two of the roads leading north. At the same time, Eritrea was "taking back its homeland" and seeking independence from Ethiopia.

Foreign planes were not allowed to land at Addis, but evacuations of foreigners out of the country on EAL were numerous. Banks and official offices were closed for lack of money. Prisons were opened, and prisoners took to thievery and looting along the main road from western Ethiopia to Addis. In April our regional capital was taken by rebel fighters from both the Tigre and Oromo tribes. Soon the road was closed to all private vehicles as the takeover groups "liberated" town after town along that route.

Embassies advised nonessential staff and their families to leave. Missionaries from outlying stations took refuge in Aira until evacuation plans could be made. Some left under the cover of darkness via a five-car convoy to Addis on back roads. A week later, another four-car convoy of families left. We were two of only six expatriates who chose to remain.

Aira was "liberated" from communism by Tigre and Oromo troops. Our Aira students at the university in Addis returned home via plane to Dembi Dolo and then hitched rides or walked the eighty miles to Aira. Students from the eastern colleges of our region walked 125 miles to their homes.

The Oromo Liberation Front (OLF) declared its rule in Aira and the western regions. No buses dared drive west from Addis to our region. Conflict, however, erupted between the OLF and the new government formed by the conquering Tigre army.

In July the church's secondary school temporarily resumed to make up cancelled classes. By the time the new school year had begun in the fall, imprisoned church workers had all been released and were back at work. Non-Oromo church workers left the region due to ongoing tribal conflict.

Deserting government soldiers in search of cash for food ambushed a car of synod workers, killing three men. Robbery and pillaging were common along the roads by the retreating, defeated soldiers, far from home and walking to their home provinces. Some wounded and dying straggled to farmers' huts—all of them starving. They gave up their guns and begged for a place to hide. When the way was clear, they would move on to their homes or to find a hospital.

Social customs change

In 1975, when we moved from Oman to Dembi Dolo, a rural village in western Ethiopia, the greatest change we observed was that both genders could be together in public. Yet, there was no dating nor even hand holding among the youth. Although people were in Western clothes, girls seldom wore trousers. In very traditional homes, both boys and girls approached their fathers on their knees. Students never wrote or ate with their left hand—it being the "unclean" hand. As one girl coolly explained to left-handed me, "That's not our way."

With the fall of communism in 1991, Ethiopia moved eagerly into the world of private enterprise, albeit not into the affluent, twenty-first-century lifestyle we had seen in Oman. Ethiopia gradually adopted twentieth-century modes of trade and development. Grass roofs on housetops were replaced by tin sheets. Small shops and tea rooms were cobbled together and attached to the fronts of mud-brick homes. Over time, modern technology and global goods were evident throughout the countryside. It was not long before our village boasted a telephone in the marketplace. Students came to school with watches and cameras and wanted computer classes. New computers at the hospital forced us to add three morning hours of electric power to our usual four hours in the evening. New private colleges encouraged more of our graduated students to leave their families and villages by accepting those with lower marks than was allowed for eligibility at government colleges.

No matter how far from home the students ventured, many returned to their villages to marry partners their parents had chosen for them. The stability of their families drew them back in times of celebration and in times of crisis. Parents told children, "This is our way," a cultural expression preserved in many Ethiopians' memories and in their traditional writings.

Life in the new Ethiopia

Capitalism returned to Ethiopia as quickly as Marxism exited, and the change was dramatic. Merchants raised prices to buy second shops or business enterprises and to import a better quality and greater variety of goods. Landowners and farmers followed the merchants' example. Most men with fields began planting a few rows of coffee bushes or tobacco plants in place of the food crops needed for their families. Even the lowest workers of the social strata—potters, blacksmiths, weavers, and tanners—raised their prices. Imports, especially electronics and modern technology, carried high customs duties, and although this provided income for the government, it also put the items out of middle-class reach. Under communism, all people were equal, but capitalism divided people into the "haves" and the "have-nots."

The census of Aira in 1995 put the population at thirty-five hundred or more, reflecting an amazing growth rate. Among the newcomers were an innkeeper, who opened an overnight inn near the bus stop for the increasing numbers of travelers, and a restaurant owner, who set up her business at the same bus stop. Owners of liquor shops soon followed.

The local post office opened its long-sealed doors. The Bible school now had classes of men, some of whom brought their families with them. The hospital needed more staff for local patients and for those from outlying areas; overnight inns for the relatives who accompanied them also grew in number.

The influx of people demanded more water. Water from the deep well was not pumping fast enough; only a trickle of dirty water was getting through. The problem was solved by cleaning out the pipes. The river pump was also broken, so nonpotable water was not available to wash floors, dishes, and clothes until a new pump arrived from Germany.

Once, when our garden boy cleaned our car, he left the inside light on overnight; hence, the battery died. There were no spare batteries in Aira. We had to wait for a replacement. A lack of butane tanks for stoves and refrigerators meant that we reserved a small, cold box for the clinic medicines needing cool temperatures. One tank of gas for the cold box lasted three months, whereas a large refrigerator used a tank in three weeks. Our kitchens also had wood stoves to minimize the demand for butane.

The photocopy machine malfunctioned, so it had to be sent to Addis for repair. Our computers were in bad shape, and lacking shops in Aira to fix these problems, it took a long time to have them transported to Addis for repair. And there were other concerns besides modernization.

The Tigre government was filling its offices with their own tribal people. It was also promoting the idea of regionalization, with each region consisting of only one tribal group.

The Orthodox Church tightened its hold on parishioners after a census was taken "for the sake of obtaining burial spaces for every member." The church returned to the ancient Ge'ez language in place of Amharic and encouraged families to expel evangelical members from their homes.

Islam was luring young people away from villages, offering scholarships "abroad"—usually in neighboring Muslim countries. There were also promises of work and money. Once the buses carrying Ethiopian children crossed the border, however, boys were circumcised, given Muslim clothes to wear, and either put to work in the fields or conscripted to augment Arab armies. This might last for a year before they received any promised education programs, other than the required Quran schools. Meanwhile, girls often became maids for Muslim households.

With the nation waking up from the stultifying "sleep" of communism and the exhilarating, frenetic growth that followed, infrastructure could not keep pace. Updating basic amenities, like getting a flight out of the country on short notice, would lurch along in fits and starts. Never was this more acutely manifested for us than when news came about the death of our oldest son, Dirk.

Dirk was studying for his master's degree at the University of Nevada at Reno and died in a motorcycle crash near the California border.[63] As we scrambled, trying desperately to get out of Ethiopia, we encountered many barriers. It would ultimately fall to my twin sister, Mary Jo, and our son, Keith, to collect Dirk's body and make burial arrangements, all of which would be done and over with by the time we got back to the United States. It made for a surreal grave visit.

Family vacations

The fall of communism brought the freedom to travel, which we did in 1992. This time was planned to be our furlough in the United States, but we added an eight-day trip to visit Keith, who now worked for Ford Motor Company in Japan, and Ardith, our daughter-in-law. Ardith had studied Japanese to get her local nursing license and work at a hospital.

We continued eastward to the United States, visiting relatives, and attending the RCA Women's Triennial, at which we were to speak. Due to my lost luggage, Mary Jo mailed some clothes for me while we were at the Montana home of Harvey's sister. The last week of vacation, our luggage finally arrived from Pakistan, where it had gone astray.

At Christmas, Keith and Ardith came to see us in Aira. Keith wanted Ardith to know where and how we lived and to see

---

[63] Dirk died in June 1991, the day before his graduation. He had lost control of his motorcycle. His roommate, who was driving behind him in a car, tried to resuscitate him, but to no avail.

Harvey's medical work. One of the Dembi Dolo students we had assisted in education, a blind English teacher in a town in our province, came by bus to be with us and Keith. Once the children had left for their onward travel to India, she also left, only to return a week later with a sprained ankle from a fall.

Apology and reconciliation

The Bethel Synod of Dembi Dolo requested we reserve Saturday, November 20, 1993, for a meeting with them in Aira. Two elders of the Bethel Church congregation in Addis and four elders from congregations of Dembi Dolo, as well as their synod president, development secretary, and vice director of their school, came to our home where our Western Synod vice president, three local Aira pastors, and our Ethiopian doctor awaited their arrival with us. Harvey and I had no idea why they were coming but hoped they did not want us to leave Aira and return to work at their hospital again.

The meeting began with prayer, after which their development secretary handed us a letter from the Western Wellega Bethel Synod to the Presbyterian Church, USA, and read it to all present. It was an apology and a gesture of reconciliation to the mission workers who had suffered under the revolution:

Dear Brothers and Sisters in Christ:

The Presbyterian Church of the USA established our church in this area beginning from 1922. The mission established the work of evangelism, education, and medical care, rendering a great work to our people. Such great work continued up to the time of the Satanic revolution which had disrupted normal development of our society, in general, and our church in particular.

During this disgusting period, some of our missionary friends, who were willing to risk their lives in service for our people, became the victims of undeserved hatred and humiliation. The sad point in this episode was that the individuals, who were brought up and trained by this church, had been instrumental in persecuting our church and the concerned mission workers. The church workers and members were persecuted for bearing witness for Christ, the founder of the church.

The fact that the persecution was spear-headed by the insiders who were sharing from the same table of Christ should have not surprised us. The first persecution on the person of Christ started with such persons about two thousand years ago, and such irony is to be expected. As a result of this persecution, our church had lost many of its concerned, true friends.

As the missionaries were forced to leave, some of the schools were confiscated, while clinics and a hospital were nationalized. Ultimately, the church had lost its identity. Its properties were looted, and church buildings were used as dance halls, stores, meeting places for social affairs, etc. The indigenous church members were either imprisoned and tortured or were forced to flee the country.

The seventeen years of Communist rule had robbed the people of the sense of Christian concern and reason. A great apology should have been extended to the concerned missionary friends and the Presbyterian Church itself on behalf of all the ill-mannered Communist groups of our community for the wrong done. The apology has been long overdue because the church had been closed down for most all of this time. When it did open, the political conditions of the period did not allow us to improve or strengthen our traditional relations. But now this opportunity has come, and it is never too late to apologize. We feel it is our responsibility to apologize and to establish the spirit of reconciliation when there is a time and a chance to do so.

Of those missionary friends subjected to the humiliating persecution, Mr. Deeter (builder), Miss Jo Ann Griffith (teacher), Dr. Harvey Doorenbos and his wife were those to be remembered with honor as the true soldiers of Christ. We give special thanks to Miss Griffith and the Doorenbos family for staying on in our Synods up to the present time and giving exemplary service—even to those who had been persecuting them.

Therefore, we extend our greatest apology to the above mentioned and others concerned, as well as the

Presbyterian Church USA, for all the offenses they have faced during the persecution. Furthermore, we thank you for your great service and thank God who has made us one in Christ Jesus for the service of his church and for this opportunity of apology and reconciliation.

After reading the letter, the president of Bethel Synod read 2 Corinthians 5. Then an Addis guest, a rich Dembi Dolo merchant, whom the local revolutionaries had stripped of all possessions, gave a history of the mission work from 1922 onward and of his trials after we left Dembi Dolo. His son, who had been a student of mine, was one of the student agitators.

Harvey responded with words of forgiveness, emphasizing that we were privileged to stand beside our brothers and sisters in Christ during their trials. He repeated what he had often said: "We foreigners experienced little of what the local people suffered." I spoke briefly, quoting the Genesis passage in which Joseph comments to his brothers, "You meant it for evil, but God meant it for good." The "you" I translated as the government.

One of our Western Synod pastors, who had suffered much in prison, spoke of his great surprise to hear the body of Christ apologizing for its government's actions. He was truly awed by the meeting, whose purpose none of our people had had an advanced hint of. The first ordained pastor in Aira spoke briefly of healing through forgiveness.

Many pictures were taken, and our signatures on a list verified our presence. We proceeded to dinner, and I promised to make a copy of the letter and send it to every missionary who had worked in Dembi Dolo during the period of revolutionary zeal. Each person needed to hear the apology; who were we to be the sole recipients of a letter also intended for others?

The Dembi Dolo delegation was relieved to know the letter would get to all our former colleagues. Whatever sad or difficult memories the letter might evoke for each colleague, we trusted those memories might be eased by the loving apology these new leaders of Bethel Synod humbly presented through us.

Juxtaposition of cultures

For our family, going to Ethiopia in 1975 produced the expected culture shock. Surprisingly, returning to the United States for a short home leave in 1993 also produced the feeling of traveling through a time machine to another world.

On Saturday, we left Ethiopia with images of barefoot farmers plowing their fields, guiding oxen pulling a single plowshare; their wives bent over cooking fires in small mud huts with thatched roofs, busily preparing the one big meal of the day; and their daughters gathering firewood or carrying large water jugs on their backs to use in meal preparation. There was no electricity, gas stove, tap water, telephone, radio, car, or refrigerator in their homes.

On Monday, we were walking on Michigan's concrete city sidewalks. We had to learn how to turn on the motion-controlled water faucets in public washrooms, and we observed grocery checkout clerks looking for UPC codes instead of price tags. Office buildings harbored fax machines, computers, and Xerox machines, and homes had washing machines and dishwashers. Our trip became a cultural experience in reverse.

The changes might be equivalent to when electricity came to rural housing, city gas lines replaced wood stoves, a TV replaced the home's only radio, and tractors left horses and mules idle in their pastures. We had moved through a time machine in our lifetime. How long would it take for Africa to make the same moves?

Change did not come easily to Ethiopia, and when it did, it could be a mixed blessing.

The new hospital we were building was scheduled for completion in eight months; it took three years. Imported equipment arriving by ship was stored until customs duties were negotiated. Months passed before the material was finally delivered with a large storage bill attached. Arranging transport was filled with fraught—governmental needs had priority. When our truck and shipment arrived, the floor-polishing machine was missing its polishing stone. To add to the challenges, no cement was available for the machine's use. With the passage of much

The new Aira hospital under construction, 1989

time, a new shipment delivered all the items needed for a polished floor.

Nearby Aira, the Lutheran World Federation built an irrigation dam. This "Food for Work" project paid workers with bags of grain. Some two thousand people, mostly women and youth, volunteered to construct an earthen dam. Young men dug out dirt that others, in a slow-moving line, hauled from the excavation site to the dam's fill-in site. The continuous procession of people was awe inspiring.

The completed dam provided irrigation for fish farms and fields, and its resulting lake was stocked with fish. The benefits, however, were offset by an increase in malaria due to the year-round supply of standing water for mosquitoes to breed in.

Our new school replaced only twelve classrooms of the old school, adding one building for three science laboratories and two more for administration and a library. But the number of students grew significantly: twelfth grade increased by eighty new students and eleventh grade by an additional 120 students. Lower classes were even more crowded. Bible classes had been banned by the Marxists, but with their downfall, Bible classes could resume.

Nationwide, there were sixty thousand secondary students but space for only three thousand in the limited university programs.

The Health Assistant School that trained nurses selected only eighteen candidates from tenth grade applicants. The small size of their class was due to a lack of teachers and hospital beds for training.

Self-serving political power plays, tribal fidelity, unpredictable famines and flooding, and warring rebel and tribal factions impeded progress and inflicted heavy costs. A glaring difference between Africa and the West is in relationships: Africans place personal relationships—to people, community, family, tribe, and clan—above all other priorities, even to the disregard of work commitments. Will the West have the patience to wait as Africa grows at its own comfortable pace?

After retiring in 1999, we returned to Aira in 2003 as volunteers to the same hospital and school. Amazingly, the town boasted of a post office and twenty-four-hour electricity. Again in 2007, we returned to find a town with phone and email service, paved roads, and all types of vehicles. Development would come to Ethiopia in its own comfortable time.

Aira Hospital inauguration, 1993

Though it was a long time in coming, we were able to celebrate the opening of the Aira Hospital in 1993. Days before the inauguration, the details all fell into place for guests, transportation, and canvas shade for the outdoor "floor" of the old Outpatient Department (OPD). Schoolchildren cleaned up their rooms, and women prepared spices for the feast. Some men had brought carrots and potatoes from Dembi Dolo two weeks earlier. Using the storeroom under our house, we had opened the potato bags and spread them out. The carrot bags had no room to be spread out, so most of them had rotted.

We cleaned houses for guests, borrowed hospital linens to make up beds, lent dishes from our houses, cleaned the compound yards and sidewalks, instructed thirty-five youth chosen to be guides, set up a windsock at the airstrip, and other minutia. Friday morning the loudspeaker system was installed, and bunting was hung on the speakers' platform.

Friday afternoon, cars began arriving, greeted by our youth guides at every gate and at the bus stop in town. As guide leader and chairman of the reception committee, I was at the main gate most of the afternoon. Our personal guest, the former president of the whole church, now eighty years old, came later in the afternoon without his wife but with two young men. We gave them our two bedrooms and took the two living room couches for ourselves.

Not all invited guests arrived, but other people came uninvited. One bus brought many alumni from our secondary school, but fortunately they stayed with relatives, so we did not have to house them. During the night, it rained, and that helped to settle the dust on paths and roads.

Saturday morning's activities went well, and the general impression of the guests was admiration that we could put together such a program and provide hospitality in such a small, rural community. After breakfast, the guides and I again stayed at the main gate to welcome arriving guests, sell brochures for the day, and answer questions.

At 8:45 a.m., the first MAF plane landed on the airstrip, and cars went out to meet the distinguished passengers, including the architect of the school, hospital, and housing buildings. At nine o'clock, a second MAF plane landed with more guests from afar. One of the planes then flew off to Gimbi town, where a larger plane had brought six more guests (including the minister of health and the US ambassador) to be shuttled to Aira. Their arrival signaled the start of the program.

Harvey gave a brief speech and served as host to our US ambassador most of the time. Unexpectedly, Harvey and I were called up to receive traditional Ethiopian garments and gold rings.

To end the program, the minister of health cut the ribbon at the hospital's entrance, and Harvey led the VIPs on a tour of the facilities.

The feast extended to Sunday when all the boys who had worked for the contractor were fed, and then all the women who had worked for the feast sat down to eat. In this way, the

Ethiopian eating-order custom was kept. These kitchen-working women had not even had a chance to see the program on the other side of town.

Touring historic northern Ethiopia, 1993

In 1993 Sisters Helena and Leena (Finnish and Swedish nurses with the Lutheran Mission), Harvey, and I decided to tour the northern reaches of Ethiopia known for its historic sites. We left Addis in the afternoon, driving northwest to the western side of the Semien Mountain Range. Our return to the capital would be down the east side of the mountains. We planned half a day driving, half a day touring, and an overnight stay. Ascending the good road from Addis, we saw wide plateaus and oat fields. Near the Debre Libanos monastery, we stopped to photograph the scenic gorge and its massive rock cliffs.

The Debre Libano church—a modern structure—is approached through a town for the monks and their families. We passed a graveyard adjacent to the church, and before us was a cement building with three large mural panels made of colored stone pieces set over the front door. Atop the church was the typical iron Libanos cross. Inside were tall, brilliant stained-glass windows depicting many biblical characters. The floor and the altar walls were hewn from marble.

From the church we crossed a stony field and clambered up to a cave in a rocky hillside. Legend has it that St. Timotewos[64] stayed in that cave praying and meditating his entire adult life, all that time fed and clothed by devotees of the monastery. As a reward for his devout life, he received three sets of wings and is always painted with them on his back. The cave always dripped with water; only recently were a doorway and window set into a cement front.

---

[64] St. Timotewos was a renowned, historic figure in the Ethiopian Orthodox tradition; he was credited with slaying a dragon, an Ethiopian symbol of the devil. From the back of a horse, he thrust a spear into the dragon's throat. The story is similar to that of England's patron saint, St. George, who had slain a dragon.

Leaving the area, we drove a short distance to the turn-off to Fiche. There we stayed overnight in a local motel, where many truckers also stopped for rest. The room was three dollars per night, and we ate supper in the dining room. The most expensive room on our trip was twenty-six dollars, and the cheapest was one dollar.

We ate breakfast in our room since we had brought an alcohol stove and our foodstuffs and clothes in a large box on the back of our double-cabin Mitsubishi pick-up truck. The girls usually made supper and breakfast, after which Harvey would pack the large box, cover it with tarp, and then hit the road again.

The second morning, we drove through breathtaking scenery. The fields were filled with wheat, either harvested or soon-to-be harvested. Though lush greenery surrounded the mountain roads, we marveled that any crops were able to grow in the stone-filled hills and fields. We were climbing and twisting, overlooking valleys, facing sheer cliffs, and driving along endless mountain tops. High above the Blue Nile, we stopped to photograph the gorge, its river, and a bridge over it. We sipped our morning coffee, kept hot in a thermos, as we absorbed the panoramic beauty before us.

Our presence cued the soldiers from the bridge far below to hop onto a truck and come up to inspect us. After our coffee, we followed them down to the bridge, where we were stopped by more soldiers who demanded our cameras. After a tense hour of arguing, Harvey reluctantly took the film from his camera and gave it to them. Harvey hit the gas, and we sped off, not waiting for them to ask the girls for their cameras. Ethiopia's bridges had been blown up during the war by enemy troops, so the soldiers were concerned that we were taking pictures of them. We crossed over the four repaired bridges; the bigger, more strategic ones, such as we had just crossed, were well guarded.

As we climbed out of the Nile gorge, the asphalt road turned to gravel; it wound through mountains and then into wide plateaus, affording occasional glimpses of other gorges. Townsfolk along the road were poorly dressed: women wore grey dresses with blousy tops and long, bulky sashes at the waist, and mothers wore large rectangles of leather on their backs to carry their babies.

Some leather carriers were decorated with fringe, others had rows of small shells on the fringe ends that swayed and bounced with each step.

After 379 kilometers, we approached Bahr Dar in Gojjam Province, a beautiful city with wide boulevards and flowers, most likely planted during the Italian colonial rule. We were near Lake Tana, the source of the Blue Nile. Once we had settled into a cheap hotel, we were greeted by a young boy who introduced himself as a "parasite"[65] of the hotel and offered to guide us—for a small fee. Following his directions, we drove to the Teachers' Training College on the edge of town. The campus of flowering bougainvillea, "flame of the forest," trees and other beautiful flora was well laid out but in sad condition after years of neglect. We met three of my former schoolboys—two were college students and one a teacher there. They took us to the student union for coffee.

Students commented that we were in Orthodox territory, where attitudes toward evangelical Christians who tried to convert "already Christian" Ethiopians were strongly antagonistic. We sensed disagreeable reactions from the locals, partly from our religious bent and partly from their begging ways toward tourists. Our little parasite boy, an eighth grader, whose English was quite good, kept us from too much harassment. I assumed his English skill was motivated by a desire to earn some money helping tourists. We think he may have needed glasses, but we had no way of confirming it.

The next morning, we drove thirty kilometers to Tissat Falls[66] to see "the river that smokes." Five village boys became our official guides, while our parasite guarded the car for us. We walked for forty-five minutes on a stony path, using sticks to navigate and for balance on slick mud and slippery stones, with boys holding onto each of our arms. We were thankful it was not raining.

---

[65] Presumably, this was a new word to him. Like parasites that attach themselves to humans, he was similarly attached to the hotel—and became attached to us.

[66] The Tissat Waterfalls (the "river that smokes" in Amharic), 42 meters high and 400 meters wide (138 and 1,312 feet), are the source for the Blue Nile.

Margaret, Harvey, and Matthew (the mission's
driver) at Tissat Falls

We crossed a stone bridge, built in 1626, and climbed to the
top of a grassy hill, where we finally saw the falls. There were five
smaller falls of greater or lesser width and one very wide falls,
altogether about one mile wide. The sun did not come out to make
its famous rainbow at the bottom of the forty-five-meter drop of
the falls. There was a lot of muddy-brown water flowing over the
rims because it was the middle of the rainy season. After taking
photos and drinking the soft drinks the boys had carried along for
us to buy, we gingerly maneuvered back across the mud and
stones, doing our best to limit the muck to just our feet. Other
little boys tried to get us to buy pieces of fragrant bark from
frankincense trees. We resisted.

With disappointment, we decided against a motorboat trip to
the islands in Lake Tana, Ethiopia's largest lake. There are many
fine old churches and monasteries on these islands that demand
careful study of their unique, marvelous artwork. We learned,
however, of the high tourist fee associated with the tour and that
several islands did not allow women to disembark, so we decided
against venturing onto the lake. We observed that local
transportation, used for centuries on Lake Tana and the Blue Nile
River, consisted of canoe-type boats made of papyrus reeds.

We returned to our fancy Lake Tana hotel, tracking our muddy shoes on their carpets. From the windows of our dining room, we enjoyed a spectacular view of the lake while enjoying a wonderful, two-dollar noon meal. After lunch, we drove north through wide valleys, over hills, and past flooded fields. About halfway to Gondar, the road disappeared under water. Two men, up to their shoulders in water, were slogging from their homes, crossing the road with their goods held aloft. Others had already evacuated their huts, a frequent occurrence during the rainy season.

We kept climbing from the valley on a good road to Gondar, built on several small hills. Long ago, this was the capital of Ethiopia, and there were palaces to tour. Most hotels were full, so we ended up at a poor one, where the doors had no keys, and there was no water for the sink or tub. But, at a dollar each for a shared room, we did not complain. In many Ethiopian villages, merchants set up skittle bowling and ping-pong tables along the roadside for youngsters to enjoy. The noise of those games from the dining area kept up late into the evening.

In Gondar, we sensed a strong antagonism toward us. When we parked to look for bread and gather information, some young boys crowded around the car asking questions, and some even tried to scratch the Mekane Yesus Church decal off the side of the car with their fingernails. When we asked them who had taught them to hate and fear so much, they replied it was the priests. Everyone, both male and female, wore a silver cross on a string around their necks, and many women had crosses tattooed on their foreheads.

Getting underway the next morning, we washed our breakfast dishes at the hose outside, and Harvey did his share by drying them, much to the astonishment and amusement of local observers. We drove to Gondar's central hill—topped by a complex of castles—hired a guide, and toured the six stone castles and baths constructed in the seventeenth and eighteenth centuries. They were built by five kings and one queen—all within a walled area. On another hilltop, we toured yet another castle, a palace, and a royal bathhouse, which looked like a swimming pool.

The best drive was to the Debre Berhane (Hill of Light) Church. Fifteen churches had been built like it, but the pagan Queen Judith[67] had destroyed all but this one. It was a stone church with a thatched roof. An outside verandah, where the worshippers congregated, encircled the whole building, as was typical of Orthodox churches.

Exquisite artwork on the ceilings and wall panels adorned the interior. The ceiling consisted of rows of angel faces painted between the beams, each face unique. The walls depicted Bible stories, as well as biblical figures and Ethiopian priests who had become saints. A large painting of Mary and child rested against the altar area in a modest room where drums were left from the celebration of a saint's feast the previous week. We later learned that this was like the Ethiopian artwork we would have seen had we toured Lake Tana's churches.

The compounds of churches and palaces boasted trees of great girth and age. The olive trees were especially huge and reminded us of those we had seen in the Garden of Gethsemane in Jerusalem.

While Harvey drove the guide back to his post, I visited a former student now studying at a nearby medical college.

On our way again, we drove north through poorly kept towns with houses fronted on the highway. We puzzled why so few houses were made of stones when the fields were full of them. We saw a queue of people waiting to be paid for their work on a program under Orthodox sponsorship. We were to see more of these food-for-work programs under Catholic, government, World Vision, and Mekane Yesus sponsorship as well. Along the route were scores of stick homes being erected to make room for the thousands of war refugees expected to return from Sudan.

Driving higher and farther north another one hundred kilometers, we drove into mountain mists. At dusk, we checked into an out-of-the-way hotel; it was a lovely setting in the high, cold altitude. Had the weather been better, we could have seen Ras

---

[67] Queen Judith (Gudit) was a Jewish queen who ruled Ethiopia in the tenth century. She was reputed to have laid waste to Christian churches and monasteries.

Dashen, Ethiopia's highest mountain at over forty-five hundred meters (15,000 feet).[68] The town was a base camp for tourists hiking into the Semien Mountains and climbing Ras Dashen. The climb takes nine days, first by mule to the foot of the mountain, then the hike up and back down again, and then by mule to camp. Our hotel keeper said he had had four hundred tourists so far this year, over half of them Israelis.

Local women had multiple tiny braids over their scalps that ended in a fluff of ends on their napes. Their clothing was not so loose and had finely worked, embroidered edges. Heavy shawls were used to tie babies onto their backs. People in Gondar Province seemed to be better off than those of the surrounding region; perhaps tourist money boosted the economy.

We were up early the next morning; this day's trip promised varied and breathtaking scenery, and we were not disappointed. Passing through savannah, we witnessed camels nibbling acacia trees on the roadside, and small villages dotted the landscape but still no stone houses. Quail and francolin frequently darted across the road as we climbed to dramatic scenery amidst dense forests. These were dotted by long, thin waterfalls, hairpin turns in the road, and constant exclamations from Sister Leena: "This is so much like Norway!"

The forests offered no outlooks onto wide plateaus or broad vistas; distant views were not ahead but up and down as the road convoluted in tight loops. The evergreen forests, the waterfalls, the flowers, and the height and depth of the narrow gorges were awe inspiring. Without doubt, this was the highlight of our travels. We were grateful to have stayed overnight at the base of Ras Dashen, where we marveled at all this beauty through which we were driving.

Once we left Addis, we could no longer rely on our Oromo language, so we were grateful for Sister Helena's knowledge of Amharic for directions, prices, and food. It was good to have two extra drivers on these demanding roads. We met only two vehicles on this stretch: a beer truck and a truck loaded with wood and charcoal for the towns behind us where wood was scarce.

---

[68] Ras Dashen is the tenth-highest mountain in Africa.

Along the route were abandoned, burnt-out, and rusted army vehicles from the war, stripped clean of any usable parts. Most were pushed to the side of the road; some teetered on the edge of sheer mountain drop offs. Their number increased as we continued north to Tigre Province, where battles had been numerous and intense. We were reminded time and again of the cost of war in lives and equipment that the vehicles represented.

In Tigre Province, we finally came upon stone houses; some were two stories high. Grass is a common roofing material in the mountains of Ethiopia, yet many houses had tin roofs, which glinted in the sunlight even from far off. We noted farmers had cleared stones from their fields to provide larger arable plots to sow a greater variety of crops. Stones were piled around their fields or gardens to prevent animals from "harvesting" the produce. Considerable construction of buildings was evident in the towns we passed.

After another 264 kilometers, we arrived in Axum, the ancient capital of Ethiopia and apex of our circular trip. This was tourist territory; it cost twenty-six dollars for a room with a hot shower. People were riding camels; previously, we had seen camels transporting only goods.

We drove to the center of Axum the next morning and found it to be a small, tidy town. We quickly hired a tour guide and thoroughly enjoyed touring the region under beautiful, sunny skies. The Axumite kingdom predates Christianity's arrival, but Axum is where Christianity began in Ethiopia.

Kings erected three rows of obelisks and stelae with writings and pictures. During the reign of Judith, an anti-Christian Queen, some were destroyed. Foreign archaeologists had removed some of the treasures, and rumor has it that the Queen of Sheba's wealth was hidden under the stelae. A farmer had recently unearthed a stela in his field, on which were inscriptions in Greek, Sabean, and Ge'ez. The Sabean dynasty included what is now Yemen. Ge'ez is an old Ethiopian language still used by priests in their schools and churches.

One Orthodox church was now a museum housing many of the early kings' crowns, and according to local legend, it contained a lower-level hiding place for the original Ark of the Covenant, reportedly brought from Jerusalem before the city's destruction.[69] The Ark is never seen except by a twenty-four-hour-a-day, solitary, religious guardian. Once designated, a monk is its guardian for the remainder of his life, and he is brought food and clean water daily, never to leave his post in the lower level. Several crowns were placed on tables covered in red velvet and set inside the fence for our viewing from the outside. We toured a small museum where shards of broken pottery, drinking goblets of the Queen of Sheba, pottery with faces of royalty in relief, gold nuggets, and other magnificent archaeological finds were displayed.

A tour of King Caleb's[70] palace revealed excavations of several rooms, including a crypt, where his well-preserved body was found wrapped in animal skins, and a tunnel with walls of smoothly hewn granite blocks and large solid slabs across the top for the ceiling. We marveled at the labor required for such an enterprise. The domed tunnel extended 170 kilometers north into Eritrea, where its other end had been unearthed. How did they do it? What ventilation system did it have? Such questions went unanswered. With peace, hopefully, archaeologists will return to dig more deeply, and farmers will continue to unearth coins, stelae, and artifacts from their fields.

The palace of the legendary Queen of Sheba was locked, so we looked over the broken walls to see lots of grass and room dividers. There appeared to be little evidence of excavation work. Nearby, numerous short, graveyard stelae were stuck upright in a field. Everywhere, there were rocks and stones in fields, on hills, and in yards. Among those stones lay treasures, such as coins, which children and adults picked up to sell to tourists.

I do not remember seeing a single tree. They had all been used for buildings and firewood over the centuries, and new

---

[69] According to the Kibra Negast (Glory of the Kings), Ethiopia's chronicle of its royal line, the Queen of Sheba traveled to Jerusalem to partake of King Solomon's wisdom. On the way home, she bore Solomon's son, Menelik. Later, when Menelik visited his father and returned with some Israelite nobles, they stole the Ark and brought it to Ethiopia (*Smithsonian Magazine*, Dec. 2007).
[70] King Caleb reigned in the sixth century AD in northern Ethiopia (Axum) and Eritrea.

seedlings had never been planted. That is why the capital moved from Axum to Gondar, and when the trees there had been depleted, they settled again in Addis in the nineteenth century. In recent times, poor women walked many miles outside of Addis in the early morning to gather large bundles of firewood and carry them back to the city to sell. They did this every day for a pittance. Access to wood has been crucial throughout Ethiopian history.

Cacti and their prickly pear fruit lined the roads around Axum. The prickly pear is the size of a lemon and covered with thorns, easily knocked off with a small stone. The watery, refreshingly cool fruit is a safe and welcome drink for people walking by. Camels eat them, prickers and all.

Leaving Axum's sandy environs, we drove down the eastern side of the Semien Mountains. Our road twisted and turned on the eastern slopes but with a different kind of scenery. Instead of forests enclosing us, broad vistas greeted us. The land extended eastward to extensive salt flats and farther east (although small mountain ranges hid the steamy expanses from our view) to seaports on the Red Sea. Vast plateaus were formed by the Semien Mountains on this eastern side. Patches of eucalyptus trees grew where water was found.

Stone houses with grass roofs were either built into the hillsides or freestanding. Towns along our route harbored huge storehouses filled with grain stowed for times of famine or disaster. For years, Tigre and Wollo Provinces had been drought stricken and suffering severe adversities, so warehousing surplus food made good sense.

Trucks and buses used the narrow mountain road to reach Asmara, the capital of Eritrea. Bridges and embankments were protected by stone abutments built when the Italians made the roads. The drive was mostly over gravel roads that became slippery clay when wet. We took the mountain turns carefully to avoid any steep plunges. In front of us, a bus maneuvered back and forth three times to negotiate a hairpin curve.

In Axum, the honey farmers' cylindrical honey baskets—hung from acacia branches—were wrapped in cloth. In Wollo, the cylindrical baskets were a meter long and woven with vines tied around them.

Our destination, Makele, with its castle and fort, bore stark evidence of the revolution's major battles fought there. We stayed in a motel—for one dollar per room—near the Mekane Yesus Church, where a regional church conference was being held.

The following morning, we drove in more cultivated areas than we had seen previously. Our route took us through a long, low, desert-like plain, where goats were more common than sheep. No horses were seen. Three varieties of cacti, acacia trees, and shrubbery were the only green in sight. Soon, even that greenery gave way to dusty scrub on the high mountains and hillsides. These were riven by wide, dry wadis, and everywhere, there were the ubiquitous stones of northern Ethiopia. More black stones appeared among the numerous light brown ones. As we descended to more tropical environs, we began to see date palms and acacia trees with a yellow, birch-like bark among vast stretches of the more familiar acacia trees.

Clothing was different in these eastern regions of Ethiopia. Men, looking Arab-like, wore checkered wraparounds that folded up and were cooler in this climate than trousers. They carried bamboo walking sticks to steady themselves on steep paths. Women wore light cotton dresses and carried babies in shawls on their backs.

Donkeys hauled loads in oil drums cut lengthwise to make two balancing halves. As we drove into Wollo Province, we noticed that houses were again constructed more of sticks than stone, making the towns seem less well-kept and more impermanent.

Arriving in Weldiya, we settled into our lodging and then set out again to gather information about our next objective. We were intent on a visit to the carved stone churches of Lalibela,[71] which would be the grand finale of our tour. We got many differing opinions regarding the road conditions to the churches, so we decided to go see for ourselves the next morning.

At our motel, an English boy, concluding one-and-a-half years of traveling through Africa, asked to join us on our drive to

---

[71] The eleven rock-hewn churches of Lalibela, carved out of stone in the twelfth century to become a "New Jerusalem," are an important pilgrimage destination for Ethiopian Orthodox worshipers.

One of the rock-hewn churches (carved from a single piece
of rock) in Lalibela, Ethiopia. Such churches, built from
the seventh to thirteenth centuries, were an attempt to
build a new Jerusalem

Lalibela; he had missed the bus and the truck that went that day.
Later, two German boys touring Africa on a motorcycle also asked
for a ride. They had tried to get to Lalibela, but mud had clogged
their wheels, forcing them to turn back. For them, too, this was the
primary sight they had come to see. Their presence would be a
bonus if we got stuck.

It rained hard all night, so we knew we would have a muddy
road ahead of us. Neither buses nor air flights can reach Lalibela
in the rainy season, but our carload of missionaries and youth
decided to take a chance at it. We drove up and up on a good road
until we had to turn off on a narrow mud road. The car churned
through holes and mires until we got hung up on a rock in a mud
hole not too far from the village that would be our halfway point.
The men went into the muck and began shoveling and removing
rocks. Harvey went to work in shoes and all, but the youth took
their footwear off and rolled up their trousers. Several local men
helped push us out, and we continued on our way.

Stopping for tea, we learned that just beyond us the road got better; a truck, however, was stalled two kilometers ahead on the other side of a washout. It would take two hours to fill the washout with stones. If we continued to Lalibela after the repair, what else might happen during the night? It might rain and wash out the road again. The girls had to be back in Addis on Monday in order to be back in Aira for work on Wednesday, so we could not risk it. We turned back to Weldiya, greatly disappointing the three youth and ourselves.

We had no further incidents returning over the same mud holes back to Weldiya. We went back to the motel to clean ourselves up a little bit, but having already checked out, the motel management was not keen to have us use the little available water that was reserved for the paying guests. The German boys, however, were staying another night, and they let us use their facilities to clean up.

We left warm Weldiya and began climbing again on an asphalt road. Car traffic on Ethiopian roads is minimal compared to pedestrian traffic and their animals. People walk stony paths from their distant villages to smooth roads that lead to markets, everyone carrying something to be sold.

We reached the town of Dessie, one more of many relief centers during the hard times. Dessie is in the highlands, so it was cool. We went to a once-grand hotel, which looked ancient to us, and obtained rooms overloaded with furniture.

From Dessie, we had four hundred kilometers on good, asphalt road ahead of us. As we drove out of town the next morning, we were flagged down by two English boys who had not found space on any buses or cars and asked to ride in the back of our pick-up. They joined us, shivering in the damp, cool air, then burning in the sun's rays as we climbed out of Dessie into beautiful mountain scenery.

Approaching Senbeta, we saw camel trains, donkeys, and many people all walking toward town. Atop a rise, we stopped to view the spectacular sight below: the famous Sunday market, where lowland Atari people from the east came with their salt, cotton, and silver to exchange for highland goods of pottery, cloth, and other craft items. Everywhere there were animal skins, camels and donkeys, brilliant cloth and pottery, and fresh fruit—bananas, mangoes, papayas, and oranges. Tourist buses and cars were parked alongside the road, their occupants visiting the market.

The dark-skinned Atari women wore colorful cotton dresses and a red cloth piled up haphazardly on their heads. The cloth would become a shawl in the evening when the sun set, and even the desert seemed cool to those accustomed to heat. Atari women would braid their hair into many tiny, long braids. Their abundant silver jewelry—bracelets, necklaces, earrings, and amulets—was fashioned exactly like that of the Yemeni and Omani Arab women just across the Red Sea. The jewelry included the ancient Austrian Maria Theresa dollars used in the interior of Oman. They were pierced so that each coin could be threaded on a string as a necklace. The women looked very much like Arabs when compared to the highland tribes, who considered themselves "white" people.

A few local high school boys offered to guide us through the market and became nasty when we declined. "You!" "Money!" were words we got accustomed to hearing from youngsters in every tourist town, but these boys became so aggressive that they spit at Sister Leena as we pulled away.

Passing through a long, hot valley, we saw a lot of bamboo. Then we climbed higher into northern Shewa Province and noticed stacks of wheat stalks, such as we were accustomed to in the United States.

During the climb up to Addis, we could see that it was raining heavily in the distance. As we were considering how we might squeeze our two riders inside the cab with us, we were relieved to overtake a car with the Norwegian secretary and his friend out for a ride. They had space in their back seat and took the two English boys. Not long after, a heavy rain started that quickly turned to hailstones. By the time we entered the foothills of Addis, there were small piles of snow along our route. How thankful we were that the boys had dry transport. Later we learned that a bus traveling behind us had overturned in the hailstorm, and eight passengers died. God protected us more often than we knew during that trip.

Our journey ended in a light drizzle in Addis at 5:30 that evening on the ninth day; the odometer indicated that we had traveled 2,343 kilometers. We were grateful we had opted to drive and not fly; by car, we had seen many different tribes, spectacular scenery, and ancient history at our own pace.

Sentimental journeys

In 1995 we set out on a sentimental journey to visit Keith and Ardith and their new baby, our grandson Stephen, whom we were meeting for the first time in their beautiful home in Bangalore, India. It was a city we had toured with our boys when visiting them at Kodai School. Bangalore is India's "Silicon Valley," and Keith enjoyed the brilliant Indian engineers and coworkers in his office.

While in Bangalore, we took a trip up the Palni hills to Kodai, where our boys had spent their school years. We relived old memories, met a few familiar folks among the staff, and trekked popular trails the students gamely hiked every year.

Leaving Bangalore—with Keith, Ardith, and Stephen joining us—we added Oman to our sentimental itinerary. Oman was the home from which Dirk and Keith had gone off to Kodai for the first time. This detour was the result of the minister of health's generous invitation to have Dr. Doorenbos visit the "new" Oman after twenty years away, to see for himself the progress in medicine, education, and other developments.

Ironically, our old home in Mutrah had been razed a week before our arrival, and the hospital next to it would soon follow. We stayed in a lovely new hotel, and our children were guests at the seaside home of Dr. Donald and Mrs. Eloise Bosch, who had remembered Keith from twenty years earlier. While Harvey toured the new hospitals, the family and I took memorable jaunts to places we had had picnics, pitched tents, or gone swimming many years before.

We toured the date gardens at Nakhal and Rustaq, the Nizwa Fort, and the Green Mountain (Jebel al Akthar), with its fruit and sometimes winter snows. We flew to Salalah, where we dipped into the Indian Ocean and saw camel herds and frankincense trees. These places had been off limits to foreigners when we lived in Oman. Everywhere we toured, decorations and lights were strung to celebrate the twenty-fifth anniversary of Sultan Qaboos' reign. All along the roads, flags and oversized posters of the sultan's image adorned lamp posts.

Besides the tours by car and driver—kindly loaned to us by the sultan for the entire trip—we were feted on several occasions. Together with other medical personnel, we enjoyed a dinner banquet sponsored by the minister of health. We attended a Beach Club party given by former Arahma Hospital staff that included Indian medical professionals. And we especially reveled in a lovely afternoon tea party given by the Bosches for the Arab Christians and their families, which included the children of my female students of many years ago.

In February 1997, Keith and his family came from Bangalore to visit us in Aira, a highlight of the spring. In May we headed home for our last furlough. Notably, we were both recognized with the Distinguished Alumni Award at Hope College. We also attended General Synod of the RCA in Milwaukee in July, followed by a reunion of current and retired Arabian missionaries later that same month. We also joined the RCA's summer missionary conference for all missionaries on home leave.

The following year, we took our last trip to Keith's home in Bangalore, where I celebrated my sixty-fourth birthday. Keith would be transferring to Detroit in June. Our visit included a final journey up to Kodai. Keith and Ardith then joined us on our trip to an RCA gathering for all East Africa missionaries in Mombasa. Before the conference started, we toured the Masai Mara game park. Besides the excitement of seeing many wild animals from the safety of the safari vans, the quiet setting made for a relaxing two days.

Missionaries came from Sudan, Tanzania, Ethiopia, and Kenya. RCA staff came from the United States to lead the meetings. After morning sessions, the men went scuba diving; I swam in both the ocean and the pool, while Ardith and little Stephen opted for the cool shade of the pool throughout the day.

Second Nile Valley trip, 1996

May first, International Workers' Day, Sister Leena accompanied us on a short vacation to visit the Blue Nile again, as we had in 1986. Driving northwest, we were surprised to see the small homes in the distance reflecting sunlight. Then we realized that farmers now had more money from their market goods and had replaced their grass roofs with corrugated metal sheets. At a stop in Mendi, where we were to attend a Sunday wedding, we picked up a Gumuz guide who would navigate the road down for Harvey. It was rocks and stones and ruts the whole way, just as it had been a decade earlier.

The dry landscape became blacker as we proceeded into the area where farmers would burn their fields after harvest and then burn more trees to extend their tracts of land. Charred tree stumps bore witness to a once-thick forest being transformed into farmland. This traditional method of clearing land was the practice of the Oromo highland tribe, but it affected the wood supply for the Gumuz people of the valley. As we continued down, we saw not only little green flora but also lots of stands of bamboo and tall frankincense trees with their fragrant, sticky sap. In the villages, trees were bare but not burned.

A Norwegian couple who worked with the Nilotic valley people gave us a tour of their village. After an evening meal under a grass roof on poles, Harvey, Sister Leena, and the Norwegian couple slept outdoors on cots since it was very hot. I slept inside on a cot beneath a mosquito net. I minded mosquitoes more than the heat.

The house had a spacious, round, cement base, walls of split bamboo sticks, and a grass roof, and very basic appointments lined the circular walls: a double bed, a single cot, a desk and bookcase, two water barrels, a one-burner gas stove, and a hope chest. A coffee table and sofa in the center space still did not crowd the home.

An outside light and a house light were powered by a solar panel. A number of huts that housed workers, a clinic, showers, and latrines were scattered around. Breezes carried sand into the clinic and homes, but they were welcome nonetheless, especially in the afternoon and evening hours.

The next morning, the Norwegian nurse and Harvey saw patients. The nurse mentioned that many children died from pneumonia and malaria. The sun came out as they finished their work, so we walked down to the Nile River. Returning to the village, we were invited to a "feast" (beverages only) to celebrate the birth of the firstborn of a man and his third wife, who was fifteen years old.

Returning to Mendi in the afternoon, the Norwegian couple, Sister Leena, and Harvey stopped to cool off with a swim in a river.

The next day, arriving in Mendi, we participated in the wedding celebration. There were eleven cars for the wedding party and friends, a fine show of respect for the groom. He had been Sister Leena's garden boy and was now a health assistant. Monday morning, we returned to Aira with a valley patient to be operated on.

Back in Aira, Sister Leena and Harvey immediately began to take a course of antiparasitics to prevent the sickness which comes from the disease schistosomiasis. It comes from a larva in river snails that bite into skin and infect people, often fatally. Since we had been so close to the Nile River, Harvey felt that such preventative measures were essential. The medicine worked well, and neither Sister Leena nor Harvey contracted the disease.

It was not an extreme precaution to take. In June Sister Helena wrote of how sick she had been in Addis and on her trip home to Finland. In Finland they quickly diagnosed schistosomiasis and put her in quarantine, but they had no drugs in Finland for it. They had to order some from a tropical drug company. Sister Ashild wrote that she too had been sick in Addis, and she admitted that both girls had swum in a river in the Blue Nile Valley.

Mekane Yesus churches of Aira

When communism collapsed, a secret underground church community emerged. Where there had been 150 in attendance during the Communist years, now there were over one thousand, all expecting baptism and confirmation. In 1994 our congregation received 188 new members in one service alone.

By 1998 there were four Ethiopian Evangelical Churches—the Mekane Yesus (EECMY)—in Aira. The original Lutheran church, which the German missionaries had built, was located northeast of town. As hospital and school personnel increased, a church immediately east of the market was built. It was rebuilt and enlarged while we were there to accommodate the increasing crowds.

In the nineties, a third church was started southeast of the market, and a fourth church was erected on the western hill opposite the hospital compound. The first and fourth churches had loudspeakers that broadcast all day on Sunday and could be heard booming from the hilltops all the way to our end of Aira.

On Gospel Day 1997, we attended Aira's original church. The congregation had invited four churches from outlying areas, as well as Aira's other three churches. Over three thousand attended an all-day, outdoor celebration. Some sat on benches in the shade, while others stood under the covering of trees, but the majority stood or sat in the sun throughout the service.

In spite of the repeated arrests of youth and workers at prayer meetings after work hours, the churches added either an afternoon or a Saturday evening service to their program. Attendance continued to grow, as it did at the Pentecostal, charismatic house churches that enticed many young people.

Church and synod leaders claimed these new religious groups were "teaching falsely," and they wanted to excommunicate any adherents in the hospital and school. Of course, the EECMY did not like new groups "stealing their sheep," forgetting that their own church had grown out of the Ethiopian Orthodox Church's membership and from animists. The Orthodox Church not only had called that "sheep-stealing" but also had taken action against the new evangelical congregants in their beginning years.

Last Christmas in Aira, 1998

On December 23, 1998, we cut a tree in the forest and adorned it with our few decorations. We had not put out our

Advent candles, as had all the other houses. Tall, scarlet poinsettia bushes, brilliant red roses, and red-and-white-striped amaryllis decorated our yard for the holiday. Even the climate helped encourage a seasonal atmosphere, with mornings cool and crisp.

I had school on Christmas Eve and Christmas Day. On Christmas Day, I took cookies and blank Christmas cards to school for the teachers' coffee break. I gave each teacher a card to either keep for herself or to send to a family member for their Orthodox Christmas. We ate our lunch at Sister Leena's house—a dried-fruit soup and rice pudding, a traditional Christmas Eve dessert in Sweden.

In the evenings, electricity was not available until seven o'clock, so our Christmas dinner at Sister Helena's house began with candlelight, which made for a festive glow. Sister Helena's feast consisted of pork roast, a Finnish carrot-rice-beet cold dish, pickled fish, a mashed potato dish (a substitute for the traditional, mashed rutabaga dish), Swedish meatballs, miniature wieners, sweet potatoes, and Finnish bread. Dessert was a rich date pie with black walnuts that I had made for this occasion. We opened our presents at nine o'clock and were home by ten o'clock that evening.

For our Ethiopian Christmas Eve meal on January 6, Harvey and I invited Sisters Leena and Helena and fifteen of their nursing students to our home. We also invited Abebe, the wheelchair-bound colporteur[72] from the hospital—making twenty in all. The students and Abebe had a good rapport; they had pushed Abebe's wheelchair to the church for the Christmas Eve program earlier that day.

Sister Leena, Sister Helena, and I kept busy filling up the students' plates and juice glasses. Some ate an abundance of the traditional Ethiopian meal, while others, not native to Ethiopia, barely touched the "foreign" food. Roasted bones, succulent with golden marrow, were served after the main course, and many enjoyed that local delicacy. With no water in the taps, we washed hands outdoors under streams of water from pitchers.

---

[72] Colporteur: a person who distributes Bibles and religious tracts.

After dinner, we sang Christmas songs in Amharic, Oromiiffa, and English. One girl brought her guitar and sang a solo for us. Sister Helena used a video machine to show a film about Ethiopia that her mission had produced. We were thankful that neither Harvey nor Sister Leena was called to the hospital.

The lights went out as expected, but the fifteen candles bathed our happy faces in a warm glow as we finished with coffee, tea, and cookies, which disappeared quickly. Then Harvey—after a quick trip to the hospital to check on a patient—read a short devotion to end the evening. Christmas was celebrated well, and all the more so by having this joyful group with us.

On Ethiopian Christmas Day, Sisters Leena and Helena came over, and we feasted a second time on the lamb and vegetables from the previous evening. Extending the feast still further, any beggars that came to the door got the leftovers of our leftovers. Harvey spent the day at home; he and Sister Helena were on call, allowing the Ethiopian staff to attend services. The morning church service was five hours long because a drama presented by the youth went on and on, until a pastor finally intervened and cut them off. Again, we were thankful that neither Harvey nor Sister Helena was called to the hospital.

At the hospital's Christmas party and for the students we entertained in our home, Harvey played the cassette tape of "He Started the Whole World Singing a Song":

He started the whole world singing a song;
The words and the music were there all along.
What the song had to say was that God found a way
To start the whole world singing a song.

The students loved it and sang it over and over again. I realized it was "Harvey's song": he is an eternal optimist and would give anything to have the whole world singing instead of fighting. I translated the last line personally to mean His love through Harvey had started many a song here in Aira. Year after year, Harvey's example sang a song of faithfulness and integrity. I believe that, in watching him, people began to understand what total commitment looks like. Harvey began to use the word *discipleship*, an important dimension of his life.

The day after Christmas, we took down the tree and sorted through our decorations to decide what would remain and what would go. We planned a large sale of most items; we intended to carry very little back to our retirement in the United States.

Onesimos

In 1899 the Gospel was brought to the Oromo tribe in the Wollega region of southwestern Ethiopia. From that time on, the region was highly evangelized in spite of protests and persecution by the state-recognized Orthodox Church, Muslim traders, and political movements. The story of how the Wollega region received the Gospel begins with the story of a five-year-old Oromo boy.

The boy was taken as a slave and sold to several merchants before ending up in the port city of Massawa, Eritrea. There he was freed and joined a school for freed slaves run by the Swedish Mission. He was baptized and given the name Onesimos Nesib: Onesimos for the runaway slave in the New Testament and Nesib for a highly admired mentor. After finishing his education in Massawa, he was sent to Sweden for theological training.

Onesimos Nesib returned to Ethiopia and taught for almost twenty years in Eritrea before permission was given by the emperor for evangelical Christians to enter the Wollega area and settle there. During those twenty years, Onesimos translated the Bible into the Oromo language so it could be used by evangelists. It attracted much attention from the people, including Orthodox believers who were unable to read their Orthodox Bibles written in the priests' private language.[73]

One hundred years later, in January 1999, the Ethiopian Evangelical Church Mekane Yesus (EECMY)[74] dedicated two whole weeks to celebrate Onesimos' service among the Oromo. A tour to Wollega by our church leaders from Addis was planned to include four memorable events. Onesimos' home village erected a

---

[73] The Ge'ez language.
[74] Mekane Yesus means "Place of Jesus."

statue of him. One Bible school held a day of seminars on the history of church growth in the region. In Dembi Dolo, another Bible school, one with Presbyterian beginnings, had a day filled with speeches.

Our own synod prepared a grand celebration for the final weekend. An estimated ten thousand people attended on Sunday. Guests from other synods of the church, head offices, and European mission agencies helped to swell the crowds. The program, filled with speeches and choir songs, lasted for hours.

The Onesimos Nesib Seminary in Aira held an inauguration of their new dormitory on Tuesday. Our house guest attending the celebration was His Excellency Emmanuel Abraham, an ambassador and a minister for a long time in Emperor Haile Selassie's service. In his later years with the emperor, he became more and more involved with the EECMY church administration and became its second president, a post he held for twenty-two years. At eighty-seven years old, he was still spry and able to give speeches on any occasion.

CHAPTER 6

Kenya and New Sudan
2000-2001

Our "retirement" did not last long. We soon sought out mission opportunities, and our first volunteer work after retirement was in Chogoria, Kenya, beginning in 2000. We were to work there for six weeks and then take up more permanent positions in the newly formed New Sudan. In Nairobi, the capital of Kenya, we found lodgings at the Mennonite guest house, where we had stayed on several previous visits from Ethiopia.

We knew Nairobi well and could find our way around town quite easily. In the year 2000, however, Nairobi was an unsettled place. One morning we went downtown to purchase a Braille-friendly tape recorder for a blind girl we knew in Ethiopia. At the last shop in the row of Indian shops, we finally found one. As we left the shop, the merchant kindly warned us not to proceed farther down the street because the area was not safe. Despite his warning, on Nairobi's main street, we took money out of an ATM while many people passed close by.

Harvey and I walked from the guest house to the New Sudan Council of Churches office to obtain entrance visas for New Sudan. We also walked to a large shopping area and bought books to read while we were there. Some years later, terrorists entered the same shopping center and opened fire on shoppers. Besides buying a

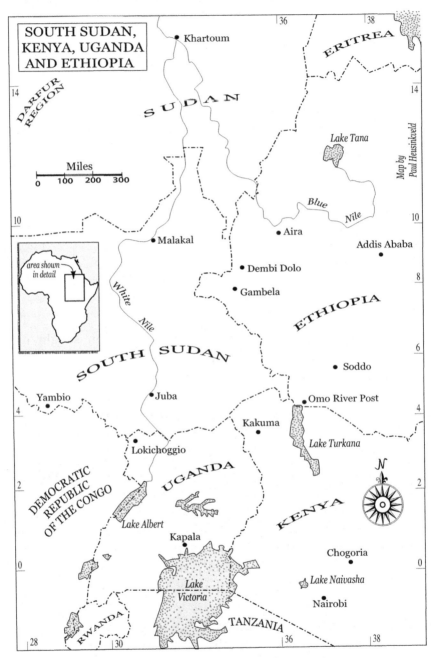

South Sudan, Kenya, Uganda and Ethiopia, with
inset map of Africa

few grocery items not found in Sudan, we also purchased a small tent and a sleeping bag.

On the Sunday we were in Nairobi, we attended the Nairobi Baptist Church and had dinner with Steve Staal[75] and his family.

After our brief stay in Nairobi, we made our way to Chogoria. Our six weeks at Chogoria took us north of Nairobi, to the east side of Mount Kenya. We lived in a guest house with other Presbyterian volunteers. The setting featured colorful flower beds and beautiful tropical birds with their delightful songs. While there, we were invited to join the RCA's East African missionaries' conference, this time held at the resort area of Lake Naivasha, Kenya.

Chogoria was a base camp, from which climbers started their climb up local mountains, but we did not have time for that. Harvey filled in for the surgeon at the hospital until a Dutch doctor arrived for a one-year assignment. Harvey also handled the gynecological cases. The staff implored him to stay longer, saying they needed him. But he had to turn down their entreaties because we had committed to go on to New Sudan.

Chogoria hospital usually planned on a one-week stay for young Muslim boys who had undergone a circumcision. While recuperating in a large ward just for them, a Muslim mullah (teacher) taught them Koran lessons and tribal customs; the hospital provided videos of cartoons, children's films, and Bible stories; and a pastor presented Christian teaching to them. It was a mutual agreement that kept the boys in a sanitary environment while their wounds healed and provided religious lessons and cultural entertainment for them. The boys enjoyed that week, and the parents appreciated the care provided in the hospital instead of a local "bush doctor."

---

[75] Steve's parents, Rev. Harvey and Mrs. Hilda Staal, spent their careers in the Arabian Mission. Steve and his brother, David, were each a year older than Dirk and Keith Doorenbos, and the boys were regular companions in Oman and Kodai.

New Sudan[76]

While in Nairobi, we met the staff from the New Sudan Council of Churches and the leaders of the Reconciliation Conference in eastern Sudan, to which I was asked to go. We also met the new Anglican bishop of Yambio, who traveled by car into Zaire and Uganda before reaching Yambio in New Sudan. He shared details of Yambio with us, mentioning that the Catholic Church had also appointed a new bishop who had been asked to oversee the Yambio Hospital on behalf of a Dutch Catholic aid agency in Nairobi.

We left Nairobi in a twin-engine airplane to the United Nations' large compound at Lokichoggio, Kenya. The compound was, in fact, an assortment of many smaller compounds that housed all sorts of aid agencies, mission and church workers, pilots and mechanics, tourists and volunteers—all under the protection of the United Nations. It functioned, in part, as a sort of transit center for people traveling into the field for work assignments or returning to their homes across the globe.

The airfield was crowded with planes, most marked with a UN insignia, since six of the biggest aid agencies to New Sudan had pulled their planes out. At Yambio there were relief centers for CARE, Christian Relief Service, Médecins Sans Frontières, and more. World Vision had been asked by the Sudan Peoples' Liberation Army to leave all their clinics and relief centers. Most provisional officials of the new South Sudan government, including the minister of health, had fled to the safety of Nairobi.

Outside the fence around the UN compounds were thousands of refugees from Sudan. Some had cobbled together corrugated metal sheets and building scraps to open little roadside shops for those who lived, ate, and survived in endless rows of open shacks in the sandy strip outside the fence. Rural refugees—

---

[76] Between 1994 and 2011, in an effort to hold the "old" Sudan together, a movement called "New Sudan" was initiated. It called for a unified, secular country. It soon became apparent, however, that this solution was not agreeable to the northern, mostly Muslim, section of the country. Civil war broke out once again, and a final division of the country resulted in 2011.

men, women, and children—waited day after day, month after month, year after year for a ride out of Africa. The Anglican and Catholic bishops of Yambio would have to travel on dangerous overland routes in trucks, buses, and cars, while we privileged few looked forward to flying in UN planes to our destinations. What a sad picture of society's inequality and inhumanity.

Inside the compound fence, life was quite stable, with two sustaining meals daily at the many open, straw-roofed canteens. Our private room was in the New Sudan Council of Churches compound. Inside the long concrete buildings were four adjacent rooms on each side, austerely furnished with a bed and water facilities. The temperature was ninety-five degrees, and any breeze that came up was suffocatingly hot and stirred up sand and dust. We spent the afternoon hours sitting and reading on our doorstep.

UN planes, loaded with aid supplies, flew to Yambio daily, but on Tuesdays, they could take three passengers to Yambio. We made sure to be aboard early on Tuesday morning. During the three-hour flight over high mountains and expansive forests, we saw only one significant town.

Sudan

In 2000 Sudan boasted around twenty-seven million inhabitants.[77] To its north, it is bordered by Egypt, and to the east by Chad. Its southern region, which counted almost seven million,[78] is bordered by Uganda, Central African Republic, Democratic Republic of Congo, Ethiopia, and Kenya. Kenya has the only nearby seaport, so goods bound for surrounding countries from Sudan have historically been transported overland to Kenya.

---

[77] Sudan was the largest country in Africa and the ninth largest in the world and included fifty-six ethnic groups, 596 subgroups, and four hundred languages and dialects.

[78] Of the seven million South Sudanese, about two million were refugees in camps outside the capital city of Khartoum in the north. Many worked as servants to the northerners, mostly Arab and Muslim. Another two hundred thousand southerners took refuge in camps in Uganda. It is estimated that almost two million South Sudanese died in the protracted civil war. That left approximately a third of the South Sudanese population still living in the south.

The UN plane flew us to an airport in northern Uganda. The road trip from the airport up into Yambio, Sudan, was difficult, necessitating an overnight stop in one of the few inns along the way. Bandits ambushed cars, and greedy border guards bullied travelers for bribes. Yambio is only a six-minute drive from the Democratic Republic of Congo (DRC), but that country was itself newly minted and still very unsettled, riven by warring factions.

In the ongoing war between the northern and southern Sudanese in the 1980s and 1990s, many young southern people fled the killing and walked the long distance east to the Ethiopian border and farther on to Kenya's Kokuma refugee camp. The mostly young male refugees who made it to America were labeled the "lost boys of Sudan" and made famous by the film *The Good Lie*.[79] Life in New Sudan was not precious—it was short. That was because of slavery, disease, war, famine, drought, conscription, prison, snakes, traditional medicine, and lack of moral discipline.

The first civil war in Sudan lasted from 1955 to 1971, the second from 1983 until 2011, at the end of which the north and south separated into two countries, Sudan and South Sudan. The Sudanese People's Liberation Army (SPLA) of South Sudan was involved in much of the fighting. The SPLA were mostly from the Nubian Mountains on the border with the north and in the Blue Nile area in eastern Sudan. Today, southern tribes carry on warfare among themselves over land, cattle, and other grievances. The war-weary southerners have a saying: "When two elephants fight, it's the grass that gets trampled."

Yambio, Sudan

At the Yambio airstrip in Sudan, we were met by the hospital doctor. Driving through town, we noticed only five cars, five motorcycles, and countless bicycles. Destruction from the first civil war was evident everywhere. The gas station, phone system, electric lines, and a TV tower had all been bombed. Many buildings had lost windows and roofs; the beautiful stained-glass

---

[79] A 2014 movie starring Reese Witherspoon and Ger Duany.

windows in the Anglican cathedral were reduced to shards clinging precariously to their panes.

A long brick building of shops in the town center and market area—all heavily pockmarked from bullets and shrapnel—had only one store front with a door still hanging on. Like most of the town's other buildings, it had no roof. A man sat on the step of one of the empty shops selling tinned margarine and bags of sugar. We could see through the missing front door out to the missing back door and beyond. There was nothing behind him; constant warfare had taken it all away. None of these war-torn structures had been repaired. Why would anyone bother? War destroys buildings; continued attacks destroy hope.

In the shops, I recognized products that must have come by truck from Uganda and produce from local gardens. Payment was made in Ugandan dollars or southern Sudanese shillings. Sudanese pounds from the north were not readily accepted. The Arabic language of the north, forced on the people of the south, was not appreciated, and so it was seldom used. Our ability to speak Arabic delighted the old ladies in the market, but the men tried to ignore all northern customs and practices.

The compound with the hospital and our living quarters had hand-pumped water from a well. Our large bedroom was in a brick-and-cement house, in which one Kenyan man (the hospital business administrator) had the other bedroom. He maintained the morning radio connection with Nairobi and related clinics and schools. Meals were prepared on a wood stove by two young girls in the kitchen, and we ate in the dining area with two more Kenyan staff members.

One was a Kenyan nurse who had her own little circular hut with a dirt floor, known as a *tukul*. These consisted of mud or cinder block walls and grass thatch roofs supported by poles all around, usually sitting on bare ground. Every blade of grass was diligently cleared away so one could see snakes and insects more readily.

The other staff member was a Kenyan Jewish hospital technician who was Israeli trained. He had previously worked in the Democratic Republic of the Congo when it was still Zaire. Our little "family" of five reportedly occupied the best renovated

A typical *tukul* of mud walls and thatched roof. Two bee-honey baskets made of woven strands are hanging in the tree. Honey is a key food and drink for rural Ethiopians

compound in Yambio. The aid agencies had their compounds in another section of town, but we seldom met those workers.

Throughout the town center and around our house and other buildings, we saw holes dug two feet deep and ten feet in diameter in the soil. Our guide said rather matter-of-factly, "That's what you jump into when the bombs drop to avoid the horizontal metal shrapnel pieces."

The town was filled with mango trees and hundreds of mangoes were there for the taking. Day and night, heavily laden branches would break off with a loud crack for lack of harvesting. The town smelled like a mango brewery, with mangoes mashed underfoot everywhere.

In the market were dried fish, monkey, snake, and wild pig. Vegetables included cassavas (a starchy tuber, dried, and ground into flour), yams, maize, cabbage, and onions. There were also palm oil, tobacco, coffee, and peanuts. Fruit included the ever-present mangoes, pineapples, bananas, and lemons. The Dinka tribe—from the northeastern part of southern Sudan—were cattle herders who introduced beef to Yambio.

A family's compound usually consisted of several tukuls. The male had his own in the center of the compound for his friends to come and visit. Each of his three wives had her own tukul with her own children born of the one shared husband. A short distance from these structures were the family graves, their earthen mounds piled up high with many stones to deter scavenging animals from digging up the bodies until the family could afford cement slabs.

Messages were sent by drums to villages farther away. Ululating, a vocalization made in the throat, resembling a high-pitched howl with a trilling quality, was a typical response to good or bad news. Ululating and shrieking were common on the night of a new moon's appearance. The day of liberation of the south from the north was celebrated annually as a three-day holiday. There were parades, drums, dancing and ululating women, sundry speakers, and many gunshots into the air. The few local Muslims were afraid to gather for Friday prayers when such crowds were out and about. To keep a low profile during these raucous events, the *muezzin*[80] did not broadcast the call to prayer, and the Muslim faithful met quietly at the appointed hours.

Medical work

Harvey immediately set to work in the "hospital." Yambio Hospital had two long, parallel brick buildings. One held the patient ward, with twenty beds on one side for males and the same along the opposite side for females. The end nearest to the hospital gate was a separate room for the outpatient clinic. The other building across the courtyard had yet to be repaired from the

---

[80] *Muezzin*: the religious leader who calls Muslims to prayer from the minaret of a mosque. Nowadays, with the introduction of loudspeakers, the call is often very loud and can be irritating to non-Muslims.

shelling, but the resident doctor had managed to fashion an office out of one mostly intact room; another room was for storage. Outside the hospital gate, a small building had been constructed by World Vision as a maternity center, but it had been closed by the government. Another aid organization built a Mother-Child Health Care clinic.

There was only one Sudanese doctor in the hospital, and Harvey had doubts about his medical training credentials and surgical expertise. The surgical work was done in a small building situated between the two parallel ones. From what we observed, there was no effort at sterilization. Blood stains on the walls, operating table, and floor gave evidence of the staff's "Why bother?" attitude, so prevalent among the discouraged and war-weary people of New Sudan.

One Kenyan nurse could hardly enforce the rules of proper hospital procedures. Harvey implemented major changes by insisting on sterile techniques, teaching proper instrument and suture use in the operating room, and encouraging aides to observe patient vital signs and record them. He taught the medical assistants and other staff daily and even instructed the Sudanese doctor when he was around.

The longer Harvey stayed at the hospital, the busier he became. Before long, there was a waiting list of surgery patients. A man pleaded for his thirty-year-old wife, who had delivered her eighth baby at hospital, to immediately be sterilized. Harvey had to deny the exasperated man's request because the hospital was under the supervision of the Catholic diocese, which was strict about no sterilizations, no family planning, no abortions, and no condoms to prevent HIV-AIDs.

One Sunday, Harvey came home for a quick, cold dinner only to turn around again and hurry back to his third emergency case. The night before, a soldier had thrown a grenade into a disco-dancing crowd, causing burns, fractures, a damaged liver, and worse. Incredibly, ten of the worst injured had walked or bicycled to the hospital. Harvey had to call the UN base to evacuate three cases, the fractures of which he had no equipment to repair.

Once we had settled in, we visited the Comboni Mission Sisters at their clinic, set off a distance, for leprosy and tuberculosis patients. One expatriate nurse spoke English in addition to the local language. She was teaching her patients how to do traditional crafts if they were not too disabled by their disease and could still paint, knit, or sew. Two other Italian nuns ran a school with the help of Sudanese teachers.

Our visit to the sisters' compound included a stop in Nzara on the way. We wandered among the ruins of a British industrial complex from earlier days before the war. The British had built a steam engine track to transport cotton collected from extensive surrounding fields, to bring palm oil to the factory, and to haul long tree trunks to be cut into wood planks for building and furniture needs. This bombed-out site had been the only industry in all of southern Sudan.

Later we visited an American couple from Hawaii who were doctors in a sleeping sickness hospital built with money from the Bill and Melinda Gates Foundation and from Doctors Without Borders. They were aided by two nurses from Russia and some local help. An open, brick building was divided into three rooms: one for recovering patients, one for sick cases, and one for the sleeping, dying cases. Two of the staff workers traveled each month over a wide area to test village children for early detection of the Tsetse Fly-borne disease to find the infected ones before it was too late to help them.

Yambio's churches

The small town of Yambio had two cathedrals, which meant each had a bishop as their leading pastor. One was the Anglican cathedral, where I taught two literacy classes for women. The other was the Roman Catholic cathedral that oversaw Harvey's hospital work. So we decided we should attend each church on alternate Sundays.

There was a difference between the two churches, in that, the large Anglican cathedral, a beautiful old monument to traditional British architecture, was only half full when we were there. The Catholic cathedral held an early service in a small chapel for about thirty English-speaking locals and expatriates. Bishop Joseph and his priests took turns leading worship services. A service for Yambio's many Catholics took place later in the morning.

On Palm Sunday, we met an American Mennonite couple after the Anglican service, when worshippers would form a circle outdoors and walk around shaking hands with each other. The couple visited us in the afternoon and shared information about their work with the UN's Operation Life-Line Sudan, a support system for all transport in and out of Yambio. They were preparing, after three years in Sudan, to go home and then return for another three years. But they had recently opted not to return to Sudan because the drive from Uganda to Yambio was not safe.

On Good Friday, the Catholic bishop and priests led a procession of church members from the airstrip where they had gathered to the cathedral. They paraded the cross ahead of the marchers who carried flowers and sang doleful songs in keeping with the holiday.

Easter Sunday, we sat in the Catholic cathedral's chapel for the early morning service. About forty-five minutes into the service, arriving worshippers for the outdoor Easter Mass announced themselves with much noise and commotion. At the conclusion of our service, we went out and watched wave upon wave of people, many carrying their own chairs or stools to sit on. They were singing and swaying and carrying flowers. Then after milling about a bit and chatting with friends, they got down to the business of finding a suitable spot for viewing the service. Once this was achieved, the crowd sat down and waited. On the walk home, we met many more worshippers dressed in their brightest colors on their way to another outdoor service. Harvey estimated over two thousand worshippers had attended that service.

Bishop Joseph invited us to supper at the Comboni Mission Brothers' compound. In addition to us, he had invited many others to the Easter banquet at the priests' compound. In a large hall, he sat and greeted the guests. Before he spoke to us, he signaled for a glass of water. Soon a servant girl came down the middle aisle on her knees, bearing the glass of water on a tray. She knelt all the way down, proffered the glass to Bishop Joseph, and then retreated to the kitchen, still on her knees. After a welcome, the bishop led us into the dining room where buffet tables were laden with food, both local and imported. It was a great feast; we had little idea what we were eating, but it all tasted good.

Education in Yambio

Every day in southern Sudan, on my way to teach English to local women, I passed by a primary school, bright with daylight both inside and outside the one-room building. Built with large windows for long-gone panes and without a roof, the light filled every corner. The roof and all the glass panes had been destroyed during an air raid, but little children streamed in single-file from the village, seemingly oblivious to the history of violence once visited upon the structure.

Every child carried a small square stool atop their head to serve as their seat in the classroom. They set their stools down and opened small notebooks on their laps. The teacher had received a fourth grade education and imparted all of his wisdom to these small ones. As if in a gesture of consolation from the earth below their bare feet, velvety grass sprung up inside the structure after the rains, determined and lush to the point that it required frequent cutting. This was their school.

The Comboni brothers, like us, were foreigners and used English at their secondary school for boys. They taught in a tukul that was open, with waist-high, cinder block walls and a grass roof supported by poles all around.

Inside, benches and tables were arrayed facing the ostensible front of the class. A second indoor classroom held chairs, desks, typewriters, and books for the students. This school was one of only five schools for ninth to twelfth grades in all of New Sudan. Two of those were in garrison towns and run by northern teachers using Arabic.

The average age of the male students, some of whom were already married to teenage girls, was twenty-two. The Southern Peoples' Liberation Army ran the government of the south under careful northern watchfulness. The army conscripted boys, including twelfth grade graduates from the southern tribes. Thus, finishing school was not always desirable, and boys nearing graduation frequently ran to Uganda to avoid conscription. They would have to repeat the eleventh and twelfth grades in Uganda before entering university there. No one in the south qualified for Sudan's one university in the north where the southerners were not wanted.

The Comboni brothers' secondary school included three boys from Darfur, in western Sudan. Each year, those boys set out on foot for Yambio from their homes in Darfur, about five hundred miles away, a journey that took almost a month, and every boy carried a large bag of harvested corn kernels to be cooked for their one meal per day. Each one also drove a cow to sell at the Yambio market, the money from which would cover school fees and supplies, clothes if needed, and additional food items.

The Comboni brothers told us that, one year, when the three boys showed up, they told of how a fourth boy had separated from them and was set upon by bandits who had killed him and taken his cow. The three boys went to Yambio marketplace daily in the hopes of finding a man returning to Nubia who could carry the message of the fourth boy's violent demise to his family.

The Anglican bishop, whom we had met in Nairobi, came to our guest house during our first week in Yambio to ask me to assist in the school for women in his congregation. They wanted to improve their limited English in order to read the Scriptures in church as the men did. I spent one hour daily with each class of women, who were otherwise taught by two young ladies from Kenya. They had an English-language curriculum for me to follow, and I added Sunday school songs that the women enjoyed singing. The first-year students met on the narrow porch of the women's dormitory and sat on folding chairs. The metal door with its white paint was used as a small blackboard. The class of second-year students met in a large tukul with wooden benches and tables, a large easel for the blackboard, and a thin carpet of grass underfoot.

Bishop Joseph

We invited Bishop Joseph of the Catholic cathedral and Dr. Anthony from the hospital to tea at our compound. There, the bishop told us the story of his seminary years. He was in seminary in Juba, the capital of his state, when soldiers of the northern government entered the seminary compound and began shooting. The teachers and students had little time to escape, but he crawled up to safety in the rafters. From there he watched in horror as the soldiers gunned down all of his teachers and his fellow students. After days of hiding, he was caught and imprisoned by the troops who guarded this garrison town where northerners still ruled and terrorized schools.

He also shared with us an experience from a trip to the United States years later. His American host had driven him along the New Jersey shoreline and awed him with the sight of tall buildings and homes. When he marveled at a seven-story building, his host said it was a hospital. When he expressed a hope to one day see such a fine hospital in New Sudan, his host replied with the shocking words, "It's an animal hospital for pets." The bishop was speechless, dumbstruck that money would be spent in that way, for animals. That inconceivable idea would color his opinion of Western culture for a long time.

Peace for New Sudan

While I was in Chogoria, Kenya, the RCA's secretary for African Affairs had invited me to attend the East Nile Bank's Reconciliation Conference in her stead. The conference was set up by the New Sudan Council of Churches as the next step in the People-to-People Peace Process for the South. The New Sudan Council of Churches was eager to see unity between the southern tribes to stand against the north and be in agreement when—or if—they ever became independent and opened their own embassy. The conference was to be held at an undisclosed site along the Nile in March for seven to ten days. Details about where and when were not widely publicized in an attempt to keep news reporters, the Sudan People's Liberation Army, and northern spies away from the conference.

The secretary believed it would save expenses if I attended the conference in her place since I would already be in New Sudan in March. So while I was still in Kenya, besides getting a sleeping bag and tent and a few snacks, I also acquired papers for that area of New Sudan and enough money for UN flight tickets from Yambio to Lokichoggio in Kenya, to the unknown conference site in Sudan, then back to Lokichoggio, and then home to Yambio. Not being a photography buff, the prohibition on cameras did not faze me. We were told that the plane would go when it was ready and not on any schedule.

Early in April, the radio message came: "East Nile Reconciliation Conference to be in Bor area." I said my goodbyes to Harvey and my classes and packed my bags for the regular Tuesday flight to Bor. Then word came of a special plane that would arrive in Yambio at the end of the week to pick up three passengers: a Roman Catholic delegate, an Anglican delegate, and me.

On Friday I stood with the Anglican delegate on Yambio's airstrip watching the sky and listening for engines. We saw and heard nothing, and eventually he asked what we should do. I suggested that we pray for seeds of love and peace in the tribal leaders' and soldiers' hearts.

Eventually, we returned home to unpack, eat lunch, and resume our afternoon work routines. The Roman Catholic delegate never joined us in our vigil for the plane. Harvey later explained that the delegate had complained of gall bladder pain, so Harvey wanted to send him to Uganda for an ultrasound.

Later that year, when we returned to Kenya[81] for our trip home to Holland, Michigan, we stopped at the New Sudan Council of Churches' office. I was given a pamphlet describing the success of the conference. In reading the report, it became clear to me that the languages and traditional customs would have left me unable to provide a useful, intelligible report of the conference.

---

[81] Air travel to the United States required routing through Nairobi. While in Nairobi, Harvey was informed his next older brother, Harold, had died. Margaret and Harvey were able to travel in time to attend his funeral.

CHAPTER 7

Mission to Malawi
2000-2001

Malawi is a landlocked nation that lies along the west shore of Lake Malawi (also known as Lake Nyasa), the fourth largest freshwater lake in the world. Lake Malawi is part of the Great Rift Valley system that runs from Turkey through the Levant and the Red Sea into East Africa. Lake Malawi is sixteen hundred feet above sea level.

The Presbyterian work in Malawi had its roots in the work of the Church of Scotland, the Free Church of Scotland, and the Dutch Reformed Church of South Africa. Their church synods combined to form the Church of Central Africa—Presbyterian (CCAP) in the late 1940s. PC (USA) began work in the mid-1950s, putting themselves under the CCAP umbrella. Malawi's religious statistics are roughly 55 percent Protestants, 20 percent Roman Catholics, and 20 percent Muslims.

English was the language used in the educational system throughout the British colonies in East Africa. It gave the citizens of those countries an advantage over other African countries. The literacy rate of Malawians over fourteen years of age was 75 percent for males and 49 percent for females at the end of the twentieth century.

The health statistics of Malawi were poor in 2000: life expectancy was forty-six years, average births per woman was six, and infant mortality was 189 deaths per 1000 under the age of five. Why were the numbers so dismal? Several factors were involved. Diet was crucial. The main diet was *nzima*, a stiff cornmeal mush with little else to enrich it. Small fish from the lake offered some protein, along with vegetable greens when affordable.

Teenage motherhood presented difficulties during birthing because the women were too young, and they came to the clinics too late, after home deliveries had failed. Local farming was done mostly by women because in many homes the father was off in another country or area of Malawi for work. Jobs outside Malawi paid much better, and the money was brought home or sent via remittance. All these factors conspired to undermine the health and wellbeing of Malawians.

At the beginning of the twenty-first century, the lack of doctors, nurses, and teachers in Malawi was dire. Over eighteen thousand primary teachers were still needed to begin the next school year. Volunteers, in groups or individually, came from abroad to provide short-term or two-year stints in schools, hospitals, and church outreach programs. Some were either professionals or students, and some returned to live and work permanently.

Harvey and I served twice at each of three different hospital sites: Livingstonia, Embangweni, and Nkhoma. Harvey replaced general practitioners on leave, so he had little surgery at the first two hospitals. But the work at Nkhoma meant daily surgery since he was there to replace vacationing surgeons. As a general surgeon, he easily covered all aspects of surgery, obstetrics, and pediatrics. On these visits, I found myself in the classroom as a volunteer teacher.

Nkhoma, Malawi, 2000

The Nkhoma Mission was built and served by Dutch Presbyterian Afrikaaners of South Africa, but the hospital workers were mostly from Malawi. The large compound of church and mission buildings consisted mostly of red brick buildings.

The Nkhoma missionary families had their own van for transporting the older children to a school in Lilongwe, about fifty kilometers away. It was in that van that we traveled an hour from the capital to our first assignment. Our home, while there, was the residence of a South African schoolteacher who was on leave.

The home was small and cold, so I often sat outside in the morning sun to warm up. There was no hot water, so we kept a large kettle of water on the stove for cooking and washing. We had to boil our drinking water. The water taps in the kitchen and bathroom had the hot water tap on the right and cold water tap on the left, as was the British,

Malawi

European, and South African custom, but regardless of the designation, only cold water came through the taps.

There were many one-track, dirt roads to take, and they confused me at first. Walking home one day, I started out, turned back, and tried another road. Two schoolboys came along and asked if I needed help. They led me directly to the teacher's house where we were staying, so in gratitude, I invited them in for tea. I saw the hesitant look on their faces, but they entered and sat on edge while I prepared tea and cookies in the kitchen. I sat with them as we talked and drank and ate. Their homes were at a lower altitude, and they had a long walk ahead of them to get home. One lad, as he left, turned to say thanks once again: "Ma'am, we were surprised to enter your house for we have never been in a white person's home." I welcomed them to come again, but I suspected they were not ready for such a bold action.

Sunday nights, the missionaries often met for Bible study in the combined dining and living room area of the guest house. No local Malawi couples came. A white South African missionary asked us how we managed to be so relaxed in our relationships with the local people when they and the locals seemed to have a wall between them. It was, unfortunately, the baggage of apartheid that created the chasm between the two African communities.

My tasks

In whatever country we served, providing hospitality was my number one task. Foreigner missionaries needed companionship, especially those who were alone most of the time. There were guest house residents who came unprepared for the customs and simplicity of the lifestyle imposed on them in these remote places. Local organizations could always use an extra pair of hands; native and foreign school children who struggled with lessons requested tutoring after school, and new or busy mothers needed babysitters. In all of this, I always found a place to volunteer.

One Afrikaans family had four boys, three of whom were too young to go with the older primary children to the Baptist school in Lilongwe. They had classes and a teacher in one of the guest house's large rooms. Their mother asked me to teach the youngest boy English for future usefulness. This break also gave his mother a few hours of peace and time to herself.

I went often to the market for produce: carrots, dried beans, potatoes, cabbage, pumpkin, eggplant, tomatoes, peas, okra, string beans, onions, cucumbers, and peanuts were always in abundance.

We enjoyed the tropical fruit: oranges, guava, mangoes, bananas, lemons, and limes. When shopping, we could snack on greasy puffed muffins or dried termites (a local favorite) purchased from street vendors. On Saturdays butchered pork, goat, and fish could be bought, along with the live versions in another section of the market.

There were many stalls selling clothing made in Nkhoma or Lilongwe. I enjoyed seeing the piles of foreign clothing available to the locals or maybe catching sight of an attractive sweater or skirt for myself. Often these bales of clothes had been imported as charitable donations for the poor but were bought by merchants at the port and sent to markets throughout the country to be sold for a profit. The port workers took the merchants' money, the merchants took the vendors' money, and the vendors took money from the poor.

Harvey's work

It was convenient for Harvey to have the guest house so close to the hospital. He went every morning at 7:30 to receive the night-shift activity report. Then he made rounds in the surgical ward. During the Christmas holidays, the surgery ward was not so busy; many patients wanted to be at home, so they delayed surgery until the holidays passed.

Elective surgeries were scheduled for Tuesdays and Thursdays until evening. Emergency and inpatient surgeries were done during other daytime hours. The hospital had enough doctors and clinical officers but lacked nurses, which made patient care difficult. The wards were so crowded that men, women, and children often slept on the floors. In these wards, nursing help was so scarce that family members had to step in. Harvey's concerns about the shortage of nurses on the wards and the surgeons' long days were readily acknowledged by all, but few viable solutions existed due to lack of trained staff.

The Nkhoma surgeons took turns once a week tending to patients at the American Baptist Clinic in Lilongwe. This service afforded the clinic surgical capability for less intensive surgeries and provided income from those patients. Harvey would take his turn at this service and bring back to Nkhoma the fees collected at the Lilongwe clinic. Private patients came to Nkhoma Hospital if surgery was needed.

The American Baptist Clinic was on the same compound as the primary school for missionary children in Malawi. Either a mother or the driver from Nkhoma drove the van of children down in the morning and returned with them at in the afternoon. Most of the older children went to Kenya to attend Rift Valley Academy, a secondary boarding school with students from several East African countries.

Malawi's "brain drain" of trained medical staff was more pronounced than in many other African countries. Nurses and doctors were well trained and spoke English fluently, which made them very employable. The government did not prohibit going abroad, partly because workers in other countries sent home large remittances to their families. Hard currencies, like US dollars, earned by expatriate workers, helped the government more than any other source of aide. Despite that welcome relief, we still heard many expressions of exasperation that America paid the government of Malawi nothing to compensate for its cost of training these medical workers.

Nkhoma's market

Our house was only three blocks from the central market. Having little else to do, I regularly walked to the market to shop. The market began with the butchers' tables. Meat displayed for sale was mostly pork and goat, brought to market alive, lashed to bicycle handlebars.

A few small shops were next with grocery items in some, pots and pans and dishes in others, and tables loaded with basic sundries interspersed. A large, covered pavilion with cement blocks for table supports held produce. Farther on, women sat on mats selling woven baskets, spices, and grain, including *nzima*. Nzima was eaten at every meal, ground into a stiff mash, not unlike grits.

Beyond the shops was a large area with big piles of used clothing on the ground, wrinkled but sorted for men, women, and children. Beside the clothing were tailors' goods, hanging on horizontal wooden poles. Also displayed were lengths of factory-dyed *chitingi* cloths that women wrapped around themselves, covering waist to ankle in vivid, bold print. A second cloth secured babies against their mothers' backs so hands could remain free for work. Nearby were potters' wares, blacksmith shops, and carpenters' working spaces.

Merchants and shoppers could buy snacks for their noon meals from vendors along the paths. There were greasy potato fries and *manzini*, deep-fried dough. A delicacy was fried termites; they came out of the ground only at certain times of the year, making them a seasonal treat. I found the miller's shelter and bought forty-five pounds of corn to have ground. That would give our household a good supply of cornmeal for our daily breakfast mush, cornbread, and corn crackers. I usually bought those items on Saturdays, when Harvey could help me carry them home.

Nkhoma stories

The church's school for boys had a dorm for students from far away. The coed government school was in another area. There were riots between the schools when government boys came to the church's dorm to protest our teachers' interest in their female students and to threaten our boys. Our boys' response was to smash windows and doors at the government school. This rioting occurred during exam week. "Exam fever" was a patent delay tactic that occurred with maddening predictability in several of the countries I taught; the students simply were not ready to sit for exams.

A second riot in the week resulted in our boys again damaging a government teacher's home and setting fire to his stored crops. They then entered three other teachers' homes, smashed the school's assembly hall windows and most of its three hundred plastic chairs. Both schools invaded the other's dorms and took wallets and goods.

In retaliation, government boys broke windows at the mission school. The library windows had all been smashed during the first rampage, so teachers had already moved the books to safe storage until the rioting stopped and police could investigate. It was easier to clean up at the private school. Our boys had taken a much greater revenge on the government facility.

Harvey went to the hospital Sunday morning expecting to find wounded students. None of the boys showed up; most had gone to traditional healers with their wounds in order to avoid the police. A government group took hostage one of our first-year students and kept him on the mountain all night with a machete at his neck. He was released unharmed the next day.

As boys chased boys through town, my neighbor suggested I not attend church but stay in the house. I was grateful for her advice since Harvey was at the hospital.

Synod guest house

During our first visit to Nkhoma in 2000, we were put in the house of a schoolteacher who was on home leave to South Africa. During our second visit to Nkhoma in 2006, Harvey was expected to take the place of Dr. Ter Haar for his four-month leave, but instead of moving into their residence, we were housed in the synod's large guest house.

Electricity was often a problem. Our laundry was done for us, but it did not get finished if the electricity had stopped. We often had candlelight suppers with the help of one gas burner. Wood for cooking fires was scarce. At one point, we went four days without water. When someone finally thought to pay the bill, there was plenty of water.

One week the cook planned for a group of eight in the guest house, but because the roads were impassable, no one came. Rain often upended everything. The missionary children who went to school in Lilongwe had no lessons for two days. A mother had driven them to school in Lilongwe and set out for their return trip to Nkhoma at 2:00 p.m. They were stuck in mud four times and arrived home at 5:30 that afternoon. At the hospital, the surgical floor was flooded. Programs were cancelled, and my trip to market was in rain and mud.

The roads entering the market center and going to the hospital, school, and Bible school destinations were lined with trees. But by the time we arrived, over two hundred trees had been felled to widen the dirt roads for vehicles. Townspeople argued and fought over the limbs and branches, while lumbermen sawed away at long trunks to make planks for building projects. A felled tree in Dr. Ter Haar's yard took down wires and kept us from using their computer for several days. Our email reception was good, but outgoing emails had to be written on the Ter Haar computer.

The muddy paths were a frustrating problem, but rain was needed due to long-term drought conditions. Nowhere in Malawi could ground corn be found, so the essential staple, *nzima*, could not be made.

Weekend getaway

The Nkhoma Synod had a small compound on Lake Malawi with a few cottages for staff and missionaries needing a break from work. It was also the site of missionary conferences and parties. One colleague had offered us his pick-up truck and sent us off to the lake for a weekend of rest and touring.

When we arrived, colleagues from Nkhoma were already making dinner in their cottage next door and invited us to join them. The fire we sat around for dinner helped keep the mosquitoes at bay, but the blowing sand stung our faces and sifted down into our hair.

The Lake Malawi area was one of the sites Dr. David Livingston had considered for a mission station in the nineteenth century, but he had to abandon it because of the calamitous and persistent malaria that had killed off so many of his entourage. A tragically large cemetery of his colleagues and their families was left behind when he pulled up stakes at the lower end and moved his group farther up the lake. There, too, he left a cemetery of deceased colleagues. Eventually, he moved his shrinking group to an even-higher altitude and established the settlement that would become Livingstonia. To reach the village of Livingstonia, the drive required twenty-two hairpin turns—a head-spinning, nausea-inducing experience to be sure. But the journey was worth it for the magnificent view of the lake twenty-five hundred feet below and, even more so, for the lack of mosquitoes and malaria.

One weekend, we drove south on the major highway from Lilongwe, the business capital, toward Blantyre, the political capital. Our destination, a Catholic compound at Mua, was along the way. When we arrived in Mua, we found a miniature zoo, an art craft center, and a fascinating museum, displaying cultural, historical, and religious masks.

The museum consisted of three attached tukuls with African masks hung on the walls. In each tukul, the masks were for different purposes: wars, religious rites, and storytelling. Interestingly, we found only one happy mask in the whole museum. Most had evil, mad, scary, unhappy faces, used in animistic rituals and healings but never in churches.

The KuNgoni Art Craft Center specialized in carving but also included painting, pottery, weaving of local grasses, and beadwork. Carving was common in Malawi; its artisans were particularly skilled at creating three-dimensional art. Painting internal and external walls, as well as weaving reed screens and ceilings, were used to decorate churches. Paint was an expensive medium, thus paintings by Malawi artists were not readily found in tourist shops.

The Nkhoma church

The synod in Nkhoma had put up a cluster of tukuls near the hospital gate as a nutrition clinic for women and children. Nearby, another cluster of mud huts housed children who had lost their parents to HIV/AIDS. Each tukul had a "grandmother" assigned to care for up to eight children. The grandmothers often had been widowed by HIV/AIDS. The synod provided food, school supplies, and clothes for each hut. In this way, the synod helped to form new families.

The church was always full for its three-hour service. We foreigners usually took seats on the stone benches at the back and not among the Malawians who sat in rows in front of us with women on the left and men on the right. Many choirs participated, including the deaconess choir that wore uniforms of white blouses and head scarves and black skirts. Some sang a cappella, and others were accompanied. On any given Saturday, the church could see three or more weddings.

One Saturday I watched as five newly married couples left the church, having had one ceremony for all five. Some of those couples had cars to parade in, while others had to walk from the church. The pedestrian brides cleverly took the colorful *chitingi* and wound it around their long white skirts so that they would stay clean and presentable while participating in their public wedding parade.

Our work with the synod, the hospital workers, and the Malawians was very pleasant. Unfortunately, some of the Dutch South Africans felt a wall in their relationship with the locals. The synod and others expressed their uneasy relationship with some Dutch missionaries. It was hard for us to witness the impact of apartheid in a country other than South Africa.

Embangweni, Malawi, 2001

In 2001 Harvey and I resettled in Embangweni to volunteer in the hospital and school. Unlike Nkhoma, Embangweni lies on a flat plain, surrounded by distant hills. The red brick buildings spread out on the plain with a church at its center. The church's stained-glass windows were beautiful but in need of repair. There was the hospital and its guest house, the pastor's and missionaries' homes, a guest house for short-term visiting volunteers, a primary school, a nursery school, and the synod offices.

The Robert Laws Secondary School, with its separate dormitories for girls and boys, lacked teachers for even some basic subjects. The idle metal and woodwork shops had no teachers or electricity to run the machinery. The school's assembly hall had only ten benches, so students brought classroom chairs into the hall when there was a gathering. The assembly hall also served as the dining room; five tables were spread around so students could stand and eat. Nonetheless, the choir's delightful singing at morning chapel was inspiring.

On the edge of the synod's property was a primary boarding school for deaf children. The school was well equipped and endowed by a grant from the United States. Some of these children formed a bell choir and accompanied the hymns every Sunday at church. Colored notes on the music sheets cued them when to ring their bells. The deaf children also provided a choir number for the service. The school was well run by a staff of eight.

I was asked to teach English to the third form (eleventh grade) in March, and in May I substituted for the second term in first form Bible and geography and in third form for geometry. My role as a serious teacher set a standard for observant teacher colleagues. Indeed, the students commented at term's end:

> "You were always on time and remained in the class the whole forty minutes!"
> "Your lessons were always prepared, and homework was always corrected!"
> "We appreciated the individual attention you gave us, encouraging us to answer your questions!"
> "Hard though it was, we were eager to attain your standard of 50 percent for passing, not just our usual 30 percent!"

The small community of Embangweni was an active one. We had a government secondary day school, a Catholic church, an Assembly of God church, and a Seventh-Day Adventist church. Our market was always busy with trucks and cars and good-sized shops doing robust business. Being close to the capital offered the opportunity for many goods to be bought there and brought to Embangweni.

One of the grim imports into Embangweni was AIDS. The gardener at the guest house took two days off to receive callers who came to mourn his daughter's death and burial. Some months earlier, she had returned to her family with her two little ones. Both children died shortly after their arrival, passing before she did. The gardener, resigned to their fate, reported this to us, saying, "I guess the same disease took them all." That disease was HIV-AIDS.

Harvey's medical work brought all kinds of tragic situations. A woman brought her child to the hospital for a check-up. She told Harvey she had had five sets of twins and five single births, but this was the only child still living. Childbirth, malnutrition, and disease had taken the other fourteen children. Though her case was quite extreme, she was not the only one to suffer such tragedy.

One week an unexpected American arrived who needed Harvey's medical attention. Missionaries from Zambia had brought him across the border and returned the next week to pick him up. They gave us two live rabbits for his stay. He was an impatient man, the overseer of native workers at a Zambian mine. Besides Harvey and me, there was only one other couple in the guest house when he joined us, but his churlish behavior and drinking caused friction amongst us all.

Holy Week

In April the Embangweni church sent us farther north for a Holy Week visit to the CCAP hospital and mission work in Ekwendeni, another plateau area. This put us much closer to the synod headquarters in Mzuzu, situated along Lake Nyasa's west shore.

Smaller than Embangweni, and just off the main highway north, Ekwendeni's activity was slower than that of Embangweni. The hospital was not busy with medical cases or surgeries. For us, it was sort of a vacation week, with time to visit the Mzuzu's mission station, its synod, and the missionaries there. We enjoyed a Bible study with the small missionary group and were invited to dinner once or twice, which was most welcome since we had not put in a large grocery supply.

The local custom on Easter morning affected us deeply with its joyful reenactment of the resurrection. At three o'clock Easter morning, folks gathered in the dimly lit church. Two women walked to the cemetery to meet an elder there who proclaimed, "He has risen!" All three then returned to share the joyful news with the congregation waiting in the church, where candles were lit, bathing the faithful in brilliant light.

Then, singing and dancing and ululating, they carried lanterns to inform all the people in town of Christ's resurrection and to collect coins as they went from house to house. The English service began at 8:00 a.m., followed by a Communion service for over eight hundred who had brought their Communion eligibility cards with them.

Following the regular message, the 12:30 p.m. Tumbuka-language Easter service included a baptism of adults, babies, and children. It was a long service but with a good crowd. Malawi's educated folks learned English in the church schools, so the English service was much larger in attendance. Easter Monday, we returned to Embangweni, where the workload increased greatly in May, our last month.

Second tour to Embangweni, August—November 2004

We left the United States in July to attend the wedding of Harvey's godson in Norway. Thomas was born in Ethiopia to an Ethiopian father and Norwegian mother. The wedding, in a country church built in 1724, was followed by a reception in the town hall.

We traveled south of Oslo, where several mission colleagues from Ethiopian days had gathered, and then continued to Sweden to meet with more colleagues from our Aira years. There we stayed with Sister Leena who had worked in Aira the same years we had and retired when we did. She was our wonderful neighbor those years, a true "sister" through good and not-so-good times. We still communicate via email and Skype.

Once again, the large mission guest house was our home in Embangweni. There were usually other guests there as well: Americans and Brits on business trips or other fellow missionaries taking a break from their work in more remote regions. A cook prepared noon and evening meals. Storks had also taken up residence in the trees on the compound—what a racket and a mess they made.

Two Irish medical students, Jonny and Declan, came during this second Embangweni tour to experience medical work in Africa. Although one was a Protestant and the other a Catholic, they were the best of friends throughout the years of Ireland's hardships. They enjoyed every day alongside Harvey, who taught them and encouraged their participation in hospital work.

One morning, Jonny and Declan got ready in their white coats for a long day working alongside Harvey. Leaving their small guest house, they walked to the hospital under the trees along the path, as was their routine. High above them a stork let go a load onto Declan's bald head and clean coat. The mess was such that he had to go back to the room and wash and change. Cleaned up again, Declan joined Harvey and Jonny for the first patient of the day: a woman with a painful, infected boil that would require lancing. With Harvey guiding the procedure, Declan pierced the boil and a putrid arc of pus spurted all over his white coat. Back to the house he went for his third shower of the morning, this time with an escort of crazed flies. He was determined to stay clean for the rest of the day.

I taught two sections of third grade English. Due to a strike the students had instigated during exam week, only the headmaster and four teachers were available to proctor exams.

The head boys in the hostel insisted they should eat in their hostels and not in the dining room. The headmaster discovered first form boys[82] were accustomed to taking meals back to the hostel. He took all their food and dumped it, leaving the younger boys hungry. In anger, the older boys called a boycott of the evening meal, preventing all boys from the evening meal.

The boys decided to vandalize the headmaster's house and administration office. Finally, they had the evening meal while the headmaster lectured them. But after supper, the older boys threw stones and used metal bars to smash windows, doors, and property. Many boys and girls ran into the forest for the night. Police found them in the morning and beat them for information.

The headmaster called the vandalism and disobedience a "misunderstanding" of the students. "The vandalism took two hours, but lessons were disturbed for a week." Fourth form complained they had had no picnic for their class and no meals in their hostel, adding that the teachers were interested only in the night school, a source of extra income.

---

[82] In non-US academic programs, first form students are typically twelve years old, equivalent to seventh graders.

About this time, the Church of Scotland called Dr. Maureen home from Livingstonia due to fatigue. She came to Embangweni to ask the synod to release Harvey from his work so he could cover for her. The synod agreed and threw a farewell party for us and for the two departing Irish students. They appreciated Harvey's daily teaching and hands-on practice of procedures.

CHAPTER 8

Arogyavaram, India
2001-2002

We flew into Mumbai and then to Chennai on India's southeastern coast. We were on our way to a new volunteer posting at the Arogyavaram Medical Centre in Madanapalle, Andhra Pradesh. Dr. John Peter and his wife, Rosalind, hosted us at their home. He was an anesthetist in Bahrain when we started our Arabic language study many years earlier. They lived in a three-story building they had bought with their dutiful remittances over the years. Each floor was for one of their two children and families, plus the ground floor apartment for themselves. Now retired, Dr. Peter had sent money from Arabia to his parents regularly, providing for their needs and his future in India. It was a relaxing weekend. We walked on the beach, attended their church, and toured the shopping area.

On Monday, Rev. Martin Weitz came to drive us to the Arogyavaram Medical Centre, the hospital of Harvey's new assignment. Our house was furnished only with a two-burner hot plate, so I used Emily Weitz's oven to bake bread, her washing machine for our few clothing items, and her computer once a week to communicate with our children. Small shops along the road outside the hospital gate offered fruit, eggs, and canned foods. To buy food and utensils for the kitchen, we ladies made a weekly

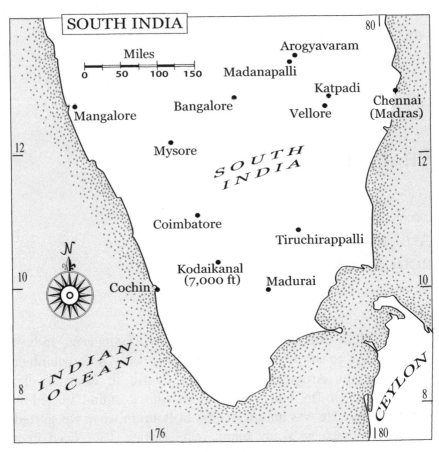

South India

shopping trip by taxi or with the hospital driver to the market in Madanapalle.

The Arogyavaram Medical Centre was in a large compound. Originally, the property had been a TB sanitarium established by the Danish Missionary Society. Now it hosted a medical center; a dentistry building; a vision center; a nursing school with living quarters; a rehabilitation and research center, with a hostel for polio children; and housing for missionaries, medical staff and guests. The chief doctor at the time envisioned the development of a medical college as well.

Nearby were a post office, a chapel, a Compassion International English-medium primary school, a Telegu-medium school, a cemetery, and the vacant buildings of a private school at

Mother Teresa's adjacent compound. Usable land was precious, made more so because the compound was a virtual obstacle course of huge rocks and boulders, some so high that they blocked the view of neighboring houses or buildings. Walking paths between homes and buildings were hewn out of the rugged terrain.

At that time, road and building laborers in India consisted of women and young children and older, weak men wielding picks and mallets, sitting on rock piles all day, breaking larger rocks into smaller rocks for the projects. It is hard to imagine the tedious, innumerable hours that they hammered the boulders into small enough pieces to clear land for building purposes. The laborers who carried boulders and large rocks on their shoulders and baskets of fine rock back and forth to the sites were mostly women.

Dr. Boman Wesley, a surgeon, was the medical director of the hospital, as well as of the compound's other programs. Harvey found very little work at the hospital. There were almost no baby deliveries and few surgical cases; most inpatients were long-term TB cases. Harvey had come to relieve Dr. Wesley, who had not had a vacation for seven years. Instead, the doctor stayed on the compound the whole six months of our time there, continuing to oversee and direct his many responsibilities.

The hospital staff consisted of Mrs. Sheela Wesley, the director of the nursing school, a radiologist, an OB-GYN, an anesthesiologist, two medical doctors, a nursing tutor, teachers, and the hospital chaplain. Staff elsewhere included a widow who directed the English School and two leaders of the Compassion International orphan charity, which had its own nursery staff.

Two doctors on the staff, a husband and wife, had a dear little boy who was the joy of their lives. He developed an intussusception that needed medical attention. How his parents anguished. Diligent monitoring and medication eventually reduced the problem. As our stay was coming to its end, Dr. Wesley had several surgical patients he needed help with. Harvey enjoyed those last busy days very much.

Thanksgiving Day we were two of a group of twelve foreigners who shared dinner at the Wesleys' house. We were also invited to the operating staff picnic. At Advent, we joined the nurses caroling through the hospital rooms and housing units. There were holiday events organized by every hospital department, children's programs and parties at the schools, and other get-togethers so numerous that one wondered who was minding the store.

We had not planned to return to the Medical Centre after our departure in December, but Dr. Wesley asked us to do so. Since we had no other work scheduled in the new year, we left, with the promise to return in February. Our trip to the airport included a stop at the potters' field, where we enjoyed watching the young male potters dancing with large silver pots (not pottery) on their heads. We flew from Bangalore to Dubai for a layover and discovered it was most assuredly not the Arabia we had known. Modern-day Dubai could not have been further from our recollection.

Return to Arogyavaram

As promised, we returned in February to India for another two-and-a-half-month stint at the Arogyavaram Medical Centre. We were put into a guest house situated near a pond. Many frogs lived there who serenaded us through the night. This new house had an oven, so I could bake bread, but I still needed to take my laundry to the Weitz's house.

The duplex where we had stayed before Christmas was now occupied by a retired couple from Iowa and a single, retired lady from Wisconsin. The women helped in the school, while the man did maintenance work for the institutions.

This second visit to Arogyavaram seems, in retrospect, to have been little work and much feasting, partying, and even traveling. In downtown Madanapalle, an inauguration of the renovated Mary Lyon Lotts Hospital's women's ward and OPD[83] was an evening of speeches, ending with a splendid late dinner. On our compound, the tenth graders held a farewell party that included a drama by the students. The youth held its annual Youth Celebration, where a long program was performed. About this

---

[83] Outpatient dispensary.

time, the schools started to shutter up at noon, sending the children home during the heat of the day.

For one week, the church held evangelistic meetings in the evenings. Many women attended the service on the Women's World Day of Prayer at St. Luke's Church. On Palm Sunday, everyone was given a palm branch to wave as we processed around the church before going in for the service. After the service, the pastor's family hosted a tea party for all. On Easter Sunday, we were at church before sunrise for a service of joyful singing and long scripture readings. Our house was directly across the street from St. Luke's Anglican Church compound, where we went occasionally for special services. But our regular Sunday worship in English was with the nursing and lab technician students in the compound chapel.

For my birthday, on March 28, I asked Harvey to take me to Vellore Medical School and Hospital; he had visited there twice when our boys were up at Kodaikanal School. A car and driver took us and the Weitzes to visit Vellore. On the way, we stopped at Katpadi Industrial Institute, where missionary friends of ours had lived.[84] Then we moved on to visit the Christian Medical Hospital in Vellore. After an excellent tour of the seven-story hospital, we had a birthday dinner in a local restaurant. It was a most pleasant and memorable birthday.

Senses in India

India is a land where the senses come to life. Vibrant sights and sounds are everywhere: muezzins calling people to prayer from the tops of minarets; street vendors braying about their wares; men spitting dark brown betel nut juice on the walkways; motorcycles weaving through crowded traffic; car horns protesting motorcycles and pedestrians; wedding parties playing music; police blowing their whistles at the tangled traffic; passers-by deliberating in the staccato patois of Indian-accented English; snake charmers piping their magic; flip-flops slapping on

---

[84] Harry and Janet Pofahl lived near Kodaikanal, where Dirk and Keith were in boarding school. Harry often checked up on the Doorenbos boys.

pavement; decorated statues of Hindu gods being lofted high on men's shoulders and marched about; brilliantly hued saris swishing by, gracing women with flowers braided in their hair and red *bindi* dots on their foreheads; wooden *tikka ghari* wheelbarrows, full of colorful goods clattering along; brightly painted oxen plowing the fields and pulling carts in busy streets; hyenas whooping eerily from dusk to dawn; elephants padding along noiselessly in the streets, despite their ponderous bulk and unperturbed by the business all around; aggressive monkeys stealing food from children and merchants alike; laundry men beating clothes on rocks in *dhobi khanas*;[85] men and women gathering at neighborhood water taps for morning ablutions; sacred cows ambling in traffic; sunrises and sunsets startling all with their suddenness; patties of cow dung drying in the sun, soon to be used for cooking fires; temples and idols abounding; discarded plastic bags snagging in trees and blowing in circles by dusty winds; men clutching their course cloth *lungis*[86] above their knees and jogging beside their bullock carts; tin shacks resting precariously on mud; straight-backed women carrying loads of twigs and branches to laundry on their heads; *tuk-tuk*[87] motorcycle taxis racing by on their assignments; and, everywhere, flies settling on children's eyes—all of which lend to the cacophony that constantly reminds one of the crowds and vitality of India.

---

[85] *Dhobi khana*: a stream or river where laundry was washed. Clothes were soaped, beaten against rocks to get the dirt out, and then rinsed in the flowing water.

[86] *Lungi*: a long, loose strip of cloth wrapped around the waist and extending down to the ankles. Most often worn by men.

[87] *Tuk-tuk*: a three-wheeled vehicle, usually powered by a small motorcycle engine, used as a taxi in many parts of the world, also commonly called an auto rickshaw in India.

CHAPTER 9

West Africa, Liberia
2002

In 2002 Harvey was asked to fill a surgical vacancy at Phebe Hospital in Liberia, West Africa. It was an opportunity to visit one of Africa's western countries.

Liberia and its neighboring country, Sierra Leone, were nations established by freed slaves. In the nineteenth century, England had brought many redeemed slaves, those freed from bondage by outside help, to the west coast of Africa. The freed slaves formed the country they called Sierra Leone, with the capital of Freetown. Liberia is a country where America sent thirty-four redeemed slaves to be resettled in their ostensible ancestral homeland to join with the native Liberian population and produce a government resembling America's. They called their new country Liberia, "land of freedom," and its capital city Monrovia, in honor of President Monroe. In 1867 twenty thousand freed blacks sailed from the United States to Liberia, where they purchased land along the coast from the local peoples, whom they viewed as less civilized.

Of course, the rulers always favored their own tribes, resulting in tribal and rebel activity with severe consequences over many years of fighting. During WWI, the Kru people rebelled against the Americo-Liberian government in Monrovia, so the

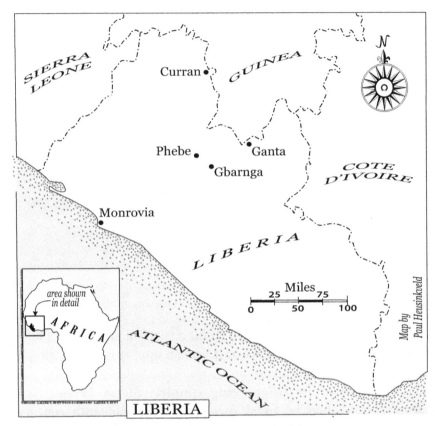

Liberia, with inset map of Africa

United States helped put down the rebellion. Because the government was so deeply in debt to foreign aid, it granted a huge land concession to Firestone Rubber Company, which developed the largest rubber plantation system in the world. Even today, wherever you travel, you can still see rubber plantations.

In 1944 William Tubman, a progressive, Liberia-born descendant of freed American slaves, became president and did a great deal to energize development throughout the country. He governed until 1971, when he was overthrown and assassinated during a rebellion. He is generally regarded as the father of the present nation. From 1971 to 2005, Liberia was unsettled by numerous rebellions, including a very serious, four-year civil war.

The country still suffers from slow reconstruction of buildings and facilities demolished in bitter civil wars. Monrovia, on the North Atlantic coast, suffers from mildew from the salty sea, long monsoon seasons, and frequent rain throughout the year. Being tropical, Liberia is a damp country, with its highest humidity closest to the wide shoreline. When we visited in 2002, water mains, sewer systems, and electricity repairs were still awaiting completion in the poorer sections of Monrovia. Homes damaged during the war and the rebellions still showed pockmarks and divots from the bullets and shells.

In 2005 we again went to Liberia to work and were there to see history in the making. With the arrest and World Court imprisonment of President Charles Taylor, the people needed a new leader, so elections were held. Of the one hundred candidates for leadership, one stood out: Ellen Johnson Sirleaf, who had spent many years in the United States. It rained for three days at election time, making over one hundred polling stations inaccessible. Bangladeshi peacekeeping troops under UN sponsorship were everywhere, keeping the election process safe. They distributed ballots, oversaw the counting of votes, transported foreign observers to villages, and used armed soldiers to protect the whole process. A wise politician, strong leader, and determined crusader against corruption, Sirleaf became the first African woman elected to be head of state.

Healthcare

During the numerous uprisings in Liberia, many people, especially educated persons, had fled. The hospitals were shorthanded, and Monrovia's medical school closed. It took six years to graduate six doctors.

Besides losing people, the damaged buildings of the medical school were looted of equipment and furnishings. Very few professors remained; those who did, usually had a private practice to support themselves. Medical students had no place for clinical training because the university hospital was closed. The six graduates did not receive medical licenses until they had completed internships for a year. The problem was where to do that. Phebe Hospital, where Harvey worked, was approved for intern training but could not provide the kind of supervision expected due to a lack of doctors.

The as-yet-unopened J. F. Kennedy Hospital, a university-related teaching facility, did open one wing because the International Committee of the Red Cross had sent an expatriate trauma team to help the government treat "emergency trauma victims," a euphemism for soldiers. The hospital had no staff to give basic medical, surgical, or pediatric care to the sick, no funds to open other wings, and no pay for specialists to treat patients.

In addition to the Kennedy Hospital, were the well-respected, albeit expensive, Catholic Hospital in Monrovia; the Phebe Lutheran Hospital, one hundred miles north of Monrovia; and a couple of smaller private hospitals. Using physicians in private practice on a part-time basis, the Catholic Hospital could keep functioning. Of some fifty physicians in all of Liberia, many worked in hospital administration, so those in actual clinical practice could not do much for a population of over three million people.

North of Phebe Hospital, the Ganta Methodist Church had a hospital. It was a lovely compound, but its buildings had suffered considerable damage from the rebels. The foundation and walls of a new hospital had been constructed before we arrived, but the hospital administrators were waiting for an American ship to arrive with the needed supplies to finish and equip it. Another hospital north of us was the Baptist Hospital in Gbarnga. Their staff was able to deal with most issues but sent difficult surgical cases to Harvey.

Harvey believed the cause of the daily mortality of the locals could be summed up with two words: "TOO LATE!" Patients were often malnourished, especially children whose emaciated bodies could not fight malaria, typhoid, meningitis, and other endemic diseases. Women with labored deliveries arrived too late to save either the mother or the baby. AIDS was rampant and complicated the healing of patients with TB and other diseases. Especially frustrating was the mistreatment of patients by local bonesetters or herbalists, whose initial folk treatment delayed proper care.

Phebe Hospital

Phebe Hospital, a 175-bed institution, had a school for training laboratory technicians, nurse anesthetists, nurse midwives, and medical interns. It was a joint venture of the Lutheran, Methodist, and Episcopalian churches in the United States. In 2002 the hospital was evacuated as Liberians fled the approach of rebel soldiers. There was much looting of furnishings and destruction of homes by the soldiers and by local people who stayed in the area.

The staff had spent hours cleaning up and repairing the hospital's damaged structures. A new building was equipped to open an eye clinic and an HIV-AIDS counseling center. We were present when the first lady, the wife of Liberia's then-president, Charles Taylor, came for the opening ceremony of that clinic. She was an active campaigner for HIV-AIDS teaching and care, so she promoted the clinic's work.

The medical staff was comprised of a general surgeon,[88] an ophthalmologist, a missionary internist, and two general practitioners. While Harvey was there, both practitioners left, one for administration of an expatriate organization and the other for graduate study abroad. The possibility of recruiting replacement practitioners was remote.

Phebe Hospital served a population of five hundred thousand, with twenty small clinics providing primary health care. The clinics primarily provided immunization of children; public health teaching, with an emphasis on AIDS prevention; nutrition for children; and malaria treatment.

Harvey's responsibility was to teach one intern surgery and the other obstetrics. The two interns also did some general practice, emergency room medicine, and anything else that came in during their night shift. Enthusiastic and hardworking, each of them presented a chapter of a textbook to the rest of the doctors twice weekly. Harvey believed this also helped remind the staff of their medical subjects from years past. The surgical intern learned

[88] This gifted surgeon was Dr. Walter Gwenigale, a Liberian who was married to an American. See page 219 for further details.

enough technique to handle hernias (a very common problem), caesarian sections, and emergency bowel surgery. The obstetrics intern enjoyed deliveries so much that he hoped to specialize in OB-GYN.

When the two interns completed their year of training, they were asked to stay on as staff. But Monrovia was a drawing card for doctors who liked city life and busy clinic work, so the interns went there. The missionary internist was not sure she would even return to Liberia after her furlough, so Harvey was urged to return as soon as possible.

The daily local market

During the week, I took the role of meal planner for the guest house and checked with the cook about what he wanted to make for lunch. Either he or I shopped daily to provide variety for our meals. On weekends, my housemates took charge of the main meal plans. I prepared the evening meal since our nurse often taught a class. She was on a vegetarian and gluten-free diet. For the remaining three of us, I picked up fresh-baked bread in the market every day.

The rebels had taken everyone's domestic animals for their food, so there was no goat, lamb, cow, chicken, rooster, or typical dinner meat to be found. The choices were large, live snails; charred antelope, hacked into big chunks, with fur still attached; hens' feet; and fish from the river. Food came to market in tubs, carried on people's heads. Baby monkeys came charred and were butchered when bought.

What was brought to the market from the sea arrived frozen. All these choices would be laid out on the grass in the sun all day. So when a merchant from Monrovia came with a large cooler of fish on ice, I took a fish from deep inside hoping that it was still cold and fit for consumption. Late in our stay, a merchant began bringing hot dogs to market from Monrovia. He would keep one out on the table for reference and the rest frozen inside. We were glad for any additional meat for our table.

One Sunday afternoon, some children were walking on the path near our house. Suddenly, they began shouting and running to pick up stones. When they killed a sizable snake, they made sure the head and poison sac were chopped off. They carried the carcass home to be cooked. What a feast awaited them that evening.

The vegetable offerings were many: cucumbers, eggplant, okra, tomatoes, squash, potatoes, and cassava. A larger roadside market provided more choices of pantry needs from Monrovia, such as palm oil, sugar, wheat flour and corn flour, relief wheat, and local rice. Oranges, avocados, grapefruit, passion fruit, and bananas were available in every market.

Walking either to the market nearby or with Harvey to a roadside market a mile from home was always a revelation. Just around our own compound, the sounds of life in Liberia were many: our Bangladeshi peacekeeper neighbors had a noisy generator, and their Muslim call to prayer rang out five times a day. Traffic noise on the compound started before sunrise and continued until well after sunset. The cacophony from the main road came from bicycles, motorbikes, cars, large trucks, and masses of people shouting and shuffling all day long.

Children passing by in school uniforms, vendors at the roadside market across from our compound, squeaking wheelbarrows of construction workers, constant sounds of pain from women in childbirth, and death wails from emergency room patients, were all part of our Liberian experience.

CHAPTER 10

Return to Aira, Ethiopia
2003

Our February return to Aira as volunteers felt like returning home once more. But changes had occurred in our absence, not only in Aira but also in Addis. Disembarking from the airplane, we entered a sleek, modern terminal building with lots of glass. The ring road for the capital city was half done. Cars, whose drivers believed they owned the road, had close calls with defiant pedestrians who crossed "their" streets by clambering over hip-high roadside fences to reach shops on the other side of the street.

In Aira, people were as bound to cellphones as Americans were; the phones were everywhere and worked better than landlines. Traditional phone connections to the country's capital and other cities were still interrupted or not even possible. Customs had changed to include a new handshake, the phrase "Help yourself" from hosts and hostesses, and loud church music.

Harvey was asked to replace the German surgeon who years earlier had replaced him. The synod had found an Ethiopian surgeon to fill her departure, but he soon learned that the salary was better in the Dembi Dolo Hospital, so he left for that posting.

We lived in our former house and worked with some of the same missionaries, as well as some new ones. The former hospital staff had grown with newcomers, many of whom had been in our school. We left in mid-June and returned by request in August to work until December.

It was a delight to once again see storks, ibis, monkeys, baboons, hyenas, and dik-diks. Fruits of the guava, persimmon, mango, lime, and papaya trees were all readily available.

Onesimus Bible School enrolled thirteen new students that year to make thirty students in all. The Aira Hospital's Nursing School enrolled nineteen new students for the next class. I taught English at both schools twice weekly. Harvey took a turn teaching the nurses some of their lessons.

I also tutored Abebe, the young paraplegic from northern Ethiopia for whom we had built a home outside the hospital gate. The home was close enough to the hospital for him to do evangelistic and colporteur work among the patients from his wheelchair. Though a northerner, he learned the local language and became very helpful to the chaplains.

New educational standards

The Education Department of Ethiopia decided to make tenth grade a final year for all but the schools' top 10 percent. The department established technical training institutes for vocational studies and two-year, teacher training colleges. A government certificate exam was given to all students of tenth grade level to determine their future course of study.

The percent of graduates from the country's large twelfth grade was very small. Those eligible for teacher training colleges was a somewhat larger percent. Except for the unambiguous failures, the rest of the students from tenth grade could attend technical training if they could surmount the disheartening obstacles of finding a training institute to accept them and of having money for travel to an institute and for tuition.

By the time of our return to Aira, many technical institutes and teacher training colleges had been built, but there were not nearly enough to absorb the enormous surge of tenth grade graduates. Secretarial colleges were built to encourage hundreds of girls to learn secretarial work. The number of these schools grew as investors built new private institutions.

This new system produced a whole new eleventh and twelfth grade curriculum, which allowed twelfth grade graduates to enter their second year of university immediately. To encourage more females among the predominately male graduates, the exam passing levels were lowered for females.

The growth of private teacher training schools demanded more teachers, which meant many teachers without four-year university degrees took these jobs. Private schools joined the government schools in expecting tuition, and parents were saddled with high tuition and boarding fees.

During school vacation, some of my former students came to see me. One fellow came from a technical school far away and told me he was in training to be a car mechanic. I asked him what a spanner or wrench was used for in car repairs. He responded that he did not know, but he had copied into his notebook a picture of a spanner that the teacher had drawn on the blackboard. The school did not have all the tools needed for actual hands-on work.

I visited one mother, dying of cancer, whose daughter had graduated from a private secretarial school. She and three other classmates had returned from that school to find no job openings in Aira. The mother had spent most of her money on her daughter's education. Harvey and I took both mother and daughter to a larger city to find work. They came back three days later by bus without any good news and even less money. The daughter, discouraged and unwilling to stay home, ran off to live with an older man. She had had secretarial training of poor standards and found no work. Sadly, she represented many students from private schools whose abilities were limited.

My schoolwork, 2003

I had plenty to do in the schools again this second time in Aira. The graduated twelfth grade had all received university or college acceptances to the many schools now available throughout Ethiopia. I began teaching English to the new twelfth graders that first semester but made sure the school understood I would be unable to teach the second semester.

I was asked to teach English to two incoming tenth grade groups, including writing and administering their final exam before I left at Christmas. The tenth grade government exam determined who continued to twelfth grade and where all other students would be sent.

I was also asked to teach ninth grade English twice a week, but it was hard to work those extra classes into my own schedule. The new ninth graders filled four classrooms, with one classroom holding ninety students, the maximum allowed in any classroom.

Many of the refugees who had been resettled from northeastern Ethiopia during the famine of 1985 were now returning by foot on the long road home. The rainy season dropped generous amounts every day and ended with plenty of water for fields and homes, but it came as a mixed blessing: the rains made for a long slippery trek on muddy roads.

Dr. and Mrs. Erikson were still having difficulty getting the papers needed to return to Ethiopia. We appreciated being in their home, which had been ours for our last years in Aira. This volunteer year allowed us to reconnect with our former longtime cook and housemaid, both having continued in the house after we left. They were still here, working for us again.

We had promised our family that we would return to the United States for Christmas, and we already had another Malawi volunteer assignment for the new year, so we left Aira, never to work there again, but we were fortunate to have volunteer work elsewhere in Ethiopia later so we could make one last visit to our Aira community.

CHAPTER 11

Return to Liberia
2005

We returned to the same guesthouse in Monrovia, with the same nurse in residence and now with an American guest. Other houses had been repaired since the most recent rebel uprising. The repairs were paid for by aid agencies wishing to rent housing for their workers. If a house was empty of its occupants during the daytime, a guard was posted inside to protect it from the thieves who looted in conjunction with the rebels.

As before, across the road was a Bangladeshi UN peacekeeping force in two repaired houses, with tents and cars, all kept within the safety of their compound, surrounded by a high barbed-wire fence. A watchtower in one corner of the property looked out over the main road traffic, active market area, and various institutions, including ours.

There was always a military patrol at the road to stop and check illegal cars, suspicious occupants, imported vehicles, and stolen goods going north. In fact, the UN checkpoints stretched northward from Monrovia to the rebel holdings and diamond mines. After that came dense forest, so most police and citizens stayed away.

On the road past our home were six houses already rented by returning aid agencies. They had cars that went out to the villages in the daytime with provisions. Most aid came by daily planes, but some arrived in trucks from Uganda. Also on that road was a large residence that housed the EU's newly established aid base and its personnel.

Electricity was available in our home from 7:00 p.m. to sunrise. That meant ironing clothes at 6:00 a.m. and using the microwave before 7:00 a.m. We had only cold water for washing ourselves and our clothes. I did everyone's laundry in the evening, but the dryer had gotten crushed in the last rebel insurgency, so clothes were hung everywhere to dry. In the doctors' residence, the interns had electricity that allowed for the use of a shortwave radio and even a working TV.

When the hospital administrator left for the United States, he left his washing machine and stove in the guest house for our use. The washer had a spin-dry cycle, which was nice because anything that expunged more moisture meant fewer days waiting for clothes to dry. That was always an achievement in Liberia's renowned humidity. All his other household items were locked up in the hospital storeroom that I had inventoried before he left. We were told to expect limited electricity until the hospital could buy a new control box and wires to replace those stolen from the pump house.

There were mosquito nets over the beds. I do not recall using such nets in any countries other than Liberia and in southern Sudan.

Since I was in the kitchen a lot, I sorted through the many boxes of food left by US volunteer groups and guests. Some of the old food was infested with insects, so I had to throw it away. But some items in tins and jars were still good and used to augment our meals and give them familiar flavors, which we always enjoyed.

Schools and churches

The medium of education at all levels was formalized American English, brought over by freed slaves and imposed on the country's schools. I visited a primary school near Phebe Hospital but did not get involved in teaching there. The students' uniforms were green skirts or trousers with yellow shirts or blouses. The girls wore white socks with an added yellow frill to dress them up. Perhaps they all had green jackets of the same material, but they certainly did not wear them in the heat. As in other countries, the students all cut their hair very close to their heads, so it was difficult to tell the boys from the girls when they were sitting in their seats.

The hospital had nursing, midwifery, and anesthesia training programs. In August the midwife students and anesthetists had a commencement ceremony. In September the nurses' class graduated a large group. Most students sought jobs in Monrovia, so the smaller hospitals and clinics could only hope subsequent graduating classes would give them a look.

The radio announced in July that all schools would stay closed until the elections were over in October. By August the government had changed its mind and broadcast that schools would open for one week in September and then close until the elections were finished.

In Monrovia there were churches of virtually every denomination and creed: Roman Catholic, Apostolic, Jesus Church, Holy Spirit Church, Bible Church, Anglican, and many others. Away from the city, there was less competition, and churches were founded by missionary and Liberian interests.

On the Phebe Hospital compound, the church's foundation and brick walls had been finished, but the roof was not. Stained-glass windows would be put in as soon as the shipment arrived. During both of our assignments at Phebe, worship on Sundays was held in the hospital's large and open outpatient department. Every seat was filled, and often more chairs were brought in and set up for back rows. Latecomers could stand outside the building's low walls to catch the service when the chairs inside were all taken.

We were privileged to be there when the harvest service offering was brought forward. Women, swaying and singing, paraded down the aisles carrying overflowing baskets, bowls, and even tubs of harvested crops in their arms. What abundance! What generosity! What praise to God!

On September 23, 2005, the community gathered for the eleventh memorial service for the one hundred people who had died at Phebe Hospital during the first rebel attacks. Twice more in the intervening years, the rebels had struck, killing staff members and looting the hospital and grounds. During the service, Dr. Gwenigale announced his intention to retire. Soon he would be chosen to be Liberia's minister of health. He agreed to the post only if he could sack corrupt government health workers and choose only honest workers for his department.

Dadabya

When I met Dadabya and heard her story, she was a nursing student at Phebe Hospital. In 1994 her family stood outside their home anxiously watching the thick black smoke rising up from the village north of their home. Soon a file of families came into view, carrying what goods they could, and shouting to run because the rebel soldiers were coming, and Dadabya's home was next. The rebels had torched their homes and driven them out.

Dadabya's family quickly gathered what necessities they could carry and said a sad goodbye to their aged, blind grandmother who could not run with them. Each one fled at his or her own speed. Dadabya with her mother and sister ended up in the Cory Internally Displaced Persons (IDP) camp outside Monrovia. Her father, other siblings, and husband with their daughter were in another camp.

As we spoke, her mother was still in the Cory IDP camp. After the war, news came to her from people who had seen her father looking well and back at his home and fields. Dadabya's daughter was found with friends, but her husband's whereabouts were unknown. She searched for her siblings and eventually found them in other camps.

In 1999 Dadabya resumed high school and finally finished in 2000. She moved to Totota IDP Camp and was chosen to study nursing at Phebe Hospital through a scholarship. Her goal was to earn enough to bring her mother, sisters, and child up north to live with her.

Doctor Gwenigale

Dr. Gwenigale grew up in Bong County, where Phebe Hospital is located. He left Liberia to attend medical school in Puerto Rico and surgical training in the United States. He married a Puerto Rican woman and started a family there. While he worked in Liberia, she stayed mainly in the Americas with the children, but they did make trips to Liberia to see his country.

On one return to Liberia, he learned of the first rebel uprising in the northern countries, including his home county. During that uprising, Sierra Leone rebels, recruited and led by Charles Taylor, then a military officer, approached Phebe hospital. They ignored the pleading staff at the door and killed all staff, patients, and the patients' attending relatives. Not only were people eliminated, but the whole hospital was razed, and supplies, medicines, furniture, machines, doors, and windows were trashed and scattered.

One of the dead was Dr. Gwenigale's mother and another was Charles Taylor's mother-in-law. All the victims were buried together in a mass grave within the circular driveway in front of the hospital entrance. Now, a monument stands there in their memory.

Aside from visits to his family in Puerto Rico, Dr. Gwenigale spent his years as a surgeon in Liberia. While the World Court tried and imprisoned Charles Taylor in The Hague, Liberian elections took place. Ellen Johnson Sirleaf, Liberia's new president, chose Dr. Gwenigale as her country's minister of health.

Our work

We arrived in 2005 to find Phebe Hospital recovering from yet another rebel attack, the third so far. The staff were reluctant to return; those who did spent much time removing all that was demolished. Machines, lights, windows, doors, pharmacy shelves, the surgical suite, the maternity ward, and much more were trashed and had to be hauled away. I joined Harvey in the hospital library cleaning and replacing medical texts and journals, which had all been pulled from their shelves.

The limited hospital staff saw as many patients as they could. There were surgery cases already awaiting Harvey's arrival. He made ward and outpatient rounds, working alongside the staff, teaching them, and generally easing their loads. Not having a working X-ray machine at Phebe Hospital, Harvey pressed the ultrasound machine into service.

The director of Ganta's orphan program came to Harvey because of a painful gall bladder problem. Harvey decided it was too risky for him to perform the required surgery, so he suggested a trip to the United States for modern surgical help. She went to the United States, accompanied by three children who were scheduled for adoption there.

A patient with a snake bite had received a double dose of antivenom at the outpatient clinic. Harvey was called to evaluate the man who, despite the antivenom, still could not breathe due to internal paralysis. Using a simple resuscitation mask to keep him breathing, the good doctor and nurses sat at intervals at the man's bedside squeezing the bag to keep oxygen flowing to his lungs. Finally, about twenty-four hours later, the man slowly began breathing on his own. It was a marvel for the family and hospital staff to see what simple, patient, and persistent medical care could do for an otherwise dying patient.

During this time, Harvey had two special visitors. His former surgical mentor from Grand Rapids, Michigan, came as part of a Rotary Club team promoting polio eradication with the World Health Organization. He had heard that Harvey was at Phebe Hospital, so he came to visit. Later, another physician from Grand Rapids, visiting the Gbarnga Baptist Hospital, came to observe the physician's assistant course at Phebe.

When I was not busy at market or during the noon hour, I worked in nine sweltering, metal shipping containers where supplies, medicines, and even bagged used clothing were stored but not sorted. With two new shipping containers in port awaiting delivery to Phebe Hospital, I worked to make order and space in our containers. Medicines required immediate attention because of their expiration date. I sent sorted and inventoried medicines to the pharmacy, nurses, and doctors, as needed. I listed the old ones for Harvey to decide to discard or keep. When he came, hopefully looking for surgical tools, he chose what was good and threw out many rusted ones. Time at the seaport and heavy rains in the interior made for necessary attention to and protection of the contents of those large containers.

Liberia was rife with uncertainties

Populations were on the move, especially to the nation's capital. The vast rubber industry was closed; diamond mines offered no work; all domestic animals were used to feed rebels, not citizens; and people had been moved to the many camps for internally displaced persons, mostly on the periphery of Monrovia. Moreover, many international relief agencies brought food, bottled water, goods, and tents to help this tropical country survive. Their focus was on Monrovia, drawing ever more people there.

Rice had long been a staple in the Liberian diet, but aid agencies brought in bulgar wheat to the camps, hoping to reduce the dependency on rice. Before long, rice was being sold in the marketplace at inflated rates, while displaced persons relied on wheat.

Three separate rebel attacks swelled the internal refugee crowds in Monrovia, leaving rural houses and village buildings to be stripped of valuables in a senseless destruction of property. Twenty-four-hour guards were employed to deter more thieving, but it was unclear who oversaw the honesty of payments to these guards.

Spoken Liberian English takes much time to get used to. Words are "swallowed" in the mouth, and the letters *l* and *r* are interchanged or dropped in pronunciation. "Put the light on the right," in Liberian English becomes, "Put the right on the light." *Th* is not pronounced when the letters occur together. In the market, "three for five" becomes "tee fo fi." "Soup" was the name for any sauce used to flavor rice; lemons are called tangerines, and "limes" is the name for lemons. This made communication, even among English speakers, difficult.

After the 1994 conflict, the government could pay workers only a third of their usual salary, so the European Union made up the remaining two-thirds. At that point, government workers had not been paid for six months, and the EU grant was being reduced by a third. Keeping workers at their jobs became increasingly difficult and made them susceptible to corruption.

Schools were not open to displaced or evacuated children who had not returned to their villages. Financing education was a significant dilemma. If the government paid fees at the village schools, and then the students fled again, a year's salary given to the schools would be lost. On the other hand, it took more money to live in Monrovia, register there for schools, and buy the children's uniforms.

Curran Hospital

The Lutheran Church had a hospital in Curran, in the far north of Liberia. It was the only hospital in South Lofa County, which had had an estimated population of two hundred thousand before the uprising. It was an area few Liberians cared to enter, but half of the citizens who had fled the rebels' takeover were now returning to build new homes and farms on the perimeter of their former homeland.

It took us three hours on rutted, pot-holed, muddy roads to reach Curran Hospital. The hospital was close to the dense forest in which the rebels had a base where they pursued their illegal work of stripping government diamond and ore mines, timber, and rubber plantations.

Edna, an American nurse, supervised the hospital workers, some of whom she had trained as midwives, nursing aides, and even physician assistants. Edna would come to Phebe Hospital when she needed supplies or a weekend of rest. One container sent to Phebe Hospital was packed about one-third full of items for Curran Hospital. Edna planned to visit us after Thanksgiving to arrange transportation of the items from our compound to Curran. She kept in touch with Phebe personnel by a satellite telephone.

The Curran Hospital had eighty beds, but the rooms had been damaged again in the third rebel uprising. Buildings, brick walls, doors, windows, roofs, and equipment all needed rebuilding. A team from the United States came for three months to help Edna with rebuilding and to work on an operating room with its accompanying ward of beds. First to be repaired was a building designated as the Outpatient Department. Another small building was repaired and served as a maternity and delivery ward.

Curran Hospital expected to get an American physician or surgeon when the next US team came to continue repairs in January. They hoped to get one wing of the hospital in shape to house inpatients. Rural hospitals had a hard time attracting physicians, but it was hoped that a rebuilt hospital would help with recruiting.

Mixing Christmas cultures

The Phebe hospital administrator asked the pharmacy and container workers to bring him bags of used clothing, toothbrushes, hand towels, and washcloths to be packaged for each staff member as a Christmas gift. Just before the new year, bales of quilts and blankets were opened and given to the staff. It was not quite blanket season at Christmas, but the upcoming January and February nights could be cold. Other nongovernmental organizations donated a good number of leftover drugs and supplies to the hospital.

Our guest house decided to invite the heads of the Bangladesh peacekeeping force over for a holiday meal to thank them for protecting us, especially when nurse Carol was alone in the guest house and they posted guards outside for her security. The peacekeepers, in turn, invited us to have dinner with them on Christmas Eve.

Liberians give presents to many people on Christmas Day. Our house bundled up little cups of raisins and peanuts in bright paper to give to children after church. Families bought new clothes and special foods for their celebration.

Christmas Day began at 4:30 a.m. with carolers singing in English and in the Kpele language while walking by our houses. Church was to start at 7:30 a.m. so women could be home early to start Christmas dinner preparations. There were only fifteen people present at the start of the worship service, but by its conclusion, there were two hundred or more. We ate wonderful leftovers from Christmas Eve dinner and then spent a few precious hours in quiet reverie, reflecting on the sumptuousness of our meal and blessings of the day.

December 26 was an official holiday. Children went to collect goodies at the gates of the NGO compounds, much like children in the United States do on Halloween.

From Liberia to Malawi via Ghana, Zambia, and Kenya
December 30, 2005—January 2, 2006

As the time approached for us to move on to our next assignment in Malawi, colleagues urged us not to fly on any airline but Ghana Airlines. Other airline schedules were not reliable. So Harvey booked us on Ghana Airlines from Ghana to Ethiopia, with a New Year's Day layover in Accra.

At Liberia's airport, we sat outdoors baking under a radiating, tin roof for an hour. Then we queued up to enter the hot, tiny airport rooms one person at a time. A half hour later, each person entered a departure lounge that was mercifully cooler than the airport's check-in rooms and capable of seating all of us inside.

Ghana's capital, Accra, seemed so up to date with its paved roads, water, electricity, and boulevards boasting of medians with palm trees and flowers such as frangipani, magnolia, and other flowering trees and shrubs. Stores, sidewalks, restaurants, hotels, and ubiquitous traffic jams made Accra a typical British capital of careful design. Our hotel was just off a busy business and shopping center, and our room had a toilet, shower, TV, and air conditioning—all for $30 USD a night.

Since the New Year's Eve service lasted until 2 a.m. the evening before, Sunday's 7 a.m. English service at a nearby, one-hundred-year-old Presbyterian church was cancelled in favor of a joint service in both English and Ghanaian languages at 9 a.m. We sat in the shade of a tree in the spacious compound around the majestic brick church, awaiting other congregants. It did not take long for them to fill the huge building with many worshippers inside and more sitting outside under tarps stretched over rows of seats at each open side door. An elderly British woman also attended the service, making the three of us the only whites in the crowd.

The wonderful service included choirs singing native numbers. A large choir decked out in robes sang to organ accompaniment as the congregation walked to the altar for the offering, followed by a young women's choir with drums and trumpets and lots of swaying down the aisles. The exuberant service lasted two-and-a-half hours.

On Monday, we walked to the supermarket for breakfast items and to restaurants for other meals: Ethiopian, Middle Eastern, Italian, Chinese, and Indian. Our visit by taxi to Accra's extensive market and shops in narrow walkways was a delight of vendors calling out their wares and merchants hanging clothes and lengths of cloth outside their shops amidst crowds of brightly dressed shoppers.

Our flight from Ethiopia stopped in Zambia, Kenya, and finally Malawi. Three Louden children (Harvey's kin) got on at Zambia. They were returning to school in Kenya after Christmas break at home. It was grand to see them again.

CHAPTER 12

Return to Malawi
February—May 2006

"The Warm Heart of Africa" is Malawi's motto, and it is indeed a beautiful country. It has every geographical and physical treasure one could imagine—mountains, plateaus, lakes, rivers, plains, and much more.

Lake Malawi is Malawi's crown jewel. When twentieth-century missionaries first saw it, they set up a mission station at its southern tip, only to find—as had Dr. Livingston before them—that their cemetery kept growing with victims of malaria, so they moved a good way north to settle on the lake's west side, but soon, they were again burying more of their own.

Eventually, missionaries ascended forty-five hundred feet from sea level to the Nyika Plateau, where mosquitoes reportedly did not live. The road up was one lane, with twenty-two hairpin turns. There they founded their Eden—Livingstonia. But by the late twentieth century, mosquitoes began appearing at higher altitudes. To ensure our health, we took a weekly malaria prevention tablet.

The first doctor's residence was a stone house, which later became a guest house. Next, a church was built of red brick and highlighted by specially designed stained-glass windows. The window over the front door depicted local Malawians receiving Dr.

Livingston when he arrived in the mid-1800s. Later, a large, two-story doctor's house was built using the same red brick. Behind us were higher mountains, which we climbed up a short distance to view the water system for the whole plateau.

Livingstonia Presbyterian Church, its guest house and synod office; the University of Livingstonia, consisting of a Teachers' Training College and Technical Training College; a secondary boarding school and primary school; the David Gordon Memorial Hospital; and a daily market with many farm goods and a few permanent shops were among the many establishments on the plateau. An airstrip, no longer in use, suggested busier times.

Livingstonia

Returning to Livingstonia, we were again in awe of its beauty, partly due to staying in Dr. Maureen's large, two-story, red-brick house. The view of Lake Malawi on the plain far below was spectacular. What a delightful scene the daily paddle steamboat made as it circled the lake's shoreline with tourists and passengers and delivered mail to homes in small coves that were easiest reached by water.

For us, living at Livingstonia was a treat, but it was not without minor inconveniences. The electricity was irregular; mornings were wet and misty; an earthquake rattled us; and postal service, via the church office in Mzuzu, took from three to five weeks to reach us.

The house creaked when the ever-present winds blew, and the roof leaked when it rained. Walking on the wooden balcony upstairs and the porch downstairs required great mindfulness to keep from slipping on the wet boards. The house was noisy with rats and mice, and the boisterous family next door was even noisier, with its children, chickens, dogs, and pigs.

At night, or when it rained, hordes of termites came out of their lairs. Our neighbor would shine a flashlight into the opening of a termite hole to lure them into a waiting wash tub. When he had filled the tub with a succulent catch, his boy would take it to market to sell. Some people ate termites raw, while others fried them to crispy deliciousness.

Dr. Maureen left many items in her freezer from markets and shops in Mzuzu. There was produce from her garden too. Because we were so well stocked, I could plan for Christmas dinner without a trip to Mzuzu.

Dan, a young, American volunteer medical student, lived with a family near us. Kevin, another American medical student, wandering through Africa, turned up in church on Christmas morning. He was passing through Malawi and was told he should visit Livingstonia. We invited both boys over for Christmas dinner, and they sometimes joined us for meals, which they greatly appreciated. Harvey enjoyed the young men's assistance in the hospital since his work was steady.

Kevin and Harvey helped me organize and catalog the secondary school's library books, which were in appalling disorder. Teaching two sections of second form English, I understood the need for orderly library resources. Before we left, over five thousand books had been reshelved.

Work at Livingstonia

Harvey was in Livingstonia to train medical students and clinical staff, to be an example of Christian faithfulness and caring as he carried out his duties, and to share night calls with the young Malawian doctor and the clinical officer.

Harvey was at the hospital when a woman arrived who had lost six of her seven pregnancies and was now expecting twins. Despite the fear of another loss, Harvey delivered two beautiful baby girls via caesarean section. The grateful mother asked Harvey to name them, so thinking of my twin sister and me, he suggested our middle names—Grace and Joy—both easily translated into the local language.

I looked for ways to help women whose societal status was very low. Females were not expected to suggest or propose a plan of action. If a woman ever earned more than her husband, he would feel obliged to leave home to save face. The synod had an employee responsible for women's work. To help local women, she taught sewing on machines donated by the missionaries. But unlike the male officers, she was not allowed use of a synod car to travel to the villages. Nor was she able to get funds to repair her sewing machines when belts or needles wore out. To compound her indignity, the male church staff expected her to be there every day to prepare and serve their morning and afternoon tea.

Initially, we were not certain what the purpose of our mission to Malawi was; in time, we learned it was not our mission, per se, but God's. Trained as a surgeon, Harvey became de facto the general practitioner and even a part-time preacher. One Sunday, the pastor was called to minister to a grieving family, so that morning, Harvey led the service, including giving the sermon.

One day, as I sorted library books, two freshmen girls sought me out. We talked as I moved about the stacks putting books away. God opened their hearts to receive Him as their Lord and Savior. They asked me to pray with them for God's help to join His family, so we huddled there and prayed for ways to seek His presence. Mission is not about Harvey and my work but about God's will being done through us anywhere in His vast kingdom, at any time.

CHAPTER 13

Soddo, Ethiopia
2006-2008

In November 2006, we answered a call for assistance from the Ethiopian administrator of Soddo Hospital. Soddo, in the hills of south-central Ethiopia, is the political center of the Wolaita Zone.

After landing in Addis, we drove west, passing lakes in the lowlands of the Rift Valley. Teff, the staple grain of Ethiopia, was being harvested everywhere. Its bright yellow fields amidst the lingering green countryside made picturesque, quilt-like patterns on the mountainsides. The flatlands were full of thorny acacia trees, agave plants, and dry riverbeds. As we climbed to Soddo at an altitude of sixty-one hundred feet, fir and eucalyptus trees replaced acacia.

Soddo was spread over the hillsides; the mountains at the city's edge and in the distance were stunningly beautiful. A deep and wide ravine cut the town in half by making a road south from the main road all the way to the lake far below. From Soddo, we could see Lake Abaya shimmering miles away in the distant southeast. The people of Soddo were Wolaita, Oromo, Amhara, Gurage, some Arabs, and many lesser language tribes.

The hospital's chief medical officer and his wife, both Americans, brought us our evening meal. They were caring for twin Ethiopian baby girls in the process of being adopted, so it was a happy, busy household that could use my extra hands. We were only three foreign couples, one of whom brought their two preteen children with them to the new hospital.

A couple and two single ladies lived at the Society of International Mission's (SIM) original compound on the other side of a deep ravine. Being only six hours by car from the capital, the hospital attracted many short-term volunteers for two- to four-week stints. The church service where we foreigners worshipped on Sundays was at the house next door. Few of us had been there long enough to understand the local language services and their two- to three-hour-long marathons, so we preferred to worship in English.

My walk to the shops was rough since the side streets were little more than gravel paths. Meat and fish shops were not near each other; both were farther than I could get to in the same day on foot. The Saturday farmers market was big and best done with Harvey on hand to help carry bags.

Many things about this countryside and community reminded us of our years in Aira, western Ethiopia. The town of Soddo, however, had a population of about ninety thousand, whereas Aira, a small rural village, still had a population of about two thousand. Even though Soddo Hospital was only two years old, word spread quickly, and patients came from far away for its quality surgery. With continuing good care, the hope and expectation was that patient numbers would continue to increase. The Christian witness in Soddo was significant; Muslims were coming to Christ, aggravating tension between the faithful of Islam and Christianity.

We had a pleasant new brick duplex to live in. The kitchen, dining room, and living room were all one room, and a master bedroom, bathroom, and smaller bedroom completed the unit. There was good twenty-four-hour electricity from the national grid and an adequate clean water supply. Temperatures during the day were in the low seventies and cool enough for blankets at night— very pleasant indeed.

Ermias

Nine-year-old Ermias (Jeremiah in English) had three siblings when his father died. His mother remarried, this time to a Muslim. Since her children were not his, he banished the four children from their home. The oldest sister could handle the next two siblings, but Ermias was too old to obey girls. One day the police brought him to Dr. Mary Anderson's home to be sent to an orphanage. Dr. Mary spent her free time teaching him to read, speak, and write in English, as well as to do basic arithmetic.

He was a quick learner, and the Andersons brought him to their home on our compound until the orphanage in Addis had all his papers and called for him to be adopted by an American family. Harvey had come to relieve Dr. Anderson who needed surgery in the United States. When the Andersons left, Ermias came to our small, spare bedroom. He was a very happy, disciplined boy who enjoyed being with us and kept reading to learn more. He moved in with two little suitcases of clothes, books, and other possessions.

When Dr. Henry Bowers and his family went to Addis for four days, they left us with a newborn orphan baby that they were feeding every two hours until he could return to the busy, local orphanage. They also left their dog, Selah, with us. What a helper Ermias was that week. He fed, walked, played with, and bedded that cute little dog in his room. The Bowers felt that Ermias would be called to the orphanage in Addis soon. "Soon," however, would turn out to be anything but.

My routine included daily homeschool lessons for Ermias, with a break for morning tea and usually a walk to the nearby vegetable stall, small shop, or bakery for bread. Ermias would speak to the merchants for me; I was pleased to find a few with whom I could speak Arabic. If our load was too heavy, we would hail a two-wheeled "taxi," pulled by a mule, to take us back to the compound.

The Bowers took Ermias to Addis when they went on another trip so he could be at the orphanage to attend his Ethiopian court case, be taken for a medical clearance, and receive his American

Embassy visa. Then his American parents would be notified that they could come for him.

Dr. Mary's work

In the months before Ermias left, we accompanied Dr. Mary into the countryside. She went bimonthly to a clinic located two hours' drive from Soddo. At the clinic, I collected money through a barred window in a small room, while the pharmacist dispensed medicine. The villagers were much poorer than the employed townsfolk, but they made money from the sale of their much-sought-after ginger crop. The ginger roots could be seen drying in the sun everywhere, set out along roadsides.

The clinic where Mary kept her supplies was very small, so she saw all her patients outside. I offered to help. I began by handing out full tins of a milk powder and medicine mix for infants to mothers in return for the empty tins received at their last visit. Then I gave out bananas from a stalk to all the patients waiting to be seen. Many adults also received special medicines and food supplements in tins. Dr. Mary saw all her repeat TB patients and gave them refills in their empty medicine tins. At this point, seeing the cobwebs, dirty floor, exam table, and benches compelled me to sweep with the empty banana stalk and then a clump of branches.

Among the waiting patients was a man whose leprosy had been arrested; a woman with a suppurating eye, for which Mary could do little but give antibiotics; and a man who complained of a toothache. There was also a man whose only good eye had turned-in eyelashes, a condition called entropion, which in Africa was often caused by bacteria transmitted by flies alighting on one's moist eyes. After seeing the crowds and taking a quick break to eat the lunches we had brought along, Mary called those last two cases inside the tiny clinic room and pulled the tooth and then operated on the eyelid.

Guess who her scrub nurse was? Me! I had never gone to clinic with Harvey in his whole medical mission career. He needed a nurse—not me. Besides, I was usually teaching in a school classroom. Nor had I ever watched him do surgery. So, with one hand, I held the flashlight steady for the doctor, and with the other, I slowly waved a paper over the patient and doctor to chase off the flies. The "pharmacist," a tenth grade boy with good English, held the eye retractor for the upper lid. And so, the operation went along.

Our trip back home was over different dirt roads than those we had taken to get to the clinic, and we bounced around a lot. A sudden downpour made the hills more slippery where the dirt road became grass. I thoroughly enjoyed my day's adventure. The gratitude of the villagers was impressive; the time spent with Dr. Mary was inspiring, and it was a privilege to see more of the area in which we lived.

On another trip, I accompanied Dr. Mary but did not work in the clinic. The road had been dug out to be an irrigation ditch, so we stopped the car, and she walked into the clinic site while I guarded the car. She returned with the waiting patients and dispensed their medical needs from the back of the car. I passed out one bun and one *samboosa* (a savory Indian pastry) to each child who showed me that he or she had been knitting as Dr. Mary had taught them to do.

Soddo Christian Hospital

Soddo Christian Hospital was a private company, like all for-profit hospitals. Its major program was to train African Christian doctors to become surgeons for Africa under the sponsorship of the Pan-African Academy of Christian Surgeons (PAACS). PAACS received most of its support money to assist the trainees from the United States, but the hospitals had to find their own means of assistance. Thus, Soddo Hospital, as a private company, was trying to become self-reliant, and although it was only two years old, it already had a significant clientele.

Harvey said, "At each hospital where I've been to work, I've compared it with Aira Hospital, and I still think Aira comes out ahead." This new hospital was built by a retired American missionary doctor, who had run the original SIM hospital before the Communists took it over in 1977, and a well-trained Ethiopian surgeon, who was from the area and worked alongside the missionary doctor. The former hospital functioned as a government hospital but was in poor condition.

Other hospitals with this same training program were also mission facilities in East and West Africa. Loma Linda University in California oversaw the medical and spiritual training being given by volunteer surgeons from outside Ethiopia, as well as the hospitals' own onsite surgeons. It was a noble goal by which private Christian hospitals could provide good surgical services while being self-sustaining.

The surgical load was heavy and kept three full-time surgeons busy, in addition to training five surgical residents. Three of the residents at that time were Ethiopian, and two were from Nigeria. Fortunately for the older surgeons, most of the on-call night work was done by the residents in training.

There was a need for a four-year commitment of a surgical director to keep the program's standards high. Dr. Anderson, an orthopedic specialist, did not want to be the director, especially when he returned to recover from his hip surgery. He asked Harvey to consider returning to the program for six months after a break in the United States.

Harvey accepted on the condition that he would not do night surgeries except for when he was called to assist the residents if they had problems. Teaching his coworkers for many years and now this PAACS program had been his delight. He was grateful not to be the hospital administrator or mechanics department overseer as he had been in the earlier years. He planned one hundred-question exams for his students, encouraged them to join him in Bible study and ethics discussions, and pushed them to share the Bible with their patients. It was a heavy duty, yet they stayed with it to graduation day.

Christmas and New Year's

Christmas 2006 passed almost without a whisper. Well, not quite, for we had brought holiday tapes and CDs along to enjoy. The Ethiopians, as always, celebrated Orthodox Christmas on January 6. Even the evangelical churches followed the Orthodox calendar. On Christmas Eve, Ermias, Harvey, and I opened our presents, one present each, plus a gift from the family next door. Harvey bought Ermias a jacket, which he proudly wore. But even more important to Ermias was the email greeting from the American family waiting for him to join them. That email included a photo of the new bicycle they had bought for him.

On Christmas Day, the family next door decided to climb the mountain close to Soddo. Harvey and I kept watch on the orphan baby they were caring for while Ermias went with them for the climb. It was a regular workday in Ethiopia for Harvey, but he managed to attend the neighbors' dinner. There were three scheduled surgical cases that day, but the day ended with eight cases in all, plus an emergency call after dinner. Christmas and New Year's Day were working days for Ethiopians and foreigners. On Ethiopian Christmas Eve, our neighbors invited us for an evening meal. On the day itself, we had our English morning fellowship next door, but we sent Ermias to the Orthodox church service, where the Christmas story was told in his language. We hoped he would keep the memory of Ethiopian Christmas in his mind when he lived in the United States. That afternoon we sent him back to the church to watch the Christmas pageant there.

When Ermias returned from church, our family and the household next door joined a feast at the home of the hospital's vice director. The feast ended with coffee: the beans were pounded to shell them, and when the shells had been removed, the beans were roasted over a fire, pounded finely, boiled in water, poured into small egg-size cups, and spiced with salt. Coffee in Ethiopian homes was not a trivial matter; it was a formal ritual, similar to the Japanese tea ceremony.

Margaret's work

My work varied with each volunteer assignment. This time, at least initially, the plan was that I would house and teach Ermias. But my opportunities kept growing. Dr. Anderson asked me to type summaries of each surgical resident's work and experience. Later, a neighbor arranged for three of her friends to meet with me at her house, and a German construction man wanted his workers to learn English. A couple from Italy wanted me to teach English to the teachers of both their vocational training school and the girls' primary school.

Ermias and I walked down the steep road to the Catholic girls' primary school compound every Tuesday and Thursday but made the uphill return in the Catholic mission's car. The girls' school had Muslim, Orthodox Christian, evangelical, and Catholic students. I met with their teachers for upgrading English and pedagogy from 3:00 to 4:30 p.m. They viewed themselves as already knowing all they needed to know, so they did not appreciate these English lessons. They were uninterested and, in fact, quite poor in their English grammar, so I quietly slipped in some grammar lessons to our conversational lessons. From 5:00 to 6:00 p.m., I taught English to vocational teachers at the technical school for young adults. How appreciative and attentive they were to learn more, since most had not finished high school. What a contrast with the Catholic girls' schoolteachers.

The half-hour wait between my classes was always spent at the Italian couple's house for refreshing drinks and fascinating talks of world news, their work, and their vision for expanding their work. What a wonderful time we shared. Each time we visited the school, Ermias enjoyed the playground equipment and was fascinated by the craft and technical classes being taught. Sometimes he spent his time in my class for vocational teachers. Four hours passed swiftly for him since he was a typical patient African.

The director of the government secondary school, just a block away from the hospital compound, asked me to teach after school on Monday and Wednesday afternoons. I taught ninth graders supplementary English lessons after their regular classes. It was voluntary for the students, so class size varied from week to week, but many students were eager to learn better English. I also gave math lessons to the girl next door.

Dr. Anderson raised the idea that I might compile statistics on a spreadsheet for all the surgical cases in 2006 and for each resident's files. The latter task required more time than anticipated since their reports were handwritten in each resident's handwriting style, which could be difficult to read. Harvey had to help me decipher the names of the doctors and the surgical work they did. This turned out to be weekend work because the original data was kept in the operating room for surgeries as they happened. To complicate matters, every date had to be translated to English dates.

With many guests visiting the compound, especially inspectors from Loma Linda University in California, we were hard pressed to find beds for everyone. We doctors' wives also shared meal preparation responsibilities among us, one of the de facto duties of wives. How grateful we were for local women and garden boys to help us.

Ermias turned ten while he was with us and did not like going back to the orphanage again because he would be the oldest child there. But the adoption did not happen, and he returned to our home in Soddo until early February when the call finally came for him. Mrs. Bowers and Harvey together walked Ermias to the bus station where a local orphanage worker waited to accompany him to Addis.

He was there for about five weeks or more to finish all the government and US paperwork before his new mother was called. She and Ermias moved to her hotel room to get acquainted and finish her paperwork. Ermias was a very patient child through all the moving and waiting he had been subjected to. In this process, we learned a lot about the measures needed to protect children worldwide from human trafficking.

To think that God would place a ten-year-old orphan, a ten-month-old orphan, and a small dog in our home at Christmas time —a time when he himself came to us. What greater task and honor is there than to care for his little ones? We were sleep deprived all the time; Harvey was at work at all hours, and I was with two children and the dog. But the privilege compensated for it. We chuckled between ourselves to wonder who would define mission work in such terms. God did, and He still does.

Neighbors

We lived in one-half of a duplex, with the other side usually occupied by guests or volunteer workers. Our neighboring house belonged to the hospital's optometrist, Dr. Henry Bowers, who had come to Soddo from Ohio. His work here was in a separate building by the main gate. It was a busy place, with many people coming for eye care.

Dr. Bowers' wife, Stephne, was a white South African. The Bowers family included a girl and a boy, adopted as infants from a Russian orphanage. Stephne homeschooled the two children, and Henry pitched in with his science and math aptitude. The children were learning to play the piano since their father was a pianist and their mother a fine singer. The family was completed by a small, white, curly haired dog named Selah, whom I cared for whenever the family left for shopping or vacation.

We went to the Bowers' house for Sunday morning service. Attendance changed weekly as the doctors rotated on emergency call, even on Sundays. We often had special group meals at their home in the large, round, open patio, with concrete walls three feet high. There was a grass roof to shade us, a barbecue fireplace for cooking our meals, and a concrete shelf to hold hot and cold dishes.

In our last weeks at Soddo, one of the Ethiopian residents training to be a surgeon moved his family into the other side of our duplex. His wife, Birtukan, was half Oromo and could talk to us in that language. She was fluent in English and a primary school teacher. Their child, Koreb, named after Mt. Horeb in the Bible, was fourteen months old at the time and very good at screaming for attention.

I took Birtukan with me to the little nearby shops and to larger shops with foreign and Ethiopian items, meat and fish shops, and the bakery. One day she asked me how to make bread and other American dishes. We also worked together making food for two groups who came to inspect the hospital and do volunteer work.

Orphanage work

When we worked in the western area of Ethiopia, orphan work was neither visible nor mentioned. When we were in the capital, however, we heard about and even met parents from America coming to adopt young ones from local orphanages.

Ethiopia was the only African country allowing adoption of their homeless children.

In Soddo alone, there were three orphanages run by local helpers but under a world agency's supervision. Newborns and tots were in one orphanage, children in another, and teens had their own place and attended secondary school. The headquarters for this work was in Addis, but supervisors came frequently to observe the work. There were other organizations from abroad also running orphanages.

Foreign doctors' wives helped when the orphanage either had a special child, had no room for one more, had lost helpers, or was otherwise overburdened. Ermias, whom we had watched until he was called to Addis, was raised in Dr. Mary's home, then in Dr. Anderson's home, and then in our home. By living with us, he learned English and math.

In addition to homeschooling her own children, Stephne Bower oversaw the work of caring for orphaned babies locally. She cared for a newborn who was underweight and needed feedings every two hours. The Andersons also cared for twin toddlers until they got accepted at the orphanage in Addis. One day Stephne took me to the orphanage for babies. It was a nice compound and a well-built structure. Inside, the cribs were crowded into the two large rooms, each crib holding two infants. Altogether there were twenty-five little ones.

The orphanage for teens was close to our compound. The Christian World Adoption Agency had responsibility for over one hundred children still living in their own homes or in foster homes. The agency gave foster parents an allowance until adoption was complete. Most of the one hundred children had already been spoken for by American couples. It was hardest to find parents for older children like Ermias.

The agency had four centers in Ethiopia for orphans, so it was understandable that it took so long for Ermias to be summoned to Addis for final clearance. Until his American mother came to take him to America, he stayed busy in the Addis orphanage teaching the younger children English.[89]

Second trip to Soddo,
November 2007–April 2008

After a few months back in the United States, we returned to Soddo in November 2007 for a second stint. This time, we were the first to live in the newly finished duplex attached to the Anderson's house. There were three of us sharing the apartment, including Heidi Zwyghuizen, the sister of our son's wife.

Heidi spent only ten days in Soddo, but she saw every missionary at their work; visited the government school, the Catholic girls' school, and vocational school at Konto; visited the hospital and the church; went to market with me; and helped sort and clean a hospital storage container in preparation for new goods coming in. She tried spicy Ethiopian food and liked it. She climbed the mountain outside town for a sweeping view of Soddo. She asked many questions and gained much knowledge and understanding.

I regretted her departure and chose to ride with her to Addis as an opportunity to be with her and pick up supplies. What a delightful ten nights we enjoyed in her company. She would demonstrate the deep impression the trip made on her by returning the following year and assisting a missionary at the Presbyterian guest house in her work among orphans and elderly who lived outside the city.

As with the prior year's visit to Soddo, we had good weather when we first arrived. Rain came mostly at night and was not heavy, but these rains enabled a second growing season every year. There was no such second chance in the one long rainy season out west, in Aira, where we had spent so many years.

Both years in Soddo we endured public electricity failures and broken water mains, but maintenance at the hospital was equally frustrating since our generator and water systems had

---

[89] Ermias was finally adopted and now lives in Idaho with his loving family and three siblings.

their own troubles. Most government and private problems were fixed in four or five days, but some issues took longer if there was a holiday or if ordered parts did not come quickly and were not the size needed.

Frustrated by email and phone-system problems, Harvey was grateful for the use of others' phones and computers until we could get one installed in our home. He received our personal email from Holland, Michigan, that way, as well as world news.

Another Christmas in Soddo

As with our previous time in Soddo, we arrived at the beginning of the Western Advent season. This meant that we enjoyed the full range of pre-Christmas events on both the Western and Orthodox calendars. For Christmas Eve, the eleven foreigners living on the compound gathered for an evening meal. I was the leader of our small worship service in the morning. The next morning, Harvey and I went off to a distant church, and Harvey preached a sermon that was translated sentence by sentence. Stephne invited all the workers and the thirty-two orphans to her outdoor *braai*[90] for Christmas supper. We kept busy holding babies.

Once again, Harvey was asked to speak on Orthodox Christmas at the first church built in Soddo. We felt very much at home in this service, which was similar to our church programs in western Ethiopia.

The church arranged for one of the hospital workers to walk us to the church. It was a strenuous walk, down into a deep ravine then up and up a steep incline on the other side. Entering the sanctuary, we found over one hundred impatient children awaiting the program's start. Despite their impatience, the service started an hour later, when the benches had filled up with adults, youth, and children. The hospital's female evangelist translated for us. Also sitting on the bench with us was the very first convert of the mission's church work. She had taught the first missionaries the local language.

---

[90] A South African barbecue.

The service began with choirs and a Sunday school group dancing to the altar with gifts. Two benches were carried in and presented by one group, a medium-sized water barrel came with another, and many bolts of cloth came with the third. Each choir sang songs, then various folks shared prayers and poems before they finally motioned that Harvey could speak. Another hospital worker translated his message into Amharic, the emperor's language, which everyone knew from school.

The room was hot and airless, and soon after Harvey concluded, a man motioned for us to leave. He had ordered a car to take us back to our compound, so we missed more singing, the procession of everyone to the altar with their offerings, and the long, drawn-out pageant yet to be performed by the youth. We were grateful to stand up after hours on hard benches. We got into the car to leave, but the steering wheel had locked up, so we set out for home on foot, down through the ravine again and up the other side. Without the protection of the escort from our earlier traverse, children on the street were bold and tiresome for much of the long walk home.

The overly exuberant, charismatic youth; the shouted prayers and thunderous preaching; the ear-piercing screech of the microphone above the clamor; the long, repetitious choir numbers shouted over the loud electronic keyboard; the hot crowded room; the incomprehensible language; and the swaying and swooning, all contributed to our desire to stay on our little compound. There, those of us who knew no local languages—guests, missionaries, volunteer workers, doctors from other countries in training—could worship in English with our small group.

Harvey's work

Harvey did hospital rounds for all patients. This was his routine seven days a week. His interest was in teaching the surgical residents and medical doctors how to manage inpatient care, with an emphasis on surgical cases.

When we arrived, there were twenty-four government-assigned medical assistants at Soddo Hospital for stints of two months at a time. They were in training to become health officers who would eventually be classified as doctors. They liked doing clinical work but were not interested in the more humdrum public health and prevention part. Harvey tried to include them whenever there was a health lecture. What level of training they received in other hospitals is anybody's guess.

A private nursing school in western Ethiopia graduated 225 nurses, of which only thirty-five were able to pass the government's exam for certification. The government was in the process of closing some of those private, for-profit schools for employing unqualified teachers who had passed students without close attention to their work or theory.

Sunday evenings the surgical residents gathered for Bible study. At one meeting, the residents complained about the work and study load, keeping records of their work, the reading required for Saturday morning exams, the end-of-year exams, and the exasperating lack of library books for such study. Harvey was generally impressed with the library but knew more books were needed.

Every day, in a gesture of sensible accommodation, doctors doing surgery would be brought a lunch from the hospital kitchen for when they had a spare moment to eat.

One evening we had just finished supper when Harvey was called to the hospital to tend to a difficult delivery. While he was there, several people were brought in with injuries from a cart accident: seven people had been crammed into a rickety, three-seat cart when the horse dropped into a deep gulley, taking cart and passengers down with it. The driver was impaled by a wooden spike; two people had bad open fractures, and one man died on the spot. Finished by two o'clock in the morning, Harvey was called back at four o'clock for another surgical case. The residents were certainly learning a few things that night.

Visiting Aira again

When Dr. Anderson returned to work after convalescing from successful hip surgery, we were given two weeks of vacation to visit our former mission station in Aira. Six of those fourteen days would be spent in buses and cars, with only five days actually in Aira and three in Addis. Our travel north and west was made quicker and more comfortable by personal friends going that way by car; unfortunately, our return east and south would be by four different buses.

To begin our trip north from Soddo, we passed the Rift Valley lakes and saw camels, an ostrich farm, flamingoes that had laid claim to a lake, and storks in the acacia trees. In Addis we stayed in the German guest house. A German missionary told us of the burning of thirteen churches far west of Aira and the murder of one of the evangelical church evangelists. There had been a lot of harassment of Christians by young hoodlums, even though congregations in that area now numbered forty-five thousand believers.

Our driver was a Norwegian missionary heading to Aira to lead the nursing school there. We stopped at the synod guest house halfway to Aira as dusk approached. Harvey and I met with a blind English teacher who had been my eighth grade student in 1977, before missionaries had to leave Communist Ethiopia. We took her to Addis at that time and settled her into a Christian secondary school. She had just one more summer term at the university to get her degree. After dinner she showed us her half-finished house; when it was finished, she told us triumphantly, she would no longer need to pay rent. She had done well for herself and her daughter, then a twelfth grade student in technical school studies.

There were over ten guests and volunteers on the Aira compound: a Swedish gynecologist, two German electricians, two Finnish water repairmen, a German doctor showing her husband where she had once worked, a German pastor at the Bible school who had worked with us in years past and returned to teach a week of theological education by extension classes, and three Ethiopian auditors from Addis going over the synod's account books.

Our first afternoon we toured the hospital, directed by Dr. Ericksen, a Swede, to which three young Ethiopian doctors had come to relieve the workload. One of them was a former student of mine who had gotten into university with our help. The hospital had a new building dedicated to eye and vision care, for which it became widely known. The waiting room was always filled with patients to be seen, operated on as necessary, or tested for corrective glasses.

We toured the secondary school where I had taught and met six former colleagues; all the rest were new and very young. I had had seventy students per room, but teachers now had ninety per room. The chemistry teacher said it was hard to demonstrate experiments so all could see. Over a third of the students were girls. The government built a new secondary school with grades nine and ten. It was as crowded as the church school. They had only one female teacher on staff.

Sunday we were at church from 8:30 a.m. until noon. The service included over an hour of prayer and praise led by two elders; it was very repetitive. The choir also sang twice, each time performing three long songs. It was great to meet the congregation again.

On Monday we visited the seminary, once only a small Bible school, now with its fifty-eight students including six females. Most of the pastors were the teachers we knew.

The next day, we decided we had visited everyone as well as every institution, so we thought about returning to our work in Soddo. In a bittersweet moment, I realized that we were guests, onlookers at the activity around us but no longer part of it. The trip helped me see it had been this way with all of our short-term, volunteer work during our retirement years. Every volunteer assignment in Africa, bookmarked by a follow-on short stay in our US home, was emblematic of life's brevity on earth.

We boarded a minibus just outside the hospital gate; some hours later, we boarded a regular bus that took us halfway to Addis that night. A three-day stop in Addis allowed us to rest up for the work at Soddo again. We went shopping, and I got my hair done—a rare treat. On Sunday we attended the International Lutheran Church service and joined our Presbyterian friends for a noon meal in a restaurant. On Monday we set out for Soddo and arrived eight hours later, grimy and dirty from the road construction and detours along the way.

Weather

The weather pattern in western Ethiopia is simple—the rainy season and the dry season—a season for planting when the spring rains came and then a dry season for harvest time.

In Soddo and the eastern areas, farmers were blessed with two rainy seasons and a shorter dry season. Around Christmas the dust was a nuisance, but by mid-January, the patter of the first heavy rain drops on hard-packed dirt ushered in an intense rainy season. Rain, wind, and rainbows made the January skies and earth beautiful. That, however, soon changed as the rain made for slippery roads and walkways with mud everywhere. For farmers, the rain produced field crops; for us, garden produce; and for all who enjoyed fruit and produce, humans and animals alike, there was an abundance of tree and ground bounty.

The nightly showers, accompanied by lightning and thunder, were always downpours that cleared the dusty air and enabled us to see the lake in the valley below. But the mud turned one little white puppy into a dirty, brown one. We covered all the new furniture in our house because of Selah, the Bowers' dog. When I returned after class, she would get so excited to see me that she would jump on my legs and skirt, leaving dirty paw prints. She got a good scrubbing on Saturday nights from Harvey, but that was not always enough.

When Stephne Bowers returned from her father's funeral in South Africa, I gladly handed over Selah, their dog. Two days later, the police went to the orphanage with eight babies they had picked up from the streets. Any baby left lying unattended for too long after its birth usually needed Stephne's immediate and vigilant care until it was strong enough to go into the orphanage for newborns.

One afternoon, after a prolonged period of clouds, thunder and lightning announced the arrival of rain that came in hail-filled torrents. Our metal windows and frames did not fit tightly, so rain seeped onto the windowsills, streaked down the walls, and made rivulets across the floor. The towels we used to sop up the water had to be wrung out many times. The hail was particularly destructive in the vegetable gardens, especially on leafy plants.

The next day, we saw the storm's damage. Men were already at work on the trench, draining the water and silt. A stretch of barbed wire fence was washed out into the road, so thorn bushes were placed there as a temporary, albeit amusing, attempt at security.

By April the rains were heavy and steady all night and into the morning hours. The afternoons dried up, and the temperature lingered in the low sixties. Walking to school downhill in the afternoon was less precarious than the morning trek, but the mud was still slippery, so I often accepted a ride from the school driver back up the hill after class. We always removed our muddy shoes at the door, but the Ethiopians did not do that.

Once April's rains started and crops could be planted, farmers began plowing their fields. Rich farmers first plowed with their oxen and then loaned their teams to neighboring farmers who had none but had saved enough throughout the year to gratefully pay for the rental of the beasts.

Religious life

Since we Westerners could neither understand nor speak Amharic, the official language of the country, we gathered Sunday mornings at one of the doctors' homes. The Nigerian surgical residents in training attended most Sundays with us. The message was often a video or recording from the United States.

Every Sunday, we were treated to all-day religious services broadcast over loudspeakers from the evangelical, Catholic, and Orthodox churches. In similar fashion, on Fridays loudspeakers broadcast Muslim services from the mosque. The mosque also used loudspeakers to call the faithful to prayer five times every day —at dawn, three times during the day, and in the evening.

Easter morning, we had a sunrise service outdoors and then Communion together in our neighbor's roof-covered patio. During Orthodox Lent, adherents did not eat meat, so butcher stalls were closed. Butchers raised meat prices very high the day before Lent. That may have been a high-minded tactic meant to discourage hoarding or, more likely, opportunistic shrewdness. Nonetheless,

Muslims and non-Orthodox Christian butchers still slaughtered meat but set the prices higher for the forty days of Lent.

The Islamization of Africa had crept into many African countries. One way was through marriage of a Muslim man to a Christian girl, who was then made to be his second wife. The father would raise all male children she bore as Muslims. Another possible avenue was through the giving of first-time bank loans with no return conditions except that the recipient be a Muslim. The pro-Christian Ethiopian prime minister at the time forbade such "buying" of his people.

Goodbye Soddo

Our last week in Soddo came quickly as little tasks at school and the hospital fell away from our schedule. Our guest list kept our rooms full and our kitchens busy during the last days.

On my final day at the vocational school, students of both classes combined to have a coffee ceremony and present me a gift. They had been my best scholars in both our first and second Soddo visits. My last school day was also the day of our dinner party for the two directors. What a great school for girls and vocational school for boys they had established.

The walks down to the school were always delightful as I gazed on the lakes in the far distance. When I realized the children and mothers along the path were speaking Oromo—the language we used for greetings and small sentences in western Ethiopia— my walks became even more delightful since we could now exchange greetings.

I spent the last two weeks in neighboring gardens that had much produce to be picked. I either baked or boiled vegetables for adding to soups that the doctors in our house and next door could take from their freezers as needed.

CHAPTER 14

Beautiful Cameroon
2008-2009

Cameroon, on Africa's west coast, is simply beautiful, from its beaches to its mountains. Upon arrival in Douala, Cameroon's secondary capital, in November 2008 (we always seemed to be arriving in November), we were transported to the American Baptist guest house. At sea level, it was hot and humid, but our overnight quarters were pleasant. In fact, the next morning, we took our breakfast outdoors, under palm trees. The activity of loading and offloading freighters at the port was fascinating to watch. The scene and activity kept us happily occupied until the car came to take us to Mbingo.

The only road north on this western, English-speaking side of Cameroon is a steep ascent with a number of hairpin turns to negotiate. We wended through hills and mountains most of the way. Our destination was partway along the road that went all the long way to the Niger border. The views of the hills, mountains, and plateaus on both sides made us feel as if we were in India driving up to our children's school at Kodaikanal or in Malawi going up to Livingstonia. What awesome scenery. What beautiful memories we were adding to these special "vagabond" work trips.

Mbingo rests on a plateau with mountains and valleys around it—our everyday scenery. Each morning we were greeted by mountains shrouded by dust or mist, but in the dry season, the

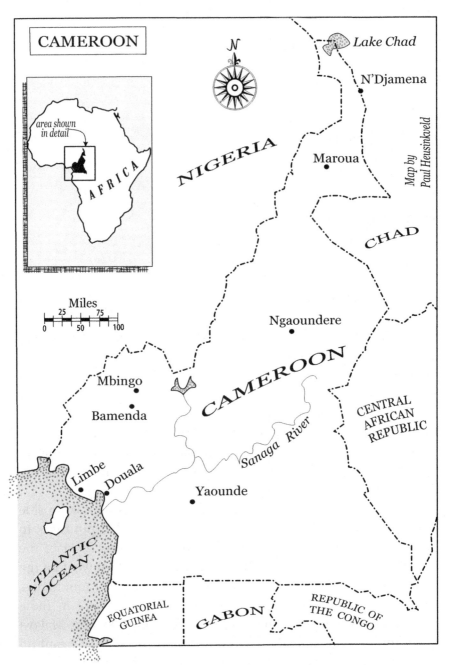

Cameroon, with inset map of Africa

mist steadily retreated up the mountainside. To the east, a mountain had a thin waterfall cascading down its steep slopes. Fog erased the valleys during the rainy season. When the dry season came, there was so much more to behold, such a feast for the eye. Harvey took a ninety-minute walk after work each day when he could get away. He tramped through the forest paths and the main road's secondary dirt paths. The good, asphalt road was so steep that I could not walk it for long.

At the school end of our compound were steep paths down into the valley, lined with crops along the way. Men went down to farm and cut the tall, dry grasses that they tied into tight bundles and carried on their heads to the Saturday market. These were sold to make roofing thatch. In the dry season, after harvesting, and in anticipation of the changes rain would bring, farmers burned the fields to remove roots and use the ash for fertilizer.

In February I daily swept my front and back porches and the sidewalk down to the dirt path to keep the ash from getting carried into the house. There was relentless dust and sand from Sahara Desert sandstorms to try to keep at bay. I used a surprisingly effective broom like my neighbors'—a sheaf of stiff grass bound tightly together. On weekend evenings, the electric bulbs of our porches attracted an endless horde of grasshoppers, termites, locusts, praying mantises, and crickets. Children laughed and darted around as they captured these delicacies for their families or to sell at market. The insects started coming out as the rainy season approached, usually in March. The rains began sparsely, bringing mostly humidity and heat, but by April they came in more steadily, cooling off the land.

New routines

Our first lodging was the guest room of the Sparks[91] family home, a home they had designed and built at the edge of the

---

[91] Dr. Steve Sparks was an American missionary surgeon with the Baptist Mission. He worked with the Pan-African Academy of Christian Surgeons (PAACS), which had the goal of training and discipling one hundred African surgeons by 2020. PAACS is a ministry of the Christian Medical and Dental Associations.

plateau. East of them, a waterfall cascaded down a mountain across a narrow gorge, and south of them, down a hill, was an airstrip where farmers let their cattle graze. Our assignment was to take over Dr. Sparks' work, his house, and the dog's needs whenever the family was away. Their two younger boys lived in Mbingo with their parents, while the two older girls were at boarding school in Youande, Cameroon's principal capital.

The mission's primary school was on the compound, and the mission's secondary school sat right next to the government secondary school on a flat area below the airstrip.

At the market, across the main road from the hospital compound, stalls, cement storerooms, and huts lined the roadside; they were utilized by merchants who came from outlying areas and local merchants who preferred to store their goods overnight rather than carry them up and down the mountain every day. A dozen stalls along the driveway leading to the compound sold various sundries for families and patients at the hospital. These patients' families lived in a row of mission rooms during their stay at Mbingo. I often went there to pick up items, thus avoiding the steep road to the market.

A maid came daily to help with housekeeping and meals. She also went to the market to have our corn supply ground at the mill. Corn was the local food staple, and a shortage of it was always a concern, sometimes causing riots to break out in city centers. While she did her chores, I sometimes spent mornings hulling rice, grain by grain.

Our new house was finally finished, and we moved in a week after our arrival. There were four large, fragrant frangipani plants between our home and the neighbors' homes. Many times, it was necessary to chase away four-footed kids who ate the plant leaves and two-footed kids who came to sneak a whiff of the plants. But how heartwarming it was to watch the children, with their eyes squeezed shut and noses turned up, smiling broadly as they inhaled deeply of the perfume. Upon seeing me, they would squeal merrily and scamper away.

The house was a few steps from the main road, so we often had people passing by. Occasionally, Muslim men would come to the hospital from their large community farther up the mountain.

They came either walking or on horses, which they tethered to trees in the meadow near the hospital. One day the main road was a noisy place as cattlemen from the north herded ninety cattle through town to the slaughterhouse down the steep, winding road. We never saw mules, donkeys, or sheep, and we certainly never saw pigs, which Muslims, like Jews, consider unclean.

There was always bread in the market, so I did not bake my own. Occasionally, the other doctors' wives and I went to Bamenda by car and bought things not available in Mbingo. Bamenda was a large town and the location of the church headquarters for our area. It was below our plateau on the main road and boasted better shopping and more everyday conveniences than we had. But Mbingo afforded us an amazing view of the world.

Christmas and New Year's

The two weeks before Christmas, we enjoyed wonderful music during morning chapel service at the Mbingo Baptist Hospital. Each day's morning service was led by English carols sung by one of the hospital's departments. The staff of each ward was large, so it made for a good choral group. Harvey and I went to the services just to enjoy the music.

In the afternoons during the holiday season, each department entertained patients with carols and a Bible reading, closing with a meditation. I especially looked forward to the practice sessions every morning as new groups got ready to sing; the hospital chapel was not far from our house, and lively strains of their warm-ups carried on the breeze.

We invited four missionary guests, away from their families, to share Christmas Day dinner with us. Later in the evening, in another missionary family's home, we had dessert and caroling. As with Christmas, there was a New Year's Eve service and a morning service the following day. Another of the missionary families hosted the whole mission group for a delightful New Year's Eve event, so we opted for the morning service on New Year's Day.

Weather on the mountain plateau was delightful. The mountains were steep, so it made even small excursions challenging. It was looking like January would be a busy month for

Harvey. He had just two weeks until the surgical residents and their administrator would travel to Kenya for a medical conference. But the surgery schedule at the hospital continued unabated for him and a volunteer doctor who had recently arrived from Alaska for a month.

Meanwhile, I kept the "home fires burning." That included a helper three times a week to whom I taught new recipes to expand her range as a cook. She made corn muffins for her son who came to greet me at morning coffee.

Church

Sunday services were the most interesting and colorful and full of praise to God. The choir did manage to walk in sedately once or twice in my recollection, but usually they shuffled and sashayed down the aisle to their own anthem or the congregation's hymn. When the choir stood to sing, a young man jumped into the aisle and danced and twirled to the music. Preaching was in the local language and when translated proved to be very biblical. The second Sunday, we heard of the Great Commission and were reminded that "No one has an excuse!"

One Sunday, individuals brought gifts to the front of the church, and the congregation followed with their offerings. A retired director began the procession with his own gifts and, turning to the congregation, asked all retired workers to stand and make themselves known. He spoke with heartfelt sincerity of their years of experience and integrity, declaring with conviction: "Retirees are like tires worn out but with new bindings on them." The congregation nodded their heads in admiration. Entire plantain stalks were carried forward by two or three men, for that fruit was especially unwieldy and heavy. Chickens bounced down the aisle in baskets, while banana stalks and produce were carried in on women's heads.

Between the dry season and the rainy season, there was an interval around Christmas called the "little rains." The wind was strong and lashed windowpanes with rain, and anybody caught outside was drenched. But many braved the pelting to get to church for the joyful experience of Christmas season.

Christmas Eve turned cold once the sun went down and the mountain winds picked up. The evening service lasted over three hours due to the many choir groups, soloists, and drama groups, each taking their turn. Christmas Day had a shorter and less intense program to allow families some time together. We invited six foreign guests for a festive lunch at our house. In the evening, all the foreigners were asked to bring a dessert to another family's dinner party where carol singing around the piano and warm fellowship brought the day to a wonderful close.

Margaret's work

No one assigned me any long-term tasks, which was just as well because I did not want to take another teacher's job away. The director of the Baptist primary school on our compound suggested I help her label books and reshelve them in the library, for they were often on the wrong shelves. I enjoyed doing that three mornings a week.

Harvey and I visited the government secondary school down the steep main road about a mile away. A church secondary school had just been built next door to the government school, so we visited them both. They lacked equipment and books, but far more alarming was their lack of qualified teachers. Both schools were built parallel to the hospital's grassy airstrip. The students enjoyed the distraction of the occasional landing or take-off of an aircraft out on the strip.

One day I had a tour of the hospital and found myself in the hospital's library. It held both medical volumes and books for patients and their relatives. There were books left behind by missionary wives who had homeschooled their children, novels left by departing missionaries, and used books sent from churches in America.

Choosing a book, I took it to the librarian, Mr. John, to sign out. He introduced himself, and I shook his hand, only to realize he had no fingers. He had been a leprosy patient before the disease was arrested and was now employed as librarian. Looking down at his feet, I saw one had been replaced by a wooden peg, attached to his lower leg. He moved about seemingly unfettered by the heavy contraption.

Mr. John not only cared for the books but also ran the copy machine—of which he was very protective—for any medical staff needing copies. He was grateful when I volunteered to work with him in the library, labeling the books and putting them where they belonged. Together we devised a shelving system to simplify the method of finding books and returning them to their places. When that task ended, he asked me to teach him to use the computer with only the five fingers on his left hand.

Mr. John was always happy and helpful, ever ready to learn new ways to serve others. Weekdays he was in the library from seven until five; weekends, he cleared the hospital conference room so his congregation could meet there for their worship service. He was the janitor, treasurer, and usher for his church.

Most of all, Mr. John was a witness for Christ to the many users of the library. People stopped in to receive his helpful advice, his books, and his friendship. He was a kind and generous worker at both hospital and church.

In all the schools, we saw the joy of the Cameroonian people shine through. In the church and church schools, we saw a remarkable depth of faith and sincerity of witness in their work and in their relationships.

Hospital work

The Mbingo hospital was a large complex backed up against a cliff. It was always busy; surgical cases were on a one-week, sometimes two-week, waiting list. The staffing was robust, but short-term medical volunteers always found plenty to do. Most came to work for three to ten weeks. Specialist surgeons came frequently enough to increase the hospital's inpatient population. An orthopedic surgeon with his wife and a Cameroonian American cardiovascular surgeon came for the doctors-in-training program to teach their specialties.

The church oversaw the medical and educational work of the mission. Nonmedical and noneducational staff were asked to be hosts for the volunteers. Besides hosting volunteers, the staff also helped to find lodging for patients' relatives who had accompanied their kin and arrange for patients to pay off their hospital debt by cutting grass, chopping wood, and doing other chores. While they worked off their bills, these former patients were housed in a facility beside the hospital that provided simple rooms and a kitchen shed for communal use.

I went several times to visit the lady in the room closest to our house. She was awaiting a new prosthetic limb for her amputated leg. She went to the therapy room in her wheelchair using a ramp that bridged the dirt path from her door to the pavement. She spoke English well and showed me her French Bible, so she also knew French. She had twins at home, and her roommate had just birthed triplets.

From my front door, I could hear voices at the hospital's entrance; the hospital's morning chapel, with its amplified singing and speaking voices; and taxis driving up to the hospital circle to let off or pick up patients throughout the day, with the accompanying bickering and haggling over the fare. The gravel path in front of our house led to the taxi stand. Usually, the trunks of the taxis were loaded to overflowing with bananas, so they remained open but secured with ropes. Taxi rides going up the steep road, loaded like that, were always at risk of losing some of the cargo crammed in the trunk. Going down, of course, gravity worked to keep the cargo in place.

One morning the hospital recognized the retirement of nine faithful workers. Over one thousand guests came to the 10:00 a.m. ceremony that finally got underway at eleven o'clock and finished at two thirty. After the ceremony, there was picture taking, gift giving, and a feast of food, including deep-fried pastries and soda pop. After all that, guests were invited to visit the workers' homes to continue celebrating with tea, coffee, and treats. This retirement send-off was unlike anything I had ever seen, certainly nothing like the cake and punch in the conference room with one's coworkers that we regarded as typical in America.

On International Leprosy Day, twelve patients with leprosy graduated from their treatment programs either cured or in remission. When leprosy patients finished their long course of treatment, they were considered cured, were given a certificate of health, and could return to their families. While taking their medicines for a year or two, the patients would cut grass, chop wood, and do other chores around the compound.

The president's wife helped celebrate the occasion. After a short ceremony, she personally gave each graduate a gift of rice, flour, sugar, oil, pots, and other small items. Most of the graduates would join a village built by Mbingo Hospital for such rehabilitated citizens. The church service began at nine o'clock, with the government program held outdoors under canopies. At one o'clock the special guests left so the local people finally got a chance to eat.

The doctors in surgical training worked hard to study, take Harvey's weekly tests, and do hands-on surgical training. Harvey sometimes brought the students home for evening discussions on medical ethics.

Harvey was asked to come to Mbingo to fill in for Dr. Sparks, the director, to keep the surgical training on schedule. The director was often away, so Harvey's presence was a "comfort blanket" for the doctors in training. Dr. Sparks had kids in school in Douala and visited them when possible.

Harvey's engagement allowed Dr. Sparks to take off for two weeks to join a mission volunteer group from his home church, join Baptist missionaries for their annual convention week, and share in the teaching of African doctors in Nairobi. These doctors were enrolled for two weeks in surgical training given by surgeons coming from America, who not only taught technique but also shared in Christian discipleship and witnessing.

Three guest doctors came to Mbingo expecting to give lectures to the resident doctors, but they were quickly put to work filling in for the residents and director who were attending the Baptist convention. They joined Harvey in regular and emergency surgery and in the daily afternoon OPD clinic. No one doubted the lectures they planned to present were valuable, but the duties they picked up were invaluable. It was a busy, meaningful time for the visitors and an experience they would not soon forget.

The hospital served all of northern and western Cameroon, so February's schedule was chock-a-block with elective surgery cases. The hospital charged the patients high fees, and they also paid high fees for taxis, food, and rooms. But the hospital's reputation was strong.

Unusual medical cases

One day Harvey worked on a four-year-old boy who had swallowed lye two years earlier, resulting in extensive scar tissue and stricture of the esophagus. He was admitted and stayed a month because of vomiting blood. An X-ray revealed he had swallowed a coin that was lodged above the stricture site. Harvey spent two-and-a-half hours trying to remove the coin with inadequate tools. He finally got it out, but two days later, because of the previous damage to the child's esophagus, there were signs of an esophagus perforation. The boy ran high fevers and faced more complications. Reluctantly, Harvey put the child in the care of a new surgeon volunteer since our time in Cameroon was over. Harvey would have liked to have sent the child to a pediatric surgeon, but none were available. Cases like this were unnecessarily complicated for the doctors because they lacked the proper equipment.

A young man with a broken leg from a motorcycle accident went to a local healer for help. The treatment he received was a compress of dirty rags and "healing herbs" on the wound. When that failed, as happened with frustrating regularity, the family brought the wounded man to Mbingo hospital, where the compound fracture was reset and the wound cleaned. After three days, the man developed tetanus symptoms and was put on tetanus medication until he stabilized. In the middle of the night, he died suddenly during a procedure to suction secretions from his throat. Harvey seldom saw tetanus in African patients. Many countries held campaigns to eradicate it by immunization, especially for young people and pregnant women.

Mothers typically carried their young on their backs as they worked. One mother put her baby down in a just-burned field. As the mother worked, the baby crawled after her and entered a section where the ashes were still smoldering, severely burning his hands and feet. His fingertips slowly sloughed off, and new skin eventually covered them, but both his feet were badly burned, requiring painful daily debridement and dressing.

There were rewards for the doctors and nurses when their patients healed. Many patients or family members paid their hospital fees and showed their gratitude by willingly staying on to do chores. The amputee patients stayed longer to get adjusted to their crutches, walkers, or new prosthetics.

Leaving Cameroon

In the lead-up to our departure, we tied up loose ends. We entertained the residents and their wives at a dinner and social gathering at our home. Eighteen guests were invited since Harvey thought the residents needed more fellowship opportunities that included their wives.

When it was time to leave, we arranged to journey by bus from Bamenda to Limbe with a Baptist group headed to a retreat. We planned to take a taxi to the airport the next afternoon. That gave us a day in the seaside city of Limbe. The Atlantic Ocean beach looked delightful and inviting; watching the waves and pondering the ocean's vast expanse made our hearts yearn for loved ones beyond the horizon. The emptiness of the distance between us was both unsettling and awe inspiring.

In retrospect, I believed our Mbingo experience was less rustic than our previous years in Africa. In Mbingo there was a middle-class mentality. There was an expectation of entitlement among people dependent on the prosperous hospital or, in the case of merchants, on salaried workers. One had to leave the plateau to find Cameroon's poor. On the plateau, workers were forever receiving relatives who were in need—usually of money. One thing that hit me shortly after arriving was how, at the small market near the hospital and along the roadside stalls in the bigger market, people could be found snacking all day long. Every day one could see folks standing and munching or walking along, snacks in hand, popping something in their mouths. I do not recall seeing that anywhere else; most did not have the blessing of a steady income.

CHAPTER 15

Harvey's Zambia Trip
2009

We left Cameroon and settled into our home in Michigan once again. Two months later, in late May of 2009, Harvey was asked to come to Zambia and cover a surgeon's one-month home leave. Mukinge Hospital was located on a hill above the plains. Harvey spent his time there seeing patients in the surgical clinic and doing procedures on the days the surgery suite was open. Work got off to a slow start at first since there were so few patients coming to the hospital. Work steadily increased during June, but there were no night calls.

All mission hospitals were included under the Zambian government's health department as far as funding was concerned. The funds were from England and the Netherlands, but the government hospitals took the greater share. Eventually, the funds for all hospitals decreased significantly, to the point where high government officials investigated and found that millions in funds had been inexplicably "lost." Unsurprisingly, the two European donors stopped sending funds.

In his emails to me, Harvey detailed his surroundings, especially noting the native flora; he knew that was a favorite topic of mine wherever we wandered. In June temperatures usually hovered around seventy degrees, while nights cooled down to the upper forties. Three large flame-of-the-forest trees were just beginning to bloom in June. Beautiful purple jacaranda and frangipani trees were in bloom, as well as flowering bushes everywhere. The trees and bushes afforded the houses some privacy on the large compound.

The hospital compound residents consisted of one single man; one married man, whose wife was briefly in the United States; and a couple with three children. The SIM offices were on a different compound, where housing included one family with three children, an accountant, a South African secretary, and one woman who ran the programs for women. These missionary workers got together every Friday night for a potluck supper at the SIM compound.

I was not with Harvey for that trip, but I knew he was in good hands. There was a church in the village with a small congregation that Harvey attended. The sermon was in English, but everything else was in Kekaunde.

CHAPTER 16

Third Trip to Soddo
February—March 2010

Our third trip to Soddo was to be our last overseas tour. We were there to cover surgical work while Dr. Paul Gray, Dr. Anderson, and the three African doctors in surgical training attended the two-week medical conference in Kenya. When we worked in Aira, Harvey had attended this conference himself almost every two years, making the journey from Ethiopia to Kenya to obtain credits for his US license. Upon their return from Kenya, the Andersons left for furlough in the United States, and Dr. Gray and his wife spent three months in language training in Addis.

The three African doctors in the PAACS training program needed to stay focused on their training in the classroom and in the operating theatre. Because it was a short-term assignment for Harvey, we did not have the opportunity to go west to visit Aira and our Ethiopian friends there.

We were assigned to the Gray's house, a large place with three bedrooms placed two on one side and one on the other. With both the guest bedroom and children's bedroom available, there was plenty of room for visitors. In fact, sometimes Paul came back when temporarily needed at Soddo, leaving the rest of his family in

Addis. The porch was delightful; we could see over the compound wall all the way down to Lake Abaya.

It was a privilege for Harvey to cover for Paul, a newly trained surgeon, not yet fully acquainted with the role of missionary doctor. Paul's role reminded us of the language study, surgery, and leadership responsibilities Harvey had during our first years in Bahrain.

Paul Gray was personable in his relationships and diligent in his medical practice. He was grateful for the two weeks in Kenya for the medical conference. He was a part of the Christian fellowship there and appreciative for all the teaching, both religious and medical. He took his turn in leading morning prayers at the hospital and participated in Sunday-morning gatherings in missionary homes.

Before we left, we invited the three surgical residents in training to a late-evening dinner. Harvey had trained them for four months, so a bond had grown among them, as well as with two Ethiopian surgeons on the hospital staff. The senior resident expected to graduate in July and planned to move out of his housing shortly thereafter; a big concern for Soddo Hospital was providing housing for doctors in training and their families.

Post-Communist development

Ethiopia had developed considerably since communism in Europe had fallen in 1999. Foreign agents and their onerous socialist agenda had collapsed. Private enterprise again became the mode of growth. Everywhere people opened shops and front-porch fruit and produce stands. New hotels, supermarkets, roads, sidewalks, and apartment buildings appeared everywhere, changing the skyline.

In Soddo the fruit and vegetable stands remained, but it appeared their owners were not making much income with the competition of the new, brightly lit grocery stores. We did not get to the farmers market but patronized many shops, both new and old, for the various items we needed. Lent having begun before we arrived, the butcher shops were closed. Our garden boy, however, could find meat in shops off the beaten path. Fish shops had refrigeration, but consistent electricity for freezers could not be counted on.

With horse-drawn carts now a thing of the past, the choices pedestrians had were light blue, electric "tricycle" taxis and larger minivan taxis, also popular in Addis.

Television and computers were new assets for businesses. In addition, cell phones, smartphones, and related technology had been brought in from Addis to these remote rural towns and villages.

The proliferation of colleges and other training centers continued the Communist-inspired goal to promote higher levels of education. It now seemed that every student wanted to go on to the next level of learning, a desire further necessitated by the higher cost of living. Unfortunately, the quality of education in technical and private schools left much to be desired. Thus, for the masses, "getting an education" did not necessarily mean better employment.

Outside of the main urban areas, the country was still oriented in agriculture. Parents, however, paid high private school fees for their children in hopes they would succeed and not have to return to the family farm. Success was now defined as doing something other than farming. This may well reflect the world's growing pains and the cities' dilemma, as well as the loss of agriculture-related jobs.

Young American guests

A young American nurse, Sophie, worked and lived on the mission compound, comprised of a church, mission offices, staff housing, and a home for children with disabilities who required short-term therapy. In addition to Sophie, two American boys volunteered at the teenagers' orphanage. The boys and Sophie often came to our home on weekends to practice guitar and keyboard, sometimes performing at our morning home services.

The mode of transport for Sophie and the boys was the motorcycle, which each had while working at Soddo. For safety, Sophie always brought her motorcycle up onto the closed-in porch if she stayed overnight. The boys always returned to their rooms in the orphanage. After a soccer game or even on dusty or muddy days, they all enjoyed showers with hot water in our home. They took advantage of the mission compound's deep well and generator to hose down their dirty bikes, especially when the town water was turned off.

One evening, while Sophie and the boys were at our house practicing their music, heavy rain started falling. Harvey was called out to the hospital, and the boys left when the rain slowed down; they had only two blocks to go, traveling on cement. When Harvey came back, he told us one of the boys was badly injured when a bus hit his motorcycle. Harvey was surprised and pleased that the injured volunteer recovered rapidly, to the point where he was able to pluckily tell everyone about the accident later that same week.

We invited the boys to supper one Saturday evening while Jen, a young Peace Corps volunteer, was staying with us for the weekend. The gathering was a send-off party for one of the boys returning to Seattle for a month. After he left, Sophie, Jen, and the remaining young man continued to make our home theirs.

A playful dog

Once again, Henry and Stephne Bowers were our neighbors. He was an optometrist, and she was the supervisor of three orphanages. Along with their two children, they had a dog called Selah. I had the pleasure of caring for Selah and walking her around the compound when the family went on trips.

One morning Selah refused to move; it seemed her hind quarters were weak, and she refused to walk. Harvey checked her out but could not detect any problems with her back or spine. We did what we could to make her comfortable and hoped for the best. It took about a week, but eventually the discomfort resolved itself, and she slowly became her old self again. I was very thankful because I could now stop worrying about how I would tell the children if it had turned out otherwise.

Dr. Ruth

The busy week of Dr. Ruth's wedding began with a bridal shower at the Norwegian doctor's house. It was an experiment, for showers are neither Norwegian, Ethiopian, nor Dutch customs. But the ladies who came enjoyed the cultural mix.

Guests began arriving: a Norwegian couple; a photographer from America with her mother and her adopted Ethiopian boy; Ruth's mother, father, and sister from the Netherlands; Ruth's adopted Ethiopian sister from Addis; and another Dutch couple with their adopted Ethiopian son.

Saturday morning the wedding began at ten thirty; the bride and groom walked down the grass "aisle" with the flower girl and ring bearer preceding them. The pulpit had roses on both sides, and the end chairs of each row sported small bundles of flowers. The hospital's big benefactor from Switzerland gave an excellent sermon on building a solid marriage. The former chaplain of SIM officiated with their vows.

The Dutch bride, Dr. Ruth, was a geriatrics specialist doing mainly pediatric work. Her Ethiopian groom, Dr. Mogus, had spent more than ten years in general practice in Toronto before returning to his homeland. A tea with treats was served at the hospital after the ceremony, and many photographs were taken. At two o'clock, we went to the convention center for the one o'clock buffet dinner for three hundred guests. Two bulls were tied at the gate, ready for slaughter if necessary.

The couple settled into Dr. Ruth's duplex, and Dr. Mogus entered surgical training with the next PAACS class at Soddo.

Easter

During Holy Week, hospital work lessened, and Harvey spent his evenings preparing a message for a Good Friday church service out of town. Good Friday morning, a hospital worker, who would be his translator, came at six o'clock to accompany him on an hour-long walk to church. The church doors were still closed when they arrived, but people began to enter the sanctuary at 7:45 a.m. When Harvey finished his message, the translator told him decisively that he could leave and quickly sat down in a nearby empty seat, making no gesture to accompany him out. After an awkward moment standing alone near the lectern, Harvey headed for the exit and walked the hour-long trek back home, alone. There was no explanation for the translator's behavior.

Easter is a big event in Ethiopian culture. Families enjoy a noon feast, usually chicken or lamb, and often share the meat and its expense with neighbors or relatives.

After we had eaten our breakfast at home, we went to our neighbor's concrete rotunda with its four-foot wall and towering thatched-grass roof overhead. After a time of singing, worship, and fellowship, we enjoyed an Easter brunch together.

Jen's story

My work consisted of tutoring five pupils in our home, four days a week after school. Additionally, the next-door neighbor's daughter struggled with math, so I helped her with that, but during our whole time in Soddo, my primary and most demanding responsibility was as hostess to the many visitors.

When we moved into the Grays' home, we soon learned that Jen, whom we had met at Dr. Ruth's wedding, would be a frequent weekend guest. She lived with a host family and was a young teacher at a rural school in a small village. She was a Peace Corps volunteer assigned to a school far outside of Soddo. She traveled to and from Soddo by bus, and sometimes we walked her to the bus station at the edge of town if it was getting dark. Without any other American teacher in the area of her assignment, she enjoyed the fellowship, hot shower, familiar food, and church services every Sunday in our home.

I had prepared my birthday dinner for eight guests when Jen arrived unexpectedly. In midafternoon the Bowers family next door returned from their trip and were added to our evening meal roster. The Bowers had not told us their return date, but we shared my birthday dinner with everyone. We heard about many of the family's vacation experiences: a Tanzanian safari, days at the ocean and beach, and a Zanzibar excursion. It was a great day, but

I had to return my little furry friend to her family and would miss our daily walks around the compound.

The next morning, after church service at our house, Harvey took Jen and me to town for an Ethiopian feast. Jen picked at her food warily, for she was not too fond of the food and had on-again, off-again stomach problems. Her meals throughout the week were with her host family, and one could only wonder how she managed; she eagerly ate my Midwestern-style cooking.

On Good Friday, Jen came to town for a lunch date with an Ethiopian friend, then on to our house for the holiday weekend. It seemed that Jen had difficulty relaxing during the week in the village of her assignment and collapsed when she got to our house. The following day, fortified by some decent sleep, Jen went along with Dr. Mary's Saturday clinic to a rural area. I had been encouraging Jen to be an occasional helper for Dr. Mary, but being new to dealing with so much poverty and sickness, Jen had resisted doing so. This time, though, she went along and helped by passing out a week's supply of vitamins to each patient and handing out bananas to all—not quite as overwhelming as directly assisting Dr. Mary with patients and coming face to face with their reality.

Easter morning, Jen had stomach problems, so she missed breakfast and most of the Easter service outdoors. When she felt better, she took a three o'clock bus back to her host home, but not for long. On Wednesday Jen came by, fell exhausted into a chair, and had trouble breathing from the walk from the bus station. She had been having shortness of breath for several days, including two or three panic attacks. Her Peace Corps doctors told her to go to Addis the next day.

At five o'clock the next morning, Harvey walked her to the bus station, where he removed some of the weight in her backpack to reduce the stress on her shoulders. When she returned from Addis, she said the doctors believed the antimalaria pills triggered her panic attacks; she had not been taking them very long and needed to give herself some adjustment time. She slept well and late before going back to her home and school in the village the next day.

Jen's issues were typical of many young, ambitious volunteers who came to Africa aspiring to alleviate suffering by the practical application of their talents, whether driven by the Holy Spirit or secular altruism. The hardships of acclimatization that we missionaries took for granted and spent years adjusting to were, regrettably, very compressed for them. Much of their productive time was spent in illness, exhaustion, and culture shock.

Hospital politics

Dr. Paul Gray left language class in Addis to return to Soddo for a day. With Harvey he took the Ethiopian government medical supervisors on a tour of Soddo Christian Hospital. Both Paul and Harvey hoped the government would grant them a license to practice surgical training of doctors from Ethiopia and other African countries. The inspectors knew the hospital was very up to date and well staffed, and that it maintained a high standard of medical work.

A month later, the wonderful news came that the government of Ethiopia had licensed Soddo Christian Hospital to legally practice the PAACS program. What a joy! What a relief! For a new young surgeon like Dr. Paul, administration of the PAACS program was a heavy responsibility. But the country's accreditation of the program gave merit and gravitas to the standard of the program and attested to the doctors' qualifications and acceptance by people throughout the country. Ethiopian and foreign doctors could return to their homes, show their certificate from the Ethiopian government, and work in whichever country they chose.

Soon after arriving in Soddo, Harvey realized the surgical student named Marco from Madagascar was not fluent in English. Marco's languages were French and Malagasy, so he struggled with the lessons, lectures, and textbooks that the other students were using. Harvey asked me to tutor the young man after class, but I soon realized he could not keep up. Harvey called Dr. Paul in Addis, and together they agreed that Marco needed to return to his country, learn English, and then find a French-speaking country with a PAACS program.

At the same time, the Soddo Hospital administrator noticed that Marco's Ethiopian visa had expired and not been renewed, so he was now in Ethiopia illegally. The PAACS leaders in the United States agreed to his leaving the program, seeking English study in Madagascar, and then finding training in a French-speaking West African area. He had been in a PAACS French program in Gabon and would practice there before returning to his country.

Margaret's Soddo work

Our house was on town electricity, which failed almost daily. Three times I made bread that rose and was ready to bake just as the electricity quit. It did not taste so great. When town electricity went off, the hospital turned on its generator for hospital work only. In the evenings, the hospital could add electricity to the compound houses. To no one's surprise, the water supply was doing very well since the well had been cleaned.

One day, when rain had not made a mess of the path, I went down the hill to the Catholic compound to visit the technical school, the office workers, and the girls' classes and leaders—Dean Aklilu Petros and Deputy Dean Antonio. Girls I knew from our previous time in Soddo had moved on to higher grades, and technical students had graduated and taken up community jobs. The school had increased its number of buildings with a larger staff and student body. Being with Antonio and his wife was always so enjoyable. The school system was growing and branching out to the villages around Soddo, encouraging and implementing school building and education.

Throughout most of our time in Soddo, we had rain and often storms that caused frequent electrical blackouts. We pinned our hopes on a team of seven engineers from the United States who were coming to install a new hospital and compound generator. Their arrival had been delayed by the ash and smoke cloud spewing from a volcano in Iceland that had covered most of western and northern Europe. Flights were cancelled everywhere. When they finally resumed, the engineers arrived and did a fine job. All the compound housing was then wired to the new generator.

In April the rainy season began, and farmers were busy plowing and planting. It was not uncommon to have seeds just breaking through the soil when rains would abruptly cease for a month, and plants would wilt and die. To prevent such waste, I harvested the gardens of absent missionaries, freezing some of the produce for their use and using some at our table. The vegetable gardens and flower beds were surrounded by blooming bushes and fragrant flowers, a delight for the senses. Fruits from our compound were strawberries and passion fruit, while papaya, bananas, oranges, and limes filled the marketplace.

We arrived at Soddo in a dust storm with cool weather and more rain than usual for the dry season. We left in a strong rainy season that boded well for a successful harvest.

Goodbyes

Our turn to leave by the hospital van came as planned. Our departure was made especially memorable since Ethiopian elections were soon to be held, and protesters were already gathering in increasing numbers in the capital and other larger cities. The slow going in those crowded streets made our trip interesting but not difficult. The crowds in the capital were louder and more dramatic, but our driver knew the city well and chose a route through Addis that did not put us amid the protesters; crowds in the street can make driving difficult and dangerous.

We overlapped with the Gray family on their last night in Addis, so we invited them out for an evening meal before they headed back to Soddo. While we were in Addis, other friends— missionaries, former students, and church leaders—invited us to their homes. The Presbyterian guest house was our de facto base, as it had been on all our trips to the capital over the span of twenty-four years. It was the first place we had stayed upon arrival in Ethiopia, and it was from there that we had set off for work in the Wollega region. Now it was to be our final residence in our beloved Africa.

Knowing this was likely our last trip overseas, we flew to Oslo and met up with old friends, the Hannes. Our second day there, Dr. Hanne took us out sightseeing and then on to where her son, Thomas, and his family lived. Harvey had been asked to be her son's godfather many years before and remembered holding baby Thomas in his arms; now he was meeting this grown man's first child. Harvey was deeply touched and honored to be part of this family's life.

In Sweden we spent four days touring Gothenburg with Sister Leena. She had arrived at Aira when we did and remained there for many years, leaving around the time Harvey and I retired.

We were tourists in Gothenburg, visiting Sister Leena's church, her favorite park, the islands by ferry, and a museum that included a very damp, three-story rain forest. Touring with her felt at once familiar and strange; we fell into our usual behaviors from the many road trips we had taken over the years in Ethiopia. We laughed about those days and marveled at the contrasts, leaving us all feeling wistful and a little homesick. We left her to fly to Michigan, our new home and a very different lifestyle.

While Harvey was still in Soddo, he met a surgeon very involved in medical mission trips. Impressed by Harvey's forty-five years of work abroad, the doctor asked Harvey if he would consent to induction into the International Medical Mission Hall of Fame at the University of Toledo in Ohio. It was the doctor himself who had set up the Hall of Fame.

On the evening of Harvey's induction, three doctors were to be presented. One was a Pakistani Muslim philanthropist who did surgery in Toledo but spent every other summer in his native Pakistan aiding his people and helping others in poor countries as well. The second honoree was Harvey. The third doctor honored had recently died, so he was honored by his son's presence. All three would have face plaques on the wall, along with those of many other famous doctors.

EPILOGUE

Margaret and Harvey are humble people who play down the uniqueness of their lives and careers and think their story might be boring. I could not disagree more. Their philanthropic lives and careers were adventuresome, meaningful, productive, inspiring, and by any standard, well lived.

After reading about Margaret and Harvey's missionary years, some questions naturally come to mind. What motivated them to become missionaries? What impact did they have? What did they do after retirement?

Origin of their call

"What led you to the mission field?" I asked Margaret and Harvey. I wanted to know what had motivated them to give up a secure life in America and go to strife-torn, poor, undeveloped, and sometimes dangerous countries. What had made them brave physical hazards, political upheavals, disease, lack of sanitation, and all the rest?

Service to others is a thread that runs through Margaret and Harvey's lives and careers. The origin of this worldview can be traced back to Harvey's mother, Florence Kooi. She grew up on a farm near Fulton, Illinois, and from a young age dreamed of Christian service. Wanting to save money to further her education, she took a job with the federal government in Washington, DC, and worked there during World War I. As she became familiar with the devastating effects of the war, even from a distance, she committed herself to bringing peace to the world. After the war, with funds in hand, she enrolled in Moody Bible Institute in Chicago, with the goal of becoming a missionary. Upon graduation, she became a missionary in Managua, Nicaragua.

But when Florence's sister died unexpectedly, leaving behind four young children, Florence left the mission field and returned to Illinois to take care of them. In time, she married their father, Jacob Doorenbos, and their family eventually grew to eight with the birth of Harvey and then Polly. Although Florence had left the mission field, her passion for missions remained. The family regularly invited missionaries to stay with them, leaving a lasting impression of adventure and commitment on Harvey, who early in life had dedicated himself to missionary work.

What impact?

Asking what impact one person can have on others is a worthwhile endeavor. Such curiosity begs the question: What contribution, if any, did Margaret and Harvey make to the betterment of humankind?

It would be easy to argue that Margaret and Harvey had a significant impact on many lives in Arabia and Africa.

Margaret's contributions are not easily quantifiable, yet they are legion. She brought education to many, especially to women, teaching them to read and write. The women used the knowledge they gained to better their lives in matters of nutrition, family planning, family health care, and life's everyday problems. The women's new knowledge was multiplied exponentially through subsequent sharing with their families, relatives, and neighbors.

Harvey's contributions are more easily quantifiable. He personally facilitated thousands of clinical visits and operations, improved the health of countless thousands of individuals, and saved many lives. Some specific data attributable to Harvey's work is available from his tenure at the mission hospital in Mutrah,

Margaret and Harvey celebrate their golden
wedding anniversary in 2016

Oman, in 1973.[92] The hospital performed about three thousand
operations that year. Harvey was the lead surgeon and performed
about three-quarters of those operations.

Harvey estimates that he performed from two to six
surgeries per day during his forty-seven years of mission work.
That translates to somewhere between forty-nine thousand and
sixty-eight thousand operations over his career. Considering that
many of those patients had mothers, fathers, relatives, and friends,
the number of people touched by Harvey's work is easily in the
hundreds of thousands.

In an unassuming way, Harvey and Margaret were a gentle
presence of caring and selfless service. They were there for the
most destitute who desperately needed to know that someone
cared for them. The impact of such a presence may be difficult to
quantify, but its reality is beyond doubt.

Even their sons, Dirk and Keith, played a part in the
crosscultural aspects of missionary life, contributing to a better
and more informed world. The many cultures and religions and
the vast human need they witnessed and were immersed in as

92 Mary Bruins Allison, *Doctor Mary in Arabia: Memoirs by Mary
Allison, MD* (Austin: University of Texas Press, 1994).

children made them highly aware, international citizens who passed on that knowledge and awareness to others. Such understanding inevitably brings humans closer, engendering much-needed reconciliation.

The impact of the Doorenbos family is a cascading phenomenon—the effect is passed on and grows. For example, when a parent is healed or educated, the effect of that gift is felt by that person's family and friends and then, in turn, by their families and friends. In sum, the gift increases as it affects many lives.

The later years

Margaret and Harvey have settled in Holland, Michigan, fully retired at last. They live modestly and happily in an independent-living retirement home. When asked how they view their lives and careers in retrospect, Harvey responded, "I have no regrets and wouldn't change a thing. I loved going to work every day. It was a privilege to help people with their health."

After reading Margaret's story, I trust it is clear that one person can indeed make a difference—a tremendous difference, in fact. Such certitude should instill hope in our doubting souls.

APPENDIX

On Being a Missionary Doctor

Harvey Doorenbos reflected on his role as a medical missionary in a lecture given in 2015 to the Hope College Pre-Medical Club.

A MISSIONARY SURGEON'S 40 YEARS' EXPERIENCE

Before beginning my lecture, a brief biography is necessary.

After graduating from Hope College in 1955, I went to Northwestern University Medical School in Chicago. I received my MD in 1959 and came to Grand Rapids, Butterworth Hospital (now Spectrum Downtown) for a one year rotating internship and four years General Surgery Residency. My wife Margaret graduated from Hope 1956 and taught math in Evanston to support us through medical school.

In 1964, we were accepted by the Reformed Church in America as missionary candidates to work with the Arabian Mission.

We studied Arabic in Bahrain for a year and a half and then were assigned to work at the American Mission Hospital in

Muscat, Oman. Oman was ruled by an elderly, very conservative Muslim sultan. Oman's culture had not changed significantly for a thousand years. The appearance of the Omani men with their dark tanned full-bearded faces looked like how we imagine the patriarchs Abraham, Isaac, and Jacob probably looked like. They were hospitable, dignified, self-reliant and deeply religious.

The Sultan hesitated quite some time before agreeing to allow an oil company to enter his country. He had seen the undesirable changes in Kuwait and other countries that happened after large numbers of foreigners with their western culture and loose behavior introduced bad habits into traditional Muslim societies.

The RCA began work in Oman in 1896 and later, in 1909, opened a hospital. The first missionaries were sensitive to the culture and refrained from objectionable behavior.

These missionaries opened a school for slaves who had been freed by the British,[93] and established separate girls' and boys' schools. These projects plus the medical work gained a good reputation for our mission. History shows this approach is wise in opening doors slowly to a reception by the Muslim to hear the Gospel.

Our work in Oman was a time of great fun, busy with lots of surgery, teaching for Margaret, and developing many friendships. We came home in 1974 for a year's furlough to take additional post-residency training in surgery, again at Butterworth.

Unexpectedly, we did not return to Oman, but were asked to go to Ethiopia to fill a vacancy at a Presbyterian hospital. That was a year after a military coup deposed Emperor Haile Selassie. The new government declared itself socialist, aligned with China and Russia, and clearly opposed to America. We were warned that Christian mission work under this regime could end abruptly at any time, but that the Ethiopian Evangelical Church wanted to keep its hospitals functioning as long as possible.

The hospital in Dembi Dolo was 650 Km west of Addis Ababa by road. It was served by domestic airline planes because during the rainy season it could not be reached by road. I was the

93 The school was for a group of 18 boys captured from a slave ship.

only doctor at its 50-bed hospital my first year. The second year a Scottish doctor joined me. The government regional referral hospital was 350 Km away by road, but unreachable during the rainy season. There were two small mission hospitals along the way to that referral hospital.

The staff at Dembi Dolo hospital included a nurse and a dozen health assistants who functioned as "barefoot doctors," lesser trained than nurses. They provided nursing care to in-patients and first line treatment for out-patients. One of them learned to do common surgical procedures and was an excellent assistant for major surgery. Another provided general anesthesia. In remote mission hospitals doctors teach technical things to the interested, clever, unofficially trained workers who do the best they can under close medical supervision. Hence the traditional phrase is: "See one, Do one, Teach one."

Keep in mind I am talking about conditions of 35 years ago. Fortunately, there's been much progress in medical education since then.

Under the communist rule we experienced considerable opposition to Christianity and church work. The first two or three years under the communists, the government was concerned with consolidating itself with "reliable party members;" after it felt secure in its members, it attacked church organizations.

After two years in Dolo, we came home for a three-month furlough. During that time, schools for missionary children were closed, the hospital in Dembi Dolo was nationalized and the missionary medical staff sent away, and the Mission Aviation Fellowship was expelled from the country. Without the MAF service, many missionaries could not stay at remote stations and had to leave Ethiopia. Countryside Farmers Organizations were encouraged to harass foreigners so they would voluntarily leave.

Although we could not return to Dembi Dolo, the Ethiopian Evangelical Church asked us to work in the Aira hospital, which belonged to a German Mission. Its two doctors were conscientious objectors who refused to perform physical exams for boys drafted into the military which the government demanded. They resigned and left Ethiopia. If I agreed to serve, the hospital could stay open, otherwise it would be closed. We went, again with the understanding that long-term service might not be possible. We could be expelled in a few months, but the church wanted to show it would try to provide medical service to a remote population who would otherwise be without adequate health care.

As it turned out we stayed not just a few months but 23 more years. There were rumors the government would close the hospital, but, by God's provision, it is still open and functioning today.

Communists controlled the government of Ethiopia for 17 years until it was defeated by a rebel military group. The church went underground during the early part of that time, but gradually, there came a modicum of peaceful understanding as the government realized it could not destroy the church. Many Christian pastors were imprisoned on the grounds of anti-government activity, but there were no trials or sentences. Local officials in our region accepted our hospital as legitimate and allowed us to train health assistants if half of them would work for the government. Toward the end of communist rule, we were given official permission from the central government to replace our old inadequate hospital buildings and build new ones. We were also allowed to employ an Ethiopian physician who was trained in Russia and did not have to fulfill an obligation to work in the government to pay for his medical education.

At one regional medical meeting, Aira Hospital was honored with the certificate of being the best run medical organization in our region. The public always recognized this, but to have the government say it was a surprise.

Missionary medical work

With this brief background of conditions in Oman and Ethiopia, let me speak briefly about medical work as a missionary.

We medical professionals are a privileged group. To be trained to work in health care fields gives us a special opportunity to see God's work. Every year medical science is learning more about the great design God placed in our bodies. Studying the development of a fertilized egg growing to the birth of a newborn baby is to observe a miracle. Our creator planned our physiology delicately and we—as health workers—get to cooperate with God in caring for this body. I thank God daily for this privilege.

In missionary medicine, we get to work where there is a great shortage of health care. We use our time and training to add value to life for those who otherwise have little chance of such care.

Humanitarian work is highly respected and appreciated Donors get satisfaction that cannot be matched by money. Medically unserved people exist in every country, but proportionally the greatest need is in Africa.

Justice

Medical missionaries do humanitarian work that can be classified under the banner of social justice.

To what level should we Christians be "our brother's keeper"? Do we Americans have an obligation to Africans? We campaign for justice and equality, but health care is not distributed equally throughout the world. In America we allocate about $5,000 per person per year for health care. African countries struggle to allocate $2.00 from their national budgets for each person per year for health care. Half of humanity lives on $2.00 per person per day for all their expenses. Most have no money left for hospital expenses; thus they must forego some other essential expense to buy medicine.

Developed countries donate large sums to upgrade health care in poor countries, but that doesn't reach much of the population. Poverty is responsible for much of the poor health, while at the same time, poor health exacerbates poverty. The millennium goals, agreed upon in the United Nations, will not be reached in many African nations where some countries are actually regressing in health statistics. AIDS, hunger, food insecurity, government policies, and poor education all contribute to the poverty and poor health quagmire.

Another aspect of justice is America's practice of importing medical professionals from underdeveloped countries. And we complain that China is stealing our intellectual property.

Can you see that we ought to be accused of stealing intellectual property from Uganda when we call a doctor or a nurse from Uganda to work in America? Who provided the general and medical education to that graduate? What do we pay Uganda for releasing that skill to America?

It was called economic imperialism when rich nations took minerals and resources from poor nations. Are not the skills of people recruited to emigrate here of similar value? For individuals who come, there are salaries many times that of their home country. That's nice for them, but what does a nation lose in the move of doctors or nurses to America?

I've said we health workers are privileged to be in this profession and that we provide valuable humanitarian service by going to undeveloped countries. I must add that when we also share the Christian Gospel we are contributing something of eternal value to individuals and to the country.

As followers of Jesus Christ we experience the blessing of receiving God's wonderful news about the purpose of His creation. This purpose is redemption: bringing back to the original owner what once was his, but was lost. God created us for fellowship with Him, but He lost us when we rejected that fellowship. Jesus Christ came to earth to restore us into that relationship.

The Bible describes this story and how blessed we Christians are to know it. We believe it and can share it with anyone who doesn't know it. Knowing Christ has made a great difference in my earthly life, but the wonderful thing is that it doesn't stop with death. The Bible assures us that after this physical life we have a new life that will be more wonderful than words can describe. The greatest joy and happiness given to a medical missionary is the privilege of sharing this good news.

How do you prepare for such a privileged life?

Be well prepared in your chosen field. A vague desire to help poor people in a foreign country will not get you a working visa. You must demonstrate the requirements of a skill needed by that country.

Find a mission organization you are comfortable with that is looking for your skills. Sometimes you may contact a mission organization before you decide on a specific special training if that seems desirable to you.

In your prayers and searching of God's Word, be sure you feel this is God's will for you. It is possible you may have a real interest in mission work, but for some reasons God is not calling you to go abroad. Without a deep sense of God's call, wait until you know.

Get all the information you can get from books, magazines, the internet, talking with Christian brothers and sisters, and attending missionary meetings.

If you have or will have a marriage partner, be sure BOTH of you feel called to this path.

Be prepared throughout your career that you might be moved from place to place or country to country.

Don't be tentative about committing your whole self to obeying God's call, or disappointments may cause a failure.

BIBLIOGRAPHY

Al Bassam. *Footsteps in the Sand*. Kuwait City: Kuwait Bookstore Co., 2004.

Allison, Mary Bruins. *Doctor Mary in Arabia: Memoirs by Mary Allison, MD*. Austin: University of Texas Press, 1994.

Arabian Mission Field Reports, Arabian Mission Quarterly, Neglected Arabia. New York: RCA, Arabian Mission 1892-1962.

Armerding, Paul L. *Doctors for the Kingdom*. Grand Rapids, MI: Eerdmans, 2003.

Badeau, John. *The Middle East Remembered*. Washington, DC: The Middle East Institute, 1983.

Barker, Jeff. *Iowa Ethiopia, A Missionary Nurse's Journey Continues*. Peabody, MA: Hendrikson, 2019.

Belgrave, James H. D. *Welcome to Bahrain*. London: Augustan Press, 1965.

Bergsma, Stuart. *Rainbow Empire: Ethiopia Stretches Out Her Hand*. Grand Rapids, MI: Eerdmans, 1932.

Boersma, Jeanette. *Grace in the Gulf*. Grand Rapids, MI: Eerdmans, 1991.

Calverley, Eleanor T. *My Arabian Days and Nights*. NY: Thomas Crowell Co., 1958.

Chamberlain, Mary. *Fifty Years in Foreign Fields*. NY: Abbott Press, 1925.

Clark, Angela. *Through the Changing Scenes of Life*. Abingdon, UK: Touchpaper Limited, 1993.

Dalenberg, Cornelia. *Sharifa*. Grand Rapids, MI: Eerdmans, 1983.

Dickson, H. R. P. *Kuwait and Her Neighbors*. London: George Allen & Unwin, 1956.

Doumato, Eleanor Abdella. *Getting God's Ear*. NY: Columbia University Press, 2000.

Harrison, Paul W. *Doctor in Arabia*. NY: John Day Co., 1943.

Harrison, Paul W. *The Arab at Home*. NY: Thomas Y. Crowell Co., 1924.

Harrison, Timothy S. *Before Oil: Memories of an American Missionary Family in the Persian Gulf, 1920–1939*. Rumford, RI: Rumford Books, 2008.

Heusinkveld, Paul A. *Elephant Baseball: A Missionary Kid's Tale*. Grand Rapids, MI: Eerdmans, 2017.

Howell, W. Nathaniel. *Strangers When We Met: A Century of American Community in Kuwait*. Washington, DC: New Academia Publishing, 2016.

Mason, Alfred De Witt, and Frederick J. Barny. *History of the Arabian Mission*. NY: Board of Foreign Missions, RCA, 1926.

Mylrea, C. Stanley. *Kuwait Before Oil*. Unpublished, 1951.

Pengelley, Janet Storm. *William Harold Storm MD*. Woodlands, Australia, 2005.

Platt, Mary Schauffler. *Christ Comes to the Village: A Study of Rural Life in Non-Christian Lands*. Brattleboro, VT: The Vermont Printing Co., 1931.

Scudder, Lewis R. *The Arabian Mission Story*. Grand Rapids, MI: Eerdmans, 1998.

Storm, Harold, W. *Whither Arabia? A Survey of Missionary Opportunity*. NY: World Dominion Press, 1938.

Swart, Morrell F. *The Call to Africa*, Grand Rapids, MI: Eerdmans, 1998.

Thompson, Andrew. *The Christian Church in Kuwait*. Kuwait City: Saeed & Sameer, 2010.

Tuson, Penelope. *Playing the Game, Western Women in Arabia*. London: I. B. Tauris & Co., 2003.

Van Ess, Dorothy. *History of the Arabian Mission 1926-1957*. Unpublished, 1957.

Van Ess, Dorothy. *Pioneers in the Arab World*. Grand Rapids, MI: Eerdmans, 1974.

Van Ess, John. *Meet the Arab*. London: Museum Press Ltd., 1947.

Voss-VandeKerk, Christine. *Collected Letters 1949-1958*. Unpublished.

Westra, Richard. *Father of the Clock*. Manama, Bahrain: Union Press, 2005.

INDEX

260; in Soddo, 266; career
summary of, 278, 282
TEAM (The Evangelical
Alliance Mission), 11, 28,
55-57, 65, 77, 91, 206, 220,
222-23, 273
teff (grain), 69, 231
Telegu (language), 198
Teppi (Ethiopia), 79
Thoms, Beth, 53
Thoms, Dr. Marion, 53
Thoms, Dr. Sharon, 53
Thoms, Dr. Wells, 53-54
Tigre (tribe), 129-30, 132, 148,
150
Timket, 73, 122
Timotewos (Saint), 141
Tissat Falls (Ethiopia), 144
Toronto, 269
Totota Internally Displaced
Persons Camp, 218
Tubman, William, 204
tuk-tuk (motorcycle taxis), 202
tukul (huts), 171, 173, 177-78,
190

U
Uganda, viii, 166, 168-71,
176-78, 180, 216, 285-86
ululating, 173, 193
United Nations, 168-70, 174,
180, 205, 213,
US Navy, 6, 32

V
Vellore (India), 42, 198, 201

W
wadi, 30, 49-51
Weiss, Dorothy, 1
Weiss, Rev. Raymond, 1
Weitz, Emily, 197, 200-201
Weitz, Rev. Martin, 197,
200-201
Weldiya (Ethiopia), 151, 153

Wellega Synod, 134
Wesley, Dr. Boman, 199
Wesley, Sheela (RN), 199
Wolaita Zone (Ethiopia), 231
Wollega Province (Ethiopia),
93, 162, 274
Wollo Province (Ethiopia), 151

Y
Yahya (young man), 44
Yambio (South Sudan), 166,
168-70, 172-73, 175-78, 180
Yemen, 61, 68, 148
Youande (Cameroon), 254

Z
Zaire, 168, 171
Zambia, vii, 193, 224-25, 263
Zanzibar, 59-61, 270
Zwyghuizen, Ardith (RN), 133,
155-56
Zwyghuizen, Heidi, 242

Made in the USA
Monee, IL
14 July 2021